Great Questions God Asks

Great Questions God Asks

Questions That Unlock the Great Issues of Our Lives

KATHY CALL

Foreword by Richard J. Mouw

RESOURCE *Publications* • Eugene, Oregon

GREAT QUESTIONS GOD ASKS
Questions That Unclock the Great Issues of Our Lives

Copyright © 2017 Kathy Call. All rights reserved. Except for brief quotations in critical publications or reviews, no part of this book may be reproduced in any manner without prior written permission from the publisher. Write: Permissions, Wipf and Stock Publishers, 199 W. 8th Ave., Suite 3, Eugene, OR 97401.

Resource Publications
An Imprint of Wipf and Stock Publishers
199 W. 8th Ave., Suite 3
Eugene, OR 97401

www.wipfandstock.com

PAPERBACK ISBN: 978-1-5326-3108-5
HARDCOVER ISBN: 978-1-5326-3110-8
EBOOK ISBN: 978-1-5326-3109-2

Manufactured in the U.S.A.   10/09/17

Contents

Foreword by Richard J. Mouw | vii

I. Meeting the God Who Asks Great Questions | 1

II. God's Great Question to Adam | 12
> "Where are you?"
> A question of disclosure

III. God's Great Question to Jacob | 30
> "What is your name?"
> A question of identity

IV. God's Great Question to Moses | 44
> "Who made your mouth?"
> A question of adequacy

V. God's Great Question to Joshua | 59
> "What are you doing with your face down in the dust?"
> A question of balance

VI. God's Great Question to Elijah | 72
> "What are you doing here?"
> A question of assurance

VII. God's Great Question to Jonah | 86

    "Do you have a right to be angry?"
    A question of mercy

VIII. God's Great Question to Ezekiel | 101

    "Son of man, can these dry bones ever live again?"
    A question of renewal

IX. God's Great Question to Job | 115

    "Where were you when I made the earth out of nothing?"
    A question of perspective

X. God's Great Question to Simon Peter | 135

    "Who do you say that I am?"
    A question of faith

XI. God's Great Question to the Woman Taken in Adultery | 154

    "Woman, where are your accusers?"
    A question of release

XII. God's Great Question to Martha | 169

    "Where have you laid him?"
    A question of hope

XIII. God's Great Question to Saul | 185

    "Saul, Saul, why are you persecuting me?"
    A question of discernment

Postscript | *209*

Foreword

RICHARD J. MOUW

EACH TIME I HAVE read this book—and I have done that several times now—it has been a refreshing experience. For one thing, reading it is for me like taking a refresher course on the grand narrative of the Bible. Kathy Call begins with Adam and Eve in the Garden and concludes with the conversion of the Apostle Paul. Along the way, she creatively enters into the *personae* of specific figures in the Biblical narrative, using their stories to illuminate key themes in God's redemptive dealings with the likes of us.

Kathy's choice of which characters to reflect upon is itself refreshing. If I were given the assignment of crafting a sermon on Jesus' question to the woman taken in adultery—"Woman, where are your accusers?"—I'm not sure I could come up with more than a few acceptable paragraphs. Kathy however, has written a marvelously detailed meditation on how the Savior's question to the woman is a message of "release." I find Kathy's thoughts here deeply moving.

A key to the refreshing nature of these meditations for me is the way this book has forced me to think differently about questions. As a teacher of philosophy I have made a big thing about urging my Christians students to take questions seriously. But the questions I have focused on in my teaching have been the ones that philosophers have asked, including questions about God. In this book, Kathy has pushed me to pay attention to those questions that come *from* God. And these are questions, as she shows, that speak in very personal ways into our own souls.

FOREWORD

The Bible, as Kathy demonstrates, is full of questions that God addresses to his human creatures. And in a compelling manner, she enters into the Biblical accounts of God's questions in the ancient world only after she has given her own testimony of God's persistent probing into her own life, revealing a personal brokenness that it took some time for her to acknowledge. The beauty of what follows in this book comes from her own very real struggle to submit to the Divine Questioner.

I have been referring to Kathy on a first-name basis because she is a dear friend. As Phyllis and I have traveled with Kathy in China, we have witnessed directly how she has put her faith into practice in concrete ways through China Connection, the organization that Kathy founded several decades ago. She has supported schools for needy kids, provided the technology for bringing fresh water supplies to remote villages, served the disabled and the elderly, and much more. She has also been a popular preacher in the pulpits of China's "Three-Self Churches."

These published meditations now make the talents and sensitivities of her decades of Kingdom service available to folks here in the West. I hope that many lives will be touched by these lessons about what it means to listen obediently to questions that God poses to each of us.

I.

MEETING THE GOD WHO ASKS GREAT QUESTIONS

I VIVIDLY REMEMBER THE DAY!

AFTER YEARS OF MY reading the Scriptures, its pages suddenly sprang to life before my very own eyes. Before I could grasp what had hit me, these "ancient" Scriptures caught me up in their own momentum. So what I experienced that day turned out to be a deep personal encounter with the living God that I could never have possibly expected.

I was "on the road." Having just returned from meetings with key business prospects, I felt absolutely exhausted! Totally miserable. At that moment all I could do was to slump down with a thud on the hotel sofa, and to stare vacantly at the Minneapolis skyline. "Where are you, Lord?" I pleaded with some urgency.

Reaching into my travel bag, I groped awkwardly for the brown leather Bible I brought along. Surely the God of the Ages would meet me there on its pages. Well, such was my hope. But, having already flipped through way too many pages, and still being unable to decide where to turn next, I chose the easy way out. I simply allowed 'The Book' to fall open where it would.

But there, I quickly discovered my expectations were to be dashed.

You see, right before my eyes, staring me in the face, was a story I had never really liked. To make matters worse, it was the same unfortunate passage I had turned to the day before. What are the amazing odds of that, I asked myself? Although annoyed that apparently there would be 'no fresh word from the Lord' for me today, I surprisingly vowed to read this newly assigned passage anyway. This time, much more slowly. More openly. More expectantly. Then I waited in silence. In holy piety? Hardly! I simply had no energy left to do anything else.

And then, out of nowhere, I suddenly heard a voice. A quiet voice. Whose voice, I didn't even think to explore at the moment.

"Well, what do you think of the passage?"

This question seemingly coming 'out of nowhere' now suddenly burst in upon me. With it came no real 'sound' to help recognize it, so no recognizable voice. Nothing too dramatic. From where, I had absolutely no idea! And yet here was this 'Voice' asking for a possible response from me.

Continuing for the moment to ignore whence the question, I responded right away. And I heard myself strangely addressing my answer to God himself. And still failing to attach much awesome importance to the question from God himself, I responded honestly and freely to his specific question to me:

"Well, Lord, I suppose that, if I were a pastor, I probably would never preach on this passage!"

"Oh! And why is that?" shot back the questioner.

I thought I had just rid myself of this thorny issue. And now before I could even think of regrouping. I was somehow being pressed—no, much more like being challenged—to begin digging even more deeply into the biblical text.

Having once again done so, I again answered the Voice with a wee bit of detachment strangely at odds with my age-old fervent longing to draw much closer to my God.

"For openers, Lord, I can see some 'textual problems' in this passage." (Oh, what an ingenious dodge!) "But Lord," I continued. "Even if I were able to get beyond these 'textual problems', with whom do you expect me to identify in the story?"

"Suppose *you* choose." Ugh! He had passed the 'buck' back to me.

Perhaps I should stop here just long enough explain that this "unfortunate story" now staring me in the face was in fact Luke's faithful recitation of the demon-possessed man, a man called the "Gadarene," who 'just happened' to encounter Jesus on the road one day, as Luke details for us.

This deranged Gadarene, you see, was running around all helter-skelter most of the time, refusing to clothe himself, or even to remain at home and out of sight. No, this unorthodox man much preferred to spend lavish amounts of time and delight in frequenting the groups of putrid burial tombs set back from the roadway—yet not set back so far as to keep him away from threatening passersby by crying out at them wildly in his loud voice. And all the while, this demented, perhaps even dangerous, man constantly ripped at his own flesh with sharp stones.

"With whom do I identify, Lord? I'm not quite sure. I glanced down and, despite my beginning to feel a bit cornered, I managed to sift through his depressing story once more. At long last, with my conclusion reached, once again I looked upward. And only then did I utter words toward the Voice, words that immediately I wished I could take back!

"I guess, Lord, that I identify a bit with Jesus." I'm certainly not off wandering around burial tombs all the time. How can I possibly identify in any way with that man? I'm not at all like him!" I am ashamed to admit that, at that time, I felt supremely satisfied with my response.

"Huh! That's very strange," the dialoguer continued. "Do you perhaps recall how a young Nathaniel was once surprised when I saw him from afar under the fig tree while he was still beyond human view? Well, during the past hour or so, I have seen you too. I see you virtually 'bleeding yourself to death' in your pain. You're virtually lock-step with 'that man' in your own desperation. And, right now at least, you're struggling even to just keep hold of your right mind. No, I hardly see you clothed with my grace, my love, my forgiveness right at this moment.

Right now, could you possibly sing with appropriate gratitude, "Jesus, thy blood and righteousness my beauty are, my glorious dress; 'midst flaming worlds in these arrayed, with joy shall I life up my head?' That's hardly the settled joy you're experiencing right now, is it?"

I want you to see, my dear one, that your *outer* garments, much like your *inner* defenses, are no more than the 'emperor's new clothes' before me. What I see here before me this moment is a person who is indeed precious to me, but who, at the very same time, seems to be so very exposed, so terribly raw, and so, so vulnerable! Am I close? Has what I've just said possibly described you?"

And, the wonderful Voice continued, "I also see you feeling very much alone in your misery. Where, I ask you, are those whom I've placed around you for support? Have you received enough lately of their loving attention and affirmation? It's there, you know. Perhaps they're just a bit tardy in expressing their deeply warm feelings toward you. Is it possible that, in the press of your work and ministry, lately you've been spending too much time away from those who love you most? Isn't it possible that you've been off wandering through your own 'burial tombs' for quite a while now?"

"'Burial tombs'? What 'burial tombs?'" I couldn't imagine what the Voice could possibly wish to convey to me by his morbidly colorful description.

At that, he laughed slightly: "You see, these 'burial tombs' are where life's demons take you—there, or perhaps to those heated deserts in your life, with their vast yawning nothingness and deadly loneliness.

And aren't you dealing perhaps with some of your own similar demons today? Oh, perhaps to you, your own demons seem like a bit nicer demons. But I assure that your demons are surely as tyrannizing to you now as they once were to this Gadarene standing before you in Scripture? Demons of pride. Demons of desire for recognition. Demons of longing to be great, rather than to be the gracious servant of all. Demons of chomping at the bit to move ahead even faster than I choose to lead you. Demons of selfishness and jealously and ambition. Aren't these the very same hellish forces ripping you apart right now?

And remember where the demons take you," my questioner pressed me. "Demons take you back to those same old burial tombs again and again. There you keep repeating over and over again the very same misery over and over, time, after time, after time. I ask you: Aren't you beat up enough already? So, here's what I suggest. Just walk away free. Walk away toward *me*!" Immediately I began to experience a strange two-step process of wounding—and healing—a process I could only attribute to God himself.

All of my life now lay spread out before me in bold relief. As if now glimpsing myself in the mirror, I saw flashed before me the depth of my brokenness. My flimsy attempts to cover up before God. My desperation born of hopelessness. My hurtful tendency to withdraw from others. My sick need to repeat the painful patterns of the past by strangely continuing to hurt myself in the present. My dark, hidden side. And when my shock dissipated, I quickly discovered that I really didn't look very much different than that Gadarene from whom I was now recoiling in such disgust.

Fortunately in that moment I also saw mirrored something more, something full of pure beauty—the outstretched arms of my Savior!

With eyes of love he now smiled at me with a wee twinkle. And he seemed to offer me the glorious possibility of being set free by his grace, and then of walking joyfully and expectantly into an unencumbered future. This second picture became equally clear, and far more compelling.

My whole being began to tremble, with a mixture of horror and excitement. And when I could finally open my mouth again, I blurted out an odd mixture of shame and joy, of relief and gratitude. "Lord, I'm so sorry I have behaved the way I have! I am so sorry! So very sorry!" And at the same time, my eyes fell on that same Scripture passage I was reading: "Jesus, Son of God, don't punish me!" the Gadarene had cried out that day in his similar desperation. So we were not really so very different after all. Both of us urgently pleading for God's loving grace. Both of us, unexpectedly encountering Jesus on the road of life. And, of course, when dear Jesus draws near, all things can become new!

I later read, and re-read, this same story again. How ironic. This deranged Gadarene was at least the sanest one of his buddies that day, at least in the sense that his other unstable friends had fled before they could be fully touched. So the Gadarene alone finally grasped Jesus's own holiness, and his own uncleanness by comparison. And, because this Gadarene fully came to encounter Jesus for himself that day, this once wild-eyed maniac became truly transformed. Now sitting in wonder and freed of his demons, here he was for all to see, fully re-clothed, back in his right mind once again, and sitting peacefully and with restored dignity at the very foot of his Lord whom he loved.

Thus, as this biblical narrative concludes, the crowd somehow disappears. Jesus's disciples somehow disappear. And this dramatic story seems to end with the spotlight focused on just two people: Jesus, and this Gadarene. And yet, not so! You see, here in Minneapolis, some two thousand years later, this same story suddenly leaps from the printed page and back into human life once again. Ah, but this time the ending is revised. Now the curtain closes on three people: Jesus, the Gadarene—and me! The story of this very man I once so despised had somehow now become my very own.

Admittedly my story is strange enough that I've hesitated sharing it. But have you opened up the pages of the Bible lately? Surely my personal account is no stranger than what happened in the day-to-day pilgrimages of Abraham or Jacob or Moses, or a whole variety of less notable folk detailed in the Bible.

What I began to grasp for myself that day in Minneapolis is the incredible power coiled up in our Scriptures. Since that day long ago, I can no longer count on the text remaining safely there on the page. Now I know that, at any time, The Book can again reach out and grab me today. Its timeless message can zoom effortlessly through the all intervening centuries and cultures and languages to thrust its faithful mirror right before my very own eyes, so that what I see now revealed there is as fully pointing to me today as it once pointed to that ancient Gadarene.

So vivid, so powerful was this moment of seeing myself portrayed in Scripture that I could hardly wait to read more. If I could possibly see myself reflected in such an unlikely face as that of the Gadarene, then surely for me to come alongside other characters of the Bible would be so much easier by comparison.

It was as if I were reading the Bible for the very first time. I allowed myself to journey back through biblical days from Genesis to Revelation. I trudged right along in the weary footsteps of those who unexpectedly encountered God centuries ago. I began to join my own self with other 'selves' in ancient times who turned out to be far more like me than I had ever imagined. Now, as I dared to identify myself as completely as possible with the men and women of the Bible's pages, entire new vistas of understanding opened themselves up to me. I discovered God mirrored in fresh and exquisitely beautiful ways. And in the stories of those needy people long ago, I saw myself again and again. As you may imagine, I began to love the Scriptures as never before.

And then came yet another discovery. While Minneapolis had initially taught me the crucial role of the biblical story as a mirror for my growth, now a second key element began to emerge from that same experience, the incisive role of **God's Great Questions** that he places before you, before me.

"What do *you* think of this passage?" the mild and intriguing question had come to me that special day. So I now began to wonder: Is this one-time experience of mine at all normal? Or, might I possibly expect it to be repeated? I'm asking: Is the God we find revealed in Scripture long ago really in the habit of still addressing questions to people like me today?

Back to Scripture I headed, starting at the beginning. And what did I discover to be the very first recorded message of God to the human race after Adam's fall? While our brother Adam cowered in broken despair in the Garden of Eden, alienated from himself, from his helpmate, from his Creator, this loving God of ours took the initiative. In a dramatic move that has somehow ceased to shock us, the eternal God of all the universes then steps down from his Throne in heaven to search out his erring creature. And what does God choose to say to the errant one? In soft words brimming with invitation to begin dialogue, he simply asks Adam a question:

"ADAM, WHERE ARE YOU?"

"Adam, where are you hiding? Adam, what has gone wrong? Adam, why are you so far away from me? Adam, what is happening inside of you right now? Adam, please start speaking to me again. Adam, let me help you deal with your brokenness. Adam, where 'the heck' are you?"

Thus begins the never-ending history of conversations between God and those whose fellowship he seeks. From Genesis to Revelation and beyond, punctuating the history of the people of God, his profound questions continue to come at crucial moments, confronting the lives of some of his favorite people, people much like you and me.

Unannounced, these amazing questions came unbidden to ancient fathers like Adam, Cain, Abraham, and Jacob. To nation-builders like Moses and Joshua. To kings like David and Solomon. To prophets like Elijah, Jonah and Ezekiel. To an honest struggler like Job. To a woman like Martha. To a beloved disciple like Peter. To a persecuting zealot like Saul of Tarsus. To ordinary men and women whose names don't even appear in Scripture but whose lives are changed dramatically as they seek to answer God's question addressed specifically to them. Question, after question, after knotty question! From our God who seems to delight in asking great, catalytic questions.

Does our God ask questions to gather some information he lacks, I ask? No! Our God is already "self-defined" as all-knowing. So his questions are hardly designed to benefit him. Rather his simple non-threatening questions are designed precisely to enable the growth process and joy of each of the man or woman he continues to address.

What kind of great questions does God ask?

Sometimes God asks us **Stoppers**: questions whose answers are so blatantly apparent that we mere mortals tend to overlook them. God's question to Moses is one of these: "Moses, who made your mouth?" It's really a question followed by both a question mark and an exclamation point: "Moses, who made your mouth?!" The implication follows: "Is it not I, the Lord?" Simply by stating this obvious question to Moses, God is helping nudge him back toward the center of the solid reality he already knows to be the case.

Then there are **Overwhelmers**: questions that startle us, that flood in upon us, questions that buffet us into wave after wave of confusion. They leave us acknowledging to ourselves how intensely frail we are as human beings in comparison with our infinite God. Nowhere is this kind of question more evident than in God's response to the knotty challenges from

Job: "Where were you when I made the earth out of nothing?" This single question by God then unlocks a whole torrent of unanswerable questions reading like a whole catalog listing of man's relative impotence and lack of understanding. His unending questions, then, jolt us (uncomfortably) back to the obvious realization that you and I are indeed God's created ones as we seek to relate to God, our Creator.

And then my favorite: God's **Probers**. These questions—if we choose to accept the assignment—challenge us to struggle with some nagging issue or problem inside us that simply refuses to go away. Perhaps its paradigm is the question asked by the God-man to Jacob as they wrestle together for hours for hours at the Jabbok River: "What is your name?" Obviously, since both God and Jacob already know Jacob's name, God is searching for a much deeper response from Jacob. Or take a New Testament example. Consider Jesus's question to Peter: "And you, who do you say that I am?" What a simple and neutral invitation for him to begin sorting through all of the information spread out before him, all he has seen of this wonder-worker, all of the ramifications of this one who speaks with authority, and then to help dear Peter formulate all of this data into his own emerging, succinct statement of faith in the Son of God.

Whatever the category, however, God's great questions probe the very deepest issues of our lives. Issues like: Who we are. Who we are 'with' our brother and sister. What to do with all the brokenness in the world and in ourselves. How we know what we know. Which things in our lives are really worth valuing. And does the Almighty God of the universe care about you and me as individual persons, valued persons? How best can I seek to relate to God, to others, even to ourselves?

These questions cause us to sort, to value, to choose. They're truly *great* questions—posed by God within time, but cast in light of all eternity.

In these great questions, people of old, and we today, encounter a graciously interfering God who, fortunately, refuses to turn away from the beloved creatures that he himself created. In good times and in bad, this Hound of Heaven still lovingly dogs our steps. Just when our joy and complacency feel most soothing, he persistently comes to knock on the door of our hearts. Just when we decide we most want to be alone, he comes faithfully to meddle in the deepest privacy of our lives. Just when we think our darkness is greatest, just when we feel most stuck, just when all else fails us, this relentless God of ours amazingly breaks into our earthbound world to bring us fresh light, fresh courage, fresh hope from above. Does anyone feel like shouting "Hallelujah?"

Why God chooses a question rather than a statement, I simply surmise from observing the process and the result.

By introducing a question God continues to affirm the right he grants us at creation to choose our own way. Like us nourishing human parents, our Heavenly Father quietly hovers around us to offer us alternative ways of dealing with the problems that continue to baffle us. His questions serve as well-conceived entry points into the tangled mazes of our broken lives today. His inquiries hardly assault us, yet they implant ideas that are pregnant with divine possibilities for our continual growth and joy. So, in his continuing relationship to us in eternal love, God simply grants us safe space in which to explore God's great questions to us. Then, whether we choose to wrestle with ourselves in God's presence or not, is up to us.

Our Great Questioner is the master of timing. Because ideas can lose their effectiveness, even perish, if introduced before their time, he sometimes interjects his catalytic question at the beginning of our struggle, sometimes toward the conclusion of our struggle, at whatever point sees us best positioned to grapple with the issues.

God's questions always seek to uncover our deepest wounds and ultimately to heal them. They are questions that probe the fundamental issues of our lives and elicit answers from deep inside us, as we wrestle with right ways of relating to God, to others, even to ourselves. They're incisive questions—yet also the gracious questions of a God who loves us very, very much!

By themselves, of course, God's questions to us contain no guarantee of fruitful harvest. They merely plant a suggestion, a seed, deep within us. But if and when this seed finds fertile soil in you and me, God then enables us to break through from where we once were, to what we can still become by his divine grace. Sometimes this sorting process is easy, sometimes fraught with anguish. Yet, through this unpredictable death-and-rebirth process, you and I eventually find ourselves blossoming into the amazing person we really are, the very person our loving God created us to be.

So, then, it's the transformed person who finally bursts forth from the struggle who then becomes the "answer" to God's great question. And ultimately, you and I will find ourselves answering not **just** a question after all, but answering the very person of our loving God!

God's great seminal questions! And God's stories-for-all-time bequeathed to us in the Bible. These two powerful forces now combine to form the purpose and the context of this book.

In these pages, you and I find ourselves walking in the very footprints of twelve colorful men and women of Scripture (eight from Old Testament times and four from the New) who, at make-or-break-times in their lives, heard and responded, to God's timeless questions.

Selecting these great questions God addressed to men and women was easy. The biblical text virtually did it for me. While the Old Testament contains more significantly deep questions from God to individuals—and the ones recorded are profound and universal—these ancient accounts generally paint vivid descriptions of the person who struggles with these questions. And, while God addressed his Old Testament questions primarily to men, Jesus breaks the pattern in the New Testament times by addressing his questions to both men and women. Regardless of the gender of the participant, however, I think you'll find each question and each unfolding story applicable to both women and men.

Each biblical writer here retains the biblical first-person story-telling format. A first-person narrative allows the characters of the Scripture to leap off the page in fresh new ways. "Story" has the added advantage of allowing our own theology today to settle into its proper true-to-life place in our journeys as well. While I have struggled to be faithful to both what is written and what is implied in the original text, I have allowed the context to permit me to speak through the silences of Scripture as well. You'll find this most obvious in the crucial stories of Adam and of The Woman Taken in Adultery, where the biblical storytelling is painfully sketchy.

If you were to ask me how to best approach this volume, I would offer some practical suggestions. Plan to read each chapter in one uninterrupted sitting, followed by a period of quiet meditation. Allow your imagination free reign to paint yourself right into the scene, amid all the dust, the dashed dreams, the derring-do. After reflection, it you find yourself bothered by some aspect of the story (or of the storytelling)—and even of you don't—then pick up your Bible and read the original again for yourself.

Most important, enjoy! Have fun! Laugh! Cry! Cheer! Boo! Who knows? While you're totally immersed in the action, perhaps with David of old, you, too, will hear that prophetic voice saying, "You are that man!

You are that woman!" And in that very moment, you may suddenly find yourself face-to-face not only with yourself, but also with God!

As you read, as you begin to hear God's questions to you, I encourage you to trust yourself fully to our living Lord who loves you beyond description.

II.

GOD'S GREAT QUESTION TO ADAM

"WHERE ARE YOU?"

A question of disclosure

GENESIS 2–5

My name is "Adam." Although you and I have not met personally, you know me. We are closely related, you and I, a kinship that saddens me to say, you often cannot celebrate.

The "black sheep" of the family, some label me. And perhaps I am. I've certainly had a lot to do with shaping our human family's dark and painful history. My hunch is that at times you've become irritated with me, perhaps even angry with me, for all the grief and destruction I have unwillingly unleashed upon humankind. I can understand those feelings, I assure you.

Much as I fear your rejection, however, I want you to know me better! There may be more to my story than you've really heard before.

As I unfold my sorry tale, I encourage you to listen both with your mind and with your heart. I will try to bridge the gulf between your experience and mine as much as I can. And I urge you to stretch as far as you can toward me too.

At the outset I can tell you that, at the same time I was experiencing the excruciating pain of fallen Paradise, I was also beginning to uncover an incredible surprise!

My turn-around came because of one GREAT QUESTION that challenged me with gentleness, yet with transforming power, just when I needed it most! It was a question designed to uncover my deepest pain and to heal my deepest wound. Even now, that life-changing moment is fresh as this morning's dew. And this is what I want to share with you.

∼

On that day, we were walking and talking in the Garden with God-Friend, as we always did. When I say "we," of course I am including the Other-Adam whom I call "Eve." She's my helper. God-Friend brought here to me as a special helpmate.

I can't begin to describe to you how much these daily conversations with our God-Friend meant. He was everything to us! Each new morning we awoke with expectancy, eagerly awaiting his visit, confident he will fill our hearts afresh with great joy and excitement.

In those early days, I don't think we had much of a clue about who he was or what he was. All we knew most surely was that this 'God-Friend' was the one who introduced us to the world. It was he who hovered over us, breathing life into us, when we first awoke to the sky and earth and each other! I suppose that in some sense we understood him to be our mother and father, our Creator. And this knowledge was more than enough for us.

Each day we grew in our experience of him.

Just being with him and hearing the sound of his voice suddenly brought such depth and value into our lives, brought new insights we never could have expected, brought bursts of feeling-beyond-feeling and understanding-beyond-understanding that kept on expanding our world!

Our eyes began to widen at the lavishness of creation. Our ears began to reverberate with sounds brimming with purity, resonance, and rich timbre. Our hearts began to surge with strange new emotions welling up from the ocean depths of our souls.

How I wish I could express to you the inexpressible! I long for you to imagine yourself in our stead, to see what we saw, to feel what we felt, to place yourself amid our blissful confusion. I long for you to experience our joy and wonder as we glimpsed the cup of life brimming full before us, spilling over with wave after wave of blessing.

Most of all, I long for you to see our glorious God-Friend as we knew him. He was our source of everything. He was our fount of life, of knowledge, of truth, of beauty, of wisdom. He was our light and warmth. Sunrise.

Sunshine. Sunset. He was all powerful, yet all gentle. His unfailing arms encompassed everything in our lives.

Best of all, he was always with us! On that, we could place our full trust.

Oh, I can't begin to describe for you how naive Eve and I were when God-Friend first breathed life into us! Everything was so impossibly "new." So utterly baffling. It was if we had burst in upon some hitherto unknown scene as full-blown adults without any prior conditioning. We had nowhere to turn for reference. We had no personal history, no nourishing parents, no siblings, no childhood, no "others," not even any childish learning. We had no human history to which we could look for our assumptions. We had no divine history of the person and activity of our God-Friend. We could find nothing against which to compare our experience in this strange new world all spread out before us as a blank page. "I am, you are, he is"—at first, that's about all we knew!

Take just one simple example. Can you picture the puzzled look on my face when God-Friend brought the first animal to me? "What's this?" I asked him. "Oh, you'll discover that later. But for now you can begin by giving it a name!" "And what's a name?" I asked. And on it went! And on, and on!

Even from our creation, however, there was one thing that Eve and I did seem to grasp. We knew that in some ways we were different from God-Friend. He was obviously so much greater than we were! At the same time, we sensed that in many ways we were similar to him. When we questioned him about it, he just teased us: "Of course I fashioned you to be like me, because I **like** me. So I could think of no finer image!"

And he was right. His image was indeed perfect; it was perfectly in balance. As Eve and I stumbled through our daily tasks, we found that we admired him more and more. And we began to discover increasingly that the deep longing of our hearts was to be just like him!

Now such a desire doesn't sound so terrible, does it? Isn't that what you want, too? Don't you love and admire God so much that you want to become more and more like him?

So, after God-Friend disappeared from our sight, the Other Adam and I got to discussing in earnest: "How can we become more like him?" we dared to wonder.

GOD'S GREAT QUESTION TO ADAM

Not an easy question. It was one we kept intending to ask our God-Friend. But somehow each time he came to us, we seemed to forget about everything else but him!

Finally Eve suggested a way out of our impasse. "I have an idea. Yesterday I met the most beautiful Serpent-creature. He sounds as if he too has met God and has talked with him. Perhaps he will know the answer to our question. I think I'll go talk to him."

Hardly had these words escaped her mouth than she dashed off and disappeared. I barely noticed. I was still deep in thought, pondering how we could possibly grow to be more like God-Friend. So while I awaited her return, I continued to sit with my thoughts all a-whirr and with my back propped up against a tree.

∽

The Other Adam hadn't been around when God-Friend had warned me about the forbidden "Tree" in the center of the Garden. Of course, I was quick to warn Eve about what he had said. And since we agreed that our God-Friend was all wise, we both vowed we would never eat the forbidden fruit. Never!

But, as folk like you have since discovered, over the years since then that "there's many a slip 'twixt the cup and the lip.'

Apparently this Serpent proved strangely clever. He was as persuasive as the devil. He seemed to intuit just how much Eve and I longed to be more like God. So he assured Eve that, at the very moment we ate the forbidden fruit, we would "become as gods, knowing right from wrong." Well. What an exciting prospect!

Then the Serpent planted a troubling thought in our minds. Perhaps God-Friend was trying to withhold this good thing from us. Was that true? Could that possibly be?

There was only one way to find out. And you guessed it!

Eve came back juggling two pieces of the forbidden fruit. She tossed one to me. And without batting an eye, she began to munch on the other.

For a moment I watched her, stifling faint feelings of apprehension. But nothing bad seemed to happen to Eve. So I stuffed an apple into my mouth, too.

"Isn't this food delicious?" we blurted out at the same time. And that was true. Never had anything tasted so good. So we began to revel in our secret discovery.

Just then, I became startled by the shadow of the Serpent that loomed up behind me, so startled that I dropped the precious fruit. But when I whirled around to see, however, I was mystified! I saw nothing there. Dumbfounded, I shook my head in confusion.

Still stunned, I instinctively reached down to the ground where the fruit had fallen. Alas, the dust of the earth had already etched the marks of my teeth onto the forbidden food. Already it was turning brown. Oh well! I found I didn't want more anyway.

For a fleeting moment, I reflected on what we had done. We had eaten what God-Friend had told us not to eat. And soon I also began to wonder. What would happen now? I shuddered to think.

And had the forbidden fruit now made us wise? Oh, I didn't think I felt any wiser yet. But I guess I really didn't know. How would one know? And this doubt made me uneasy. Very, very uneasy!

Puzzled, I gradually shifted my gaze back to Eve. Hm. Somehow she looked more tired, worn, wrinkled. Her usually lustrous long hair appeared dull and frazzled. I was perplexed. What had gone wrong with my eyes, I wondered. I'd never seen her like that. Always before she had looked so perfect, so radiant—much like our Friend.

"And what ugly feet she has!" I mused as I took a long, objective look at her. "How strange that I've never noticed them before." For the first time, I felt strangely critical of her.

"And her body! Oh my God, what has happened? In spots her body looks so stretched out of shape. I still like it very much—and yet I don't like it, I think. I'm confused. I'm feeling so torn!" Then, suddenly I heard myself gasp. And immediately I turned my face the other way. But by then, I couldn't resist the urge to sneak another peek at her again. Back, and forth! Back, and forth! I felt divided! And I didn't even know which part of myself to hold onto.

Eve must have observed all of my reactions because she suddenly flung her arms across her body, screamed, and dived pell-mell into the nearest clump of bushes.

"Oh, perhaps she's playing tag with me," I mused. She and I often played tag. She'd tease me by running away. Ah, but I always knew what she wanted. More than anything she just wanted me to chase after her, to catch her, and to hold her close. What glorious joy we experienced!

"Eve? Eve?" I cried out for her with a desperation I had not felt before. I wanted to throw myself after her. At the same time, however, I felt pulled back by invisible cords that paralyzed me. All I could do was to call to her. "Eve?"

As the plaintive echo of my voice drifted away, I experienced a dreadful and ominous silence. I could hear nothing. I could see nothing. Only a slight ripple in the bushes gave any hint that the Other Adam still existed. "Eve?" "Eve?"

With all the courage I could muster, I ventured forward. One foot. Then the other foot. I could hardly understand myself! Why was I so timid? Why so obviously fearful? I'd never felt anything like this before. I loved her, yes. I wanted to go to her, yes. And I was still a strong man. So how could I explain my sudden hesitation?

Even my two steps of approach toward the bushes, toward her, apparently caused her to become frightened.

Oh, what a screech she let out! The terror in her voice stopped me dead in my tracks. What a strange new sound! But I could hardly be confused about its message. Her voice had communicated volumes!

"Adam, don't you dare approach one step farther! And don't you ever look that way at me again! You're no better. Just look at yourself!"

I glanced down.

With horror, I saw my skin blush blood-red . . . and my chest, arms, legs . . . everything. Red all over, everywhere I looked. All over I was gloose bumps and bruises. I didn't remember ever seeing these before. Had they always been there? If so, why hadn't I ever noticed them? And if not, why were they here now? But all of life's crucial "whys-and -whens-and-hows" didn't seem to matter much at this moment! More than everything else right now, I realized that I just didn't want Eve to see me like this! At this sudden realization, I remember burning hot. I could feel my skin breaking out in funny patches of water like dewdrops. In my panic and embarrassment, everything around me grew dark. My head began to swim. I felt strangely unsteady, disoriented, fearing as if I might fall to the ground at any minute. I guess I staggered just a bit.

Amused at my oversized reaction, Eve let out a huge laugh. She laughed! She laughed! Damn her! She had no right to laugh at me in my hour of agony!

She and I had laughed a lot together. That's one of the things we enjoyed most. But this strange new laughter felt very different. Eve was laughing. I was not. She was mocking me. I felt humiliated. And I felt . . . so very much alone.

Wounded by her cruel derision, I too turned and fled.

What an odd turn of events, I reflected. What had just happened? What had so quickly gone wrong? Why were we both feeling so undone? And, whatever the reason, how could I possibly remedy this strange uneasiness?

How long my numbed confusion lasted, I don't know. But for some period of time it paralyzed me into silence.

After a while, however, I began to look around creatively. How to solve my problem? I discarded this idea and that. Then I mused: "Why don't I pick the largest leaves I can find and fasten them together for a covering?" A splendid solution. And quickly accomplished.

Gloriously garbed in my new leaves, I strode back to find Eve.

To my amazement, I found her, also clothed in fig leaves! I laughed, like our first laughter. "Yes, we're a lot alike, like two sides of the same coin," I grudgingly realized. And just this thought of our emerging "alikeness" gave me some hint of hope for reconciliation.

Yet, it was so obvious that something was no longer the same between us.

What was different? I wasn't sure. No, it wasn't our new 'clothes.' No, it wasn't the fading aura that used to surround the Other Adam. It was more a brand-new awkwardness that couldn't be explained and that couldn't be bridged! For the first time in my life, I felt lonely. Very lonely. And very much undone.

~

While I didn't yet understand, I still knew that something within me had turned bitterly sour. Something within me felt terribly upended. Something seemed to have knocked me terribly "off center." Something had marred the perfection I had felt in Paradise. And worse! Something had wrenched apart our closes relationship.

Inside me, I felt a strange void that I've come to call an "ache," an inconsolable wound. "No fig leaf could possibly cover ever that," I concluded. Was there anything I could do about it? Anything? Absolutely nothing came to mind. Utter despair began to creep all over me! What could I do? What?

Worn out by trying to cope with so many strange new feelings, I lay down to sleep, to bury my growing pains. But at mid-day, sleep refused to come. I felt totally miserable. I couldn't figure out what had gone wrong? I needed to talk with someone, a friend. But who? Eve? No, I couldn't. Not yet anyway. And the Serpent? No, never again to him. Why, he'd already crossed-up our lives enough. There was left only one other!

Perhaps I could talk to God-Friend? Oh NO! Certainly not to him.

And why not to him? Because. Because God-Friend had told us not to eat the fruit. And we had done it anyway. And it was 'wrong.' Wrong? Oh! Did this mean that I now knew the difference between right and wrong? I shrank back in terror. I was afraid I already knew the dreadful answer.

As I continued to ponder my painful plight, I must have fallen off to sleep at last. In my dream, I recalled how pleasant life used to be in the Garden of Eden. I pictured that day when God-Friend first brought the Other Adam to me. What delight I had felt! "YES, YES! At last this is bone of my bone and flesh of my flesh!" I cried with delight that day. Oh, what joy we both knew. But so soon the dark shadow of the Serpent stole across the brilliant scene of my dream and, with the Serpent's presence, the light suddenly receded.

I stirred. Just a dream. Alas! I had so hoped!

In my stupor, I drifted off again. But this second time my dream found me hiding in the Garden where I thought I heard the voice of God-Friend calling out: "Adam? Where are you?"

Even in my dream I remember realizing that this was a funny thought. Didn't God-Friend know everything? If he's omniscient, all-knowing, why wouldn't he know where I am? Why? Oh, whatever! On with the dream. In my dream I saw God-Friend suddenly turn angry. Instead of being my friend, I saw him suddenly as my accuser. Never before had I heard such bellowing and scolding tones from him. "ADAM! ADAM! ADAM!"

I sat bolt upright, my heart pounding. A feeling of unbelievable dread gripped me so tightly I could not break loose.

"Adam," I tried to calm myself, "this isn't real! It's just another dream!" I lay back down with a relieved sigh. Whew! Such a terrible scene would be the worst that could ever happen. I couldn't face an angry God-Friend. I couldn't!

From the hard ground, I lifted my eyes toward the trees towering above, the flowers surrounding me, the blades of grass just bursting forth from their seed coverings beneath the soil. And the sky! So blue by day. So clear by night. This night, with its myriad of twinkling lights stretching across the heavens now seemed to paint a giant mural declaring the story of its great Creator.

I became lost in wonder. Was it really true, as God-Friend had said, that all of this was his creation? How awesome. Incomprehensible. Frightening. Intimidating!

Oh, my! How infinitely small I felt. Why had God-Friend ever come down to speak with us in the first place? Why had he ever stooped to commune daily with such creatures of insignificance? And I had disappointed him!

The magnitude of what Eve and I had done was beginning to overwhelm me. We had failed to trust God-Friend, and that was wrong. We had chosen our own way instead. Yes, we now seeing the difference between right and wrong. Yes, we were now "wise"—but only wise enough to know we had chosen the wrong way. I felt horrible! And what would be the cost of our disobedience?

"The day you eat of the 'Tree of the Knowledge of Good and Evil' you will surely die!" God-Friend had told us. Oh! So, that apparently would be our punishment. To die.

What could it possibly mean "to die," I wondered. As you can guess, a rush of unfamiliar images and feelings coursed through me. I can't quite recall what I understood at the time. But I was feeling something roughly like this:

Was "dying" to stand forever like trees stripped bare of all leaves?

Was "dying" to fall like fruit from a branch to the earth below, to rot, to be eaten by worms, to disintegrate little by little, merging with the dust from which God-Friend had made me in the first place?

Was "dying" to feel smothered, crushed, gasping for enough air to breathe? Like drowning? Or like what I'd discover later was "crucifixion", when one finally runs out of energy to gasp for enough air to refill the lungs for just one moment more?

Or was "dying" more like being cut off from all that is most meaningful—from God-Friend—from the Other Adam—even from one's own self?

Perhaps all this, and more! With overwhelming thoughts akin to these, even then I remember feeling my life begin to ebb away, with all of the energy, the joy, the eagerness to arise for work in the morning, the excitement of walking and talking with—and, most of all, with our God-Friend!

My deep ache. My inconsolable wound. My utter despair. All of this tumbled over me now, knocking me this way and that, buffeting me in dizzying confusion, pounding me into puny insignificance.

Sorrow. Anxiety. Grief. Agony. I felt them all.

Was this "understanding?" Was this "wisdom?" If so, how could I possibly give them back? Now that Eve and I had shattered our blissful innocence, how could we broken people ever be made whole again? And would I ever again be able to break loose from the dark night invading my soul?

Somewhere amid all my sorrow and despair, I finally came to a devastating conclusion: Today, for the first time, God-Friend will not come to the Garden! How can he come now? I have driven him away. I have spoiled it all. No, he'll never come back again!

For the first time, I felt a drop of water burst forth from my eye. Then another. Then stream upon stream. I couldn't stop the torrent of tears, nor did I want to. Unashamed, I poured out my sorrow—all alone.

"No, he won't come now," I could be sure of that! Oh, some small part of me was relieved. On the one hand, I would escape his wrath. But this was hardly the whole story. On the other hand, I would forever escape the presence of God-Friend! And that was too unthinkable a loss!

Dejected, I didn't know what to do. So, I slumped down to retreat into merciful sleep.

~

"ADAM? ADAM?" Somehow the tone didn't quite fit the horror of my nightmare. Another dream? No, this time it sounded more like a real voice. And this real voice issued forth a startling question:

"ADAM ... WHERE ARE YOU?"

This time I was sure I'd heard the voice clearly. Oh my God, he's here! He has come. Oh, no! I can't let him see me. I scrambled for cover.

Like a cornered animal, I plunged headlong into the nearest clump of bushes. As I did, I amazingly felt something familiar. And I encountered a familiar pair of eyes. "Oh, Eve! He has come. He's calling for you and for me. I'm so glad we can meet him together. Now neither of us has to face him alone.."

We bundled together closely, each trying to hold our breath. If only we could stop trembling. Surely if the leaves rippled around us, that would give away our safe hiding place.

"ADAM ... WHERE ARE YOU?"

Again the voice thundered. Awesome! Commanding. And Hopeful?

Was I mistaken, or did this Almighty voice perhaps have an inflection of invitation? It certainly wasn't the harsh voice of my dreams. I hardly dared believe it, but could this really be the offer of our God-Friend to continue conversing with his erring creation? Could some meager hope return to my soul at last? You'll never know how very much I wanted to believe that!

Although the voice of God-Friend wasn't far off, Eve and I remained quite safe by hiding in the bushes. Where was Adam? Covered-up. Distant enough to escape God's notice for the moment. That's where Adam was. And that's where Adam wanted to remain. Well, at least I thought so.

But in the dreadful silence, I began to recall all the blissful days when Eve used to run away from me when we used to play tag. And just like her then, I began to realize that this is what I most desperately wanted right now. I most wanted to be caught and held close by God-Friend. I feared, however, that surely this was no longer possible. Surely not after what we had done. Surely not with such a wide gulf separating "the fallen two" from their beautiful God-Friend.

His tone was firm and unbending, I could hear that. But it also held some tenderness, I believed. Or? Or was this just my wild hope?

This was my moment of decision. I could delay no more.

"Right—and wrong," I mused. I'm supposed now to know the difference. So, what is right? And, perhaps more importantly, what do I want most?

"ADAM... WHERE ARE YOU?"

Where? Still within a stone's throw of him—yet so terribly far away. Lost in a distance of my own making. Distant from him. Distant from Eve. Distant from myself. And I couldn't seem to do anything about it. I had suddenly even forgotten how to reveal myself.

But as I pondered my plight, I discovered an amazing truth. God-Friend's penetrating question had already placed its probe into my deep wound. This Holy One searched until he found my core, and was even now lancing its poison. With such perfect tenderness, he reached into my broken heart, seeking to bring me the renewed healing I so desperately needed.

To God-Friend's utter graciousness, I simply had to respond. I had to disclose myself to him, and then to trust myself to him, no matter what!

And so—startling even myself—I suddenly heard myself cry out in a loud, plaintive voice,

GOD'S GREAT QUESTION TO ADAM

"HERE I AM! HERE I AM!"

Grabbing Eve tightly by the hand, I bounded to my feet. Together we barreled our way through the bushes separating us from God-Friend. At last I was willing to reveal myself. And oh, how very good it felt!

Of course, as you can imagine, I still felt a bit afraid and confused. I didn't know what to expect from him as a result of my sin. But my mind became fixed on one thing and one thing alone, our God-Friend. I was so grateful he had come back! Even now, the process of my disclosure was working its way closer to the surface.

From God-Friend now came the second part of his question:

"YOU TWO ADAMS. WHAT HAVE YOU DONE?" (As if he didn't know.)

My words now began to rush out frantically, tumbling over each another. I suppose even then I realized how much I appreciated his great questions to us. Gentle . . . yet incisive. Easy enough to hear, yet hard enough to cut to the very heart of our problem. What gracious invitations to conversation they were! How else could I, could we, begin our confession? How else could I dare to uncover the hidden wound of my brokenness?

If you thought Eve and I had made a disaster of things before, you should have seen us now. Not a pretty sight!

Confession wasn't something we ever needed to do before. And we didn't do it well. I found it awkward. Baffling. Humiliating. Piercing through to my heart. I didn't dare look up. I didn't want to risk looking into her eyes—or worse, into HIS.

Eve and I began first by "hiding in the bushes" of our verbal cover up! We both began talking at the same time, loudly and wildly. Accusing each other. Even blaming God, can you believe it? In this ugly process, we pointed our fingers and flailed around so violently that the seams of our fig leaves finally burst apart. Our makeshift clothing of leaves drooped, then finally dropped to the ground. Finally we were undone. Totally undone! Nothing remained hidden any longer.

God-Friend let us stand before him in stark silence for a few terrible moments that seemed like an eternity.

We felt thoroughly revealed in the presence of our Friend. Alone. Uncovered. Hidden and distant no more. But after a moment, my embarrassment faded. I felt a strange sense of peace once again.

Finally I dared to look up at him. Oh, what pain etched his face! But he nodded to me. And the faint smile I had so much hoped for now enabled me to feel safe with him again—no matter what!

"WHERE WERE YOU, ADAM? WHAT DID YOU DO THAT CAUSED YOU TO HIDE FROM ME?"

"I was afraid. And that's why I hid from you, God-Friend," I finally admitted honestly. Then I realized that that this didn't explain at all what had caused me to be afraid of him. So I added, "I was driven to my desperate act of hiding because I didn't trust you as I should. I also admit that I disobeyed you. Now everything is all broken! And I have broken it!" I sobbed and sobbed all my sorrow. My disclosure was complete.

As gravity causes objects to fall toward the earth, so our sin inexorably calls forth God's judgment. Now he has no other choice: we are the ones who have chosen badly. We had "wanted it all," but we'd given little thought to the price of our disobedience. By our actions, we were really condemning ourselves. So, he had caught us red-handed. It was about that simple, about that complex!

Quietly, almost sadly, God-Friend pronounced the judgment, the "death" he had promised. "Judgment One" was proclaimed upon the Serpent whose destiny it would be to slither and slide into the Final Judgment. "Judgment Two" was upon Eve who would bear her offspring in painful childbirth. And "Judgment Three" was on me. From now on, I would toil painfully against briars and thorns and weeds to eke out an existence outside of the Garden of Eden until the time when our physical bodies would wear out. Eve and I both nodded our heads in agreement. We had truly "fallen."

In one final protest to God's judgment the rebellious Serpent, however, again tried to raise his shadow, lifting himself as high as possible toward the sky. The earth grew dark as the slender form strained upward. But at the height of the Serpent's power, stronger arms seemed to reach outward from the vertical shadow, forming what looked like a Cross. And in that instant, the Serpent's shadow suddenly disappeared!

God-Friend sighed deeply. "Now, I must activate the other plan. Now I must send the Second Adam!" That was all I heard him say at first.

But after a long pause, God-Friend turned toward Eve and me, saying: "I will make you some sturdy clothes to last you during life's difficult pilgrimage."

GOD'S GREAT QUESTION TO ADAM

I looked down. Where the Serpent's shadow had appeared, I now saw what looked like an innocent animal lying very still upon the earth. From the little animal streamed a strange reddish liquid. This poured-out wine seemed to drain the very life from that innocent creature who now lay there wasted and motionless. I felt horrified and sad for his sacrifice. A sacrifice offered up for the sins committed by Eve and me.

From this animal's slain body, God-Friend now took the skin. With gentle hands, he fitted the covering close to my naked body. You'll never know how much the touch of God-Friend meant to me at that moment, after all the horrible hours of our separation. His hands felt caressing and healing. Comforting. Soothing. Like beginning all over. The touch of Heaven! The touch of our lovely God-Friend once again!

"I didn't think I'd ever have a chance to see you again," I whispered to him as he fitted the skin-clothes on me for my journey outward from the Garden. "But why? Tell me, why did you ever decide to come back?"

"It never occurred to me not to come!" came his candid reply. "You have now learned with sorrow what terrible consequences follow from sin. But as for me, my dear Adam, how could I ever forget the one whom I created first and whom I love so much? By the way, Adam, I never did leave you, you know. It was you who left me."

A bitter-sweet reply. A never-to-be-forgotten memory!

Through all the years I never stopped pondering, "What if God-Friend hadn't cared enough about us sinners to come back to us in the Garden? I shuddered to think. And what if, even when we insisted on hiding from him, he hadn't cared enough to ask us those exposing questions!" What a God-Friend! What mercy! What love he had shown us!

And what about our future? We didn't know. Of course we knew that we would no longer be able to live in Paradise. Life for us would surely be rugged, painful, exhausting. Our days were now numbered. Still, Eve and I agreed that we were indeed fortunate people. Though utterly undeserving, we had now experienced amazing grace and love from our God-Friend!

One truth we vowed to remember forever—He really did come back! Amazing! God-Friend came. *He came for us sinners!*

~

Outside the Garden, year after year drudged on for us. Years of toil and trouble as I struggled to subdue earth's tares and thorns, trying to fulfill my role as a faithful steward of God's wonderful creation. Years of tears and pain as Eve obeyed God's command to "be fruitful and multiply," giving birth to two sons, then to others.

With these boys of ours, we again experienced heartache. With these two, we again saw the Serpent's shadow. Once again there was hiding. Once again came broken relationships: with God, with a brother. Again, God came down. And again, he spoke a question designed to help the one who was hiding to begin to disclose himself:

> "CAIN, WHERE ARE YOU, AND WHERE IS YOUR BROTHER?"

So there we were again, mired in mistrust and disobedience. Abel, our fine herdsman, killed by his jealous brother. And Cain, our fine harvester, now banished—we didn't know where! I don't know of anything that can bless or grieve the heart of a parent as much as a child, born of our flesh, partakers of our image, copiers of our weaknesses. Our children, so much like us, yet with a life independently apart! Forever tugging at our soul. Forever locked to the deepest part of our being.

But no matter how dark our days, I'd turn to Eve and she'd know what I was thinking—"It's bearable. It's bearable because his grace will be sufficient for us. And I know this because he came to us! He came, even when we gave him every reason not to come. So at this very moment, how can he be far away?"

Eve grew older, as did I. This, too, was painful. To grow weaker. To lack zest. To misplace concentration. To mix up thoughts. To erase memories. To lose power over our faculties little by little, sometimes all at once.

Through it all, we found comfort together. Somehow we sensed the presence of God-Friend even more when we two Adams were enjoying each other. That's when his image seemed to shine most brightly in our midst.

Finally the day came when I sensed that my earthly days were numbered. I suppose it was foolish, but oh, how I wished that I could walk and talk with God-our Friend once more, just as we had back there in the Garden. How I wished that he could breathe fresh life into me once more, just as he had back when he first created me from the dust. But those days were long past, I knew.

As Eve cooled my fevered body with water, I knew my time neared. What would happen to her now, I wondered. I could see that it was a troubling thought for her too. In one final painful burst of energy, I reached up to kiss Eve's cheek and whisper in her ear:

"Don't worry, dear. Trust God-Friend. He said he had never even thought of leaving us. Surely he's here now, both for me and for you. And someday, perhaps the 'Second Adam' really will come. Then hopefully man will make a better choice. For this we must pray.

But for now, just keep remembering that He came. He came! Emmanuel—God with us!"

And with the word "Emmanuel" fresh on my lips, my dusty body returned to the dust from which God-Friend formed me. But my healed soul took effortless flight to the unblemished Garden of a world beyond. He had come once more for me! And once more, I dwelt with him in Paradise.

~

Well, my dear Friend, that's my story. Not one I'm proud of. Sin, by its nature, ultimately begets ugliness and sorrow, I'm afraid. Yet I discovered that simply by uncovering the painful reality of sin in his presence, I found his healing process begin.

While I've spoken a great deal about my own failure and pain, I'm sure you realize that 'my' story is more importantly about 'God-Friend'—the God who came to us while we were hiding in brokenness—the God whose questions uncovered how far our sin had driven us, yet how near he was to heal us and whose creative love found a way forward for us, together.

I've told you my story, my Friend, to help you know our God-Friend better. In the broken world I've bequeathed to you, it is he who can make all the difference!

If you find it difficult to imagine my relatively uncomplicated world, you can understand how difficult it is for me to imagine your complicated world as well.

For example:

- I can't imagine hiding from your neighbor behind locked doors and drawn curtains.
- I can't imagine hiding your real thoughts behind formalities and superficialities.
- I can better imagine your hiding in the midst of a family where your pain and frustration drives you farther and farther away from those created to be close to you.

- But what I have most difficulty imagining is being willing to hide (dare I say it?) even in lofty church buildings where you gather alongside other "respectable people" like yourself, concealing your deep wounds, disguising your doubts, covering up from God-Friend and from others the very needs for which you come to receive help.

I guess I'm still caught in my naiveté. But I admit to being amazed at the incredible distances you allow in your life. Distances with which you've apparently become quite comfortable!

Yet my hunch is that, like me, you really despise these distances. My hunch is that you probably long to bridge the gaps that wound you. And if that's true, I feel certain that you can relate to my paralyzing tension between wanting desperately to hide. and wanting desperately to be found. Found by God. Found by others. Found even by you.

So, have we discovered some common ground, you and I?

I realize that for you to see your own face in mine may well require a bit of a miracle. Nevertheless, I keep remembering that my name is Adam—"generic human being—a mirror reflecting universal humankind of any time and place.

And so, Adam of Today, it wouldn't seem too strange to me if, when you read my story, you hear a strange echoing in your heart. And I wonder if you possibly hear God asking the question of you too.

"ADAM OF TODAY, WHERE ARE YOU?"

Still a gentle question. Still a prying question. Still an invitation to begin conversing together. In any other voice, perhaps his question would be frightening. But not in his. I attest that his question can be the beginning of your wholeness!

As you grapple with his great questions for your life, perhaps you'll discover the same amazing truth I discovered. I found that when I finally ventured forth from my makeshift hiding place and into the exposing light of his presence, I was surprised to find in him the secure hiding place I'd always sought!

As the Psalmist of old expressed on my behalf, and yours:

> "Blessed is [the adam] whose transgressions are forgiven, whose sins are covered. Blessed is [the adam] whose sin the Lord does not count against him and in whose spirit is no deceit.

> When I kept silent, my bones wasted away through my groanings all day long. For day and night your hand was heavy upon me; my strength was sapped as in the heat of summer.
>
> Then I acknowledged my sin to you and did not cover up iniquity. I said, "I will confess my transgressions to the Lord"—and you forgave the guilt of my sin.
>
> Therefore, let everyone who is godly pray to you while you may be found; surely when the mighty waters rise, they will not reach him. *You* are my hiding place; you will protect me from trouble and surround me with songs of deliverance."
>
> (Psalm 32:1–7; original word inserted, and emphasis added)

Adam of Today, may this become your experience too. And may you continue to grow in grace and in the knowledge of our gracious God-Friend!

III.

GOD'S GREAT QUESTION TO JACOB

"WHAT IS YOUR NAME?"

A question of identity

GENESIS 32

I MUST BEGIN MY story at the ford of the Jabbok River east of the Jordan, opposite Shechem. It's a deep valley carved from rugged and tall limestone cliffs. Hardly could you imagine a more imposing setting for the greatest struggle of my life.

Dark forces had driven me here.

"Between a rock and a hard place!"—that's really the way I felt right then. Boxed in by mountains. Boxed in by enemies. No way out. Below sea level at the valley's bottom, it was so unlike anything I had ever before experienced. Here at the Jabbok River was in many ways the lowest spot in my life. I didn't know what to expect. Perhaps this was even the place where I would die. Still—whatever might transpire here—I knew this was my crucial moment!

∼

I now headed down from Asia Minor toward the land of Canaan, the land promised to Abraham and Isaac, indeed the very same land confirmed to me at Bethel years ago by the God of my Fathers.

MEETING ENEMY NUMBER ONE: UNCLE LABAN

Fleeing from the land of Haran far to the north, I was trying to escape from Uncle Laban. For twenty long years I had toiled to-the-bone for him. But just recently, my allotment of our joint flock had multiplied way out of proportion to his. We both noticed this. And this caused Uncle Laban's animosity toward me to intensify. And when I finally grasped the enormity of Laban's anger, I decided that my family must leave his household immediately, under cloak of secrecy.

So I packed up my entire household—Rachel and Leah (my two wives), their two maid servants, my eleven children, my men servants, as well as my large flocks—all of the vast bounty I had amassed during my twenty years of grueling labor for my deceitful uncle. And we set off to an unknown future.

In such a large caravan, I knew we'd be forced to travel slowly. So, even with a head start of three days, I wasn't too surprised when old Laban managed to overtake us. He arrived absolutely enraged. What an ugly confrontation we had! He and I exchanged terrible words. Laban even labeled me "deceitful", can you imagine that? Finally we agreed to an uneasy peace at "Mizpah." Our vow wasn't exactly a kindly benediction, as you use our words today. Rather it was our mutual warning that, even when we couldn't keep our own eyes peeled on the mistrusted other one, the Lord himself would surely continue to "watch between me and thee!"

Whether the Lord would actually watch, I didn't know. But I knew *I* would! As Laban turned back at last toward Haran, my eyes followed him as long as they possibly could. When he and his men finally disappeared over the horizon, I heaved a huge sigh of relief.

One enemy safely behind me! I could continue on toward my destination, the promised land of Canaan.

MEETING ENEMY NUMBER TWO: BROTHER ESAU

But now I faced an even worse problem—Esau! Still hanging over my head was the twenty-year-old feud with my twin brother, a feud still simmering between us. If I knew Esau at all, I knew that he would never, never forget his vow to kill me. No, rather than let go of his rage during all of the last two decades, I felt sure he would have nourished it even more. So, whenever we would finally meet again, I feared that our struggle would probably be to-the-death.

But I had no choice now. I had to continue my journey. If I were ever to claim God's promise, I must pass through the Jabbok Valley. And this route would take me dangerously close to the territory of Esau. I pondered and pondered my decision now to continue going forward. It was a bold, dangerous move, I realized. Yet for me, I could see no other route to the blessings of Canaan, except by going through my brother Esau's land.

In spite of my looming fears, I concluded that I could no longer avoid my angry brother. After twenty long years, we would have to meet again. I hated to even imagine what our encounter would be like. As I paused to think further, all sorts of terrifying prospects came to mind. "Think hard, Jacob," I counselled myself. "Take time to craft your plan extremely carefully."

Eventually I decided that, rather than risk being ambushed by Esau, I must take the offensive. So I sent my servants ahead of me to Esau with word from me that "I have been staying with Laban and am now returning with a message to 'my lord Esau' so that I might find favor in his eyes." That's a good opener, I calculatedly laughed to myself.

But when my messengers returned, they told me that Esau was already on his way toward me. And not only Esau! With him were four hundred men. With this news, I became frantic. I now must fumble to piece together a new strategy to replace the one that had already failed.

My only solution, I thought, was to divide my family and my herds into two separate groups. So, if Esau's men attacked one of them, then perhaps the other group could escape. At least this way, I would save part of my family and part of my wealth.

But even this plan did not ease my paralyzing distress.

So I began to pray. (See my new strategy?) And I prayed something quite foreign to my nature, something that I'd never heard myself say before:

> "O God of my father Abraham, God of my father Isaac, O Lord who said to me, 'Go back to your country and your relatives, and I will make you prosper,' I am unworthy of all the kindness and faithfulness you have shown your servant! I had only my staff when I crossed this Jordan, but now I have become two groups. Save me, I pray, from the hand of my brother Esau, for I am afraid he will come and attack me, and also the mothers with their children. But you have already said, 'I will surely make you prosper

and will make your descendants like the sand of the sea, which cannot be counted.'"

(Genesis 32:9–12; NIV, emphasis added)

You see, for me to use words like "unworthy" and "afraid" and "save me" was utterly alien to my usual personality. Those are hardly normal words of Jacob! Yet faced with my growing fear of Esau, I prayed them—and I meant them. And I added "just a wee reminder of God's earlier promises to me."

On the other hand, why rely on such a prayer? Why rely solely upon God? Why assume that God would do for me what I could be doing for myself? So, since I had always prided myself on my cleverness, I now devised yet another plan to appease my angry brother.

In growing desperation, I decided to send much of my wealth to Esau as a present. Hopefully, my extravagance would purchase his goodwill. First, two hundred female goats and twenty male goats. Then two hundred ewes and twenty rams. Thirty female camels with their young. Forty cows and ten bulls. And twenty female donkeys and ten male donkeys.

I put each flock in the care of a different herdsman. To each herdsman, I gave specific instructions: "You go on ahead of me. Keep some space between the herds. And as soon as you run into my brother Esau, just say, 'All of these belong to your servant Jacob. He is now sending all this as a gift to my Lord Esau—and Jacob is arriving behind us.'" I thought that humble words like "your servant" and "my lord" might appeal to my more religious twin. Esau preferred to be treated very specially.

So that night I took my wives, my sons, my possessions—all that I had—and I sent them across the stream of the Jabbok ahead of me.

I, Jacob, was left alone on the other side of the dark Valley.

Everything I owned was now gone! All my best schemes. All my facades. All my defenses. All the possessions that possessed me. I was utterly lonely and cold. Vulnerable. Frightened to death. Desperately awaiting some miracle to save me. Even more, I desperately needed renewal deep within me.

Somehow I managed to escape my fears by falling sound asleep.

MEETING THE "*MAN*" OF GOD SENT TO WRESTLE HIM

In the darkest part of the night, I suddenly awoke. Perhaps I was startled by a sound, or a light, or a touch. I can't quite remember. I felt dazed and groggy, yet somehow fully alert and physically energized at the same time.

Gradually I became aware that I was involved in some kind of intense struggle, a struggle I didn't quite understand but a struggle in which I instinctively felt totally compelled to prevail.

My struggle in this dream seemed to center on a "man" who was wrestling with me and trying to overpower me. He was stronger than any man I'd ever known. Who was he? Was he perhaps an angel? No, surely an angel would have been too strong and would have vanquished me within minutes. Whoever this "man" might be, somehow I must press my strength to the limit in this contest for power. On and on through the night's blackness we struggled. Hour after hour. Ache upon ache. Strain upon strain.

All of my years of striving and struggling seemed to have prepared me well for this one moment. I would not allow my adversary to conquer me! I stood my ground. I held my own. Strength for strength. Blow for blow. Strategy for strategy. No one, I vowed, not even God himself, would overpower me now.

As our contest quickened its intensity, I gradually began to understand that I was not wrestling with a mere man. Surely this could only be someone like God himself. Throughout this long struggle, I kept trying to piece together what was happening, and why this unknown wrestler kept on hounding me. All the while, I kept myself striving for dominance.

As daybreak approached, "the man of God" let loose a burst of energy. In one final move against me, he wrenched loose the socket of my hip. With that, I felt my power to maneuver suddenly sapped. Now all I could do was to keep on grasping him tightly, even though now he began begging me to let him go free.

But by then, I finally saw my chance for the 'blessing' I'd wanted since my birth. So, as I kept him pinned in my clutches, I said to him: "I will not let you go . . . unless you bless me!"

And then the strangest thing happened.

The "man of God" suddenly looked at me and asked me a very simple—and what seemed to me an irrelevant—question:

"WHAT IS YOUR NAME?"

I was confused! Obviously he knew my name. He'd been sent to wrestle with me. Why would he bother wrestling with some 'nobody,' with no name?

Gradually a cold chill began to surge through my body. I pondered again God's question to me: "What is your name?" he had asked me. Since this unknown "Man" probably already knew my name, he must have been sent by God to place his own question before me.

After a good deal of "wrestling" with my confusion, I gradually began to realize that, in fact this *"Man of God"* with whom I was presently wrestling physically was God himself! And after some time of reorienting myself I finally began to hear God's Great Question to me, Jacob. So, what was my God really asking of me?

> "Tell me who you really are, Jacob! Tell me about your true character, your true identity, and your character, Jacob, that devious character within you have never truly faced. Who are you deep inside, Jacob? What motivates and energizes you; what rules your life? Only when you admit to me your true identity, Jacob, can I ever truly bless you! Only then can I even begin to change you."

What a probing question! His question was obviously designed for my benefit, not his. So, now I must ponder carefully and then choose carefully my response. After much soul-searching, I was ready to admit my plight to God.

Even from my mother's womb, I had vied with my twin brother. Esau burst into the world just ahead of me on the day of our birth. So, born first, he inherited our father Isaac's blessing. Nonetheless, I kept on struggling with him to be born first. Alas, I could barely catch hold of my brother's foot as he was born ahead of me. Hence my parents named me "Jacob"—"grasping the heel," a term that implied forever that I was a "deceiver." My brother's name, "Esau," sounds like the Hebrew words for "red" and "hairy" (in our language sounding like "the land of Edom"), an odd fact which surprisingly gives a portent of his future.

Let me digress momentarily from what I was starting to tell God. I want you to know why God called me by name when he asked a question of me. You see, our names revealed much about us Hebrews. Our names reflected events and revealed prophesies. Our names, therefore, came to determine our own view of ourselves. This was true of the names of people. It was also true of the names of places as well. That's why I was so careful all through my life to choose appropriate names for the places where milestone-events happened to me, names such as "Beth-el" ("House, of God") that special place where I lay down that night twenty years ago when I first fled from Esau, where I saw the sacred ladder that stretched between earth and heaven. There at Bethel that night, God confirmed to me his same covenant promise to my Fathers: Abraham and Isaac.

Here at the Jabbok, I had already been named: Jacob, the deceiver, the one who "grasps."

Of course, many years had passed by now. And the question reminds me of my earlier name. And in the meantime, what was I, Jacob, to continue to pour into my "name" by all the things I was doing, both bad and good? So, indeed, what really is my "name" at this point? What is my true character? What is my identity (all the accumulated characteristics of my real person)? Who am I, deep down today at the very core of my being where I made my decisions?

Tough questions! Meddlesome questions. Painful questions. I wasn't even sure I really wanted to know the answers. Much less did I ever want to reveal them to this God-man.

I had much work to do. I must find tasks that "showed" who I was. So, I began to sift through my memories, starting by recalling days long past.

First I pictured the time back in my teens when Esau had come in from the hunt, absolutely famished. I had stayed home and had prepared a tasty stew. Its aroma drove my hungry brother out of his mind. With his first sniff, he began begging me for a bowlful before he "died of starvation." Of course, he was exaggerating. But I quickly saw my opportunity. So I held out. Esau and I bargained hard. I wouldn't give in. In the ensuing struggle, Esau finally agreed to sell me his own "birthright" in exchange for one bowl of pottage. What stupidity! That was Esau. And what cleverness. That's Jacob!

Then I remembered the day when my father, Isaac, was finally failing in health. Before our father would give his final blessing to his firstborn, Esau, he asked Esau to prepare for him a special meat stew one last time. My mother overheard the conversation. Since my mother had always preferred me to Esau, so she quickly called to me. "Hurry up, Jacob! You prepare some goat stew," she urged me. "Then, just as soon as it's done, take it in to your father. Pretend that you are Esau. Then see what happens." (With Isaac's failing eyesight, we figured, he probably wouldn't know the difference. And we were right.) I wore Esau's familiar woven robe, with some goatskin wrapped around my smooth hands and chest, and offered him the favorite stew. Those simple props were enough to fool an old man on that very important day.

And when my father asked me my name that day, how had I replied to him? I said, "Oh father, I am your son, your firstborn—I am Esau!" I lied to him. Why not? That's all I needed to do to steal my brother's final blessing.

You can imagine the loud ruckus when Esau returned from the hunt, prepared a second bowl of stew, approached our father, and knelt down for Isaac's blessing. I thought my twin brother was going to split apart when Isaac told him: "Oh my elder son, I thought you had already been here. It must have been your twin brother instead. Jacob has apparently come to me deceitfully and has fooled me. I'm sorry, Esau. Your younger brother has already taken the blessing which rightfully belonged to you! There's nothing more I can do for you now."

Esau became furious! And he nailed my true character that day. He cried out to my father: "Isn't my brother rightly called 'Jacob'? Two times now he has deceived me. He has already taken my birthright in exchange for a mess of pottage. And this day he's even stolen my blessing! He has usurped both parts of my inheritance. What a deceitful cheat! (Oh, Brother Esau probably had a few more choice words to say, but fortunately we choose not to repeat them here.)

Ah, why should they complain, Jacob reasoned? I came by my scheming and striving quite naturally. As in most families, we all schemed and strived against each other. Although my grandfather, Abraham, rose to great heights of faith, I recalled how he too had lied about Sarah being his wife. My father Isaac had lied about his wife too. My, what a forked-tongued group we were! But the greatest plotter of them all was my mother, Rebekah. She pulled many a string behind the scenes. I learned a lot from her, just as she had from her brother, Uncle Laban. But all that aside, I always cherished my craftiness. After all, hadn't it gotten me everything I wanted, both the birthright and now the blessing?

But alas, my unearned victories had their price. My grasping and my deceit exacted quite a cost. They had broken my most cherished relationships. My father. My brother. My uncle.

With Uncle Laban, my mother's brother, I almost met my match. He too was a schemer, a deceiver, a striver. He was a master of unwelcome surprises. After I agreed to work for him for seven years in exchange for Rachel as my wife, Laban had the nerve to switch wives on my wedding night. Oh, what a shock the next morning. I awoke to find Leah in my marriage bed instead of Rachel. That was just too much!

But I finally got back at Laban. I'm not sure whether the God of my Fathers showed me how to do it or whether I figured it out myself. But I discovered how to breed animals selectively. Now, Uncle Laban had already agreed to give me all of the speckled goats in his flock. So I simply mated the speckled goats with the solid colored ones, an obvious process that greatly increased the percentage of speckled goats and decreased the percentage of plain colored ones. Quite a trick! And quite legal. My flocks multiplied more rapidly than I could imagine. By amassing my own fortune at my old uncle's expense, I surely did turn the tables on him. Oh, but in the process, I somehow managed to inspire Laban's wrath.

And then there was my brother Esau. My dear brother. My brother who, even after twenty years to cool off, still wanted to even the score over the rightful blessings I had stolen from him in our youth. Just another broken relationship. In some ways, my estranged relationship with Esau was in fact the most painful one of all.

Broken relationships—this was the cruel legacy of my life to this point. This was what my cumulative deceit and striving had bought me. And suddenly this realization brought me up short. For all of my struggles to grasp the blessings of man and God, where, oh where, was the real happiness I sought?

How I began to envy my forefather, Adam, way back there in the elusive Garden of Eden. How complex our civilization had become since those early and blissfully simple days. Of course we no longer dressed in fig leaves and hid in bushes. But we had developed plenty of our own ingenious forms of hiding. Besides covering up our naked bodies, my society and I had become quite adept in hiding our real thoughts and motives—indeed in hiding from each other "who we really are." And by having so many family members scattered far and wide, I had found it fairly easy to run off and hide whenever I wanted to get away. From my father. From Esau. From Laban. Even from myself.

Surely, I reasoned, there was more to life than constantly running and scheming. Something must have gone wrong. Like my ancestor, Adam, I suspect that I too had allowed my various schemes to shift my insides off-center.

"WHAT IS YOUR NAME?
WHAT IS YOUR CHARACTER?

GOD'S GREAT QUESTION TO JACOB
WHAT IS YOUR TRUE IDENTITY?
WHO ULTIMATELY RULES YOUR LIFE?"

Awesome questions. Profound in implication. Pregnant with both despair and hope. I must give an answer to the 'man of God', before he too would agree to bless me.

~

I could see a gentle aura beginning to warm the eastern horizon. Day was breaking. Nighttime was nearing an end. I could afford to ponder no longer.

My spirit groaned. I could feel something within me struggling to die. Yet at the same time, something new was desperately struggling to be born.

For the very first time in my life I managed to look deep within me. I hated everything I saw. I hated my conflict and confusion. I hated my scheming and posturing. I hated my two-facedness. I hated my terrifying fear that my many sins would someday catch up with me. Perhaps they were even now. Perhaps right here at the Jabbok River!

Ah, but I saw something else as well. As I looked within, I saw that I was finally "naming" all of my annoyingly strongest traits—all of those devious traits that grown so large that they were flooding over me in waves. Despite the incredible pain which this self-disclosure brought me, I was beginning to discover discovering at long last that I could begin to face who I really am.

"What's your **name**, my son?" I realized that this was the same question my own father had asked me some twenty years before. That day, I had lied to him. Would I lie again? Surely not! I would hide my true identity no longer.

Finally, full of chagrin, I chose to answer the God-Man in a most straightforward manner that, up to this point, was completely out of character for me. So I introduced himself:

> Sir, my name is Jacob. "Jacob" , the schemer, the striver, the supplanter, the usurper, the struggler, the liar who struggled to prevail in my own way at whatever the cost.

To my enormous surprise, the God-Man smiled broadly when he heard my response. As he looked me straight in the eye, he didn't seem shocked at all.

"Jacob," he answered me, "you have answered rightly! You see, Jacob, all these years while you have been struggling so hard to obtain the blessings of God, I have been right here with you. All along, I have been waiting patiently to bless you. But how could I possibly bless you when you would not, when you could not, confess to me who you really are? Now, finally, you have the courage to acknowledge your true identity. Your confession is true. You are indeed Jacob!"

"Jacob", he continued, you have already received the first part of my blessing. You now most surely know your identity! And because you finally know who you really are, I can now begin to change you. From now on, you no longer need to be known as "Jacob, striving to prevail." In addition to giving you a new name, I will begin forming within your new person a "new character" and a "new identity." From this day forward, "Jacob shall prevail," you will indeed become known to all as "'Isra-el", meaning, "'God shall prevail!'

Whew! What a relief! What incredible peace. No longer did I need to run. No longer did I need to prevail. At last I could shout it aloud: "I am Jacob!" And now, by his mercy, I am truly "Israel—GOD shall prevail in me!"

How ironic. It was when I thought I was most undone, I received my greatest blessing. It was when I was most mixed up, that I was turned right-side up. Through all the long tunnels of my tangled life, without my knowing it, the Hound of Heaven had quietly pursued me. Now, when I was finally ready to turn around, I looked up and what did I see? I saw my God with arms outstretched, just waiting to hand me the very blessing I'd been running after so frantically all along.

At last I finally grasped that the covenant promise of the God of my Fathers would indeed continue, through me. From my new name, "Israel", God's own people would take their national family name. And even as I was establishing my own personal identity, I could also catch some glimpse of my offspring being the fledgling people of God who were just beginning to forge their national identity.

What blessings the God of my Fathers had given me! What more could anyone possibly ask? Right with God, at last I finally knew who I was. Now I was also ready to meet my brother. And the sun rose above a limping man as I set off to find Esau.

∼

Now all my scheming plans had to change. I myself would travel before my family and herds. I would be the first to meet Esau. I would walk on bravely right through Esau's land. I would face my angry brother head-on. And no matter what happened, I was fully ready to accept it from the hand of my sovereign God who had dealt with me so mercifully.

With head held high, I began to march forward. If I had looked down, I'd have observed the funny pattern I was creating in the dust. One strong footprint. One weak one. One strong. One weak. But not this time. New "Israel" hardly noticed. My hip's lop-sided gait was a bargain price to pay for putting old "Jacob" far behind me.

When I approached Esau, I bowed to the ground seven times toward my brother. And for the first time in my life, this gesture of mine was not part of some giant scheme. Finally I was real.

As I drew myself up to my standing position, what, glorious sight was mine. Running toward me strode my brother Esau, with arms flung open wide. He threw his hairy arms around my neck. And the big burly fellow kissed me. We wept in each other's embrace. My twin and I were one again. At long last!

All of this was so much more than I could have expected! So much more than I could have dreamed. God had prevailed! There was no doubt about it.

In a moment of exquisite shalom, I confessed to my dear brother from whom I had been estranged for twenty years: "Esau, for me to see your face is like seeing the face of God himself now that you have received me with such great favor."

Joy inexpressible, and full of glory!

∼

I'd prefer to leave my story at its highest point. But I can't give you the false impression that once I had finally faced myself, everything in my life suddenly became perfect for me. Nothing could be farther from the truth. Unfortunately sin's consequences often cast a wide circle of ripples. Adam bequeathed his brokenness to his sons. My family bequeathed their worst faults to me. And I too bequeathed my off-centeredness to my sons before I could break apart this tragic cycle in myself.

While I dearly loved each of the twelve sons who grew up in my household, I hardly grasped at the time that I should be preparing them to lead each of the twelve tribes of the children of Israel. Far from preparing them for such awesome future responsibilities, the childhood heritage I gave them more often served as a stumbling block for them instead. Hardly the sterling legacy I wished for them, you can be sure!

My own jealously of my brother, Esau, also became reflected in my sons' jealousy of their too-favored little brother, Joseph. And my own desire to usurp became reflected in my sons's plan to kill this brother who might someday "rule over them." My own scheming became reflected in my sons' secret sale of Joseph into slavery so that I, their father, would never discover my children's murderous intents. My older boys, much to my regret, learned to mirror my worst qualities all too well. They shared far too much in common with unredeemed 'Jacob.' What an unfortunate legacy of a father!

Oh, but just look at my son Joseph! Fortunately, he came along a bit later in my life. In him, I began to see the results of a few good seeds planted. Of course, he had picked up enough of my own self-flattery to enjoy flaunting his grandiose dreams as a young boy in front of his older brothers. Still, Joseph grew up absorbing far more of transformed "Israel" than of old "Jacob." I'd like to think that's why, when Joseph later ruled in Egypt, he could then graciously offer food to his scheming older brothers to prevent them from starving. And I'd like to think that perhaps he had learned a little from my own struggles, struggles about how to humble himself, to forgive another, and to show everyone mercy and love. Of course I dare not take credit for his emerging identity, his character. I can only hope that my God chose to multiply the good seeds from my 'redeemed days' that I planted in order to bring forth such a flower of humanity as my son Joseph.

In Joseph I could see that at least my weaknesses hadn't ruined everything around me.

Alas, the consequences of my sin didn't only affect my children's troubles. These consequences also continued to plague me for all my remaining days.

I was surprised to discover, however, that the limp I would carry through my lifetime from the disjointed hip would become my continual joy. It kept reminding me that, at the very moment when I thought I had "prevailed", I had been beautifully vanquished by God at my strongest point. My limp was now the outward symbol of a life that had been powerfully broken, only to be born anew.

Sometimes when I reflected on all the trouble I had made for myself and for others, I wondered why God had ever bothered with the likes of me. But he had! From the moment I confessed my real identity to him, he in love and mercy cast his very own identity in terms of me. Here's an example of what I mean:

GOD'S GREAT QUESTION TO JACOB

Throughout Scriptures (the record of God's divine self-disclosure), God revealed himself and his name in many ways. Often he chose to refer to himself as "The God of Abraham, Isaac, and Jacob." This in itself I find awesome and unthinkable. But to my utter amazement, far more often God has allowed himself to become known to his struggling people across the following centuries by another, simpler name, *"The God—of JACOB!"* Amazing!

To men and women of any generation, this can only be described as Good News! Hopeful news. Absolutely incredible. And this is our God!

∼

"JACOB OF TODAY, WHAT IS YOUR NAME? WHAT IS YOUR TRUE CHARACTER? WHAT IS YOUR IDENTITY? WHO RULES YOUR LIFE?"

Perhaps God's great question may come to you today in one cataclysmic moment such as my wrestling match at the Jabbok. But even so, you will probably face many more struggles, far less dramatic struggles, along the way. You and I are not changed once-and-for-all. We are changed from one stage of glory into another. Probably much like you, I've experienced the feeling of growing two steps forward, only to fall one step back again. And the issue for me is always the same question of deep-down identity: Will God prevail in me? Will God prevail in you?

Once you admit who you really are, what will you become? Only he knows! But I can guarantee that you will become someone indescribably beautiful—because the God of my Fathers doesn't know how to make anything else.

So, may the "God of Jacob" who never changes give you his peace! And may he transform your heart and mind more fully into the image of his own likeness as seen in face of Jesus Christ!

IV.

GOD'S GREAT QUESTION TO MOSES

"WHO MADE YOUR MOUTH?"

A question of adequacy

EXODUS 3 AND 4

BY AGE EIGHTY, I had settled into a rather comfortable life of shepherding the flocks of my father-in-law. Each day was much like the other. I loved sheep, and I expected to live out my final years caring for them. And then suddenly, when I least expected it, my tranquil life as an aging shepherd changed forever.

One day, on the back side of the desert, my attention became riveted on one solitary bush totally enveloped in flames. What fascinated me was that, although tinder dry, this bush was not at all consumed by the fire. I couldn't possibly explain it! This bush so aroused my curiosity that I left my flocks behind and scrambled across the scattered desert rocks to see for myself.

As I climbed closer, I suddenly became shocked, startled, by much more than a flaming bush. Out here in the desert, in the midst of absolutely nowhere, I suddenly heard a thundering voice. Imagine that! Seemingly from the very bush that was burning, 'someone', whose voice I didn't recognize, was amazingly calling out to me. And this voice from the burning bush called out:

"MOSES! MOSES!"

GOD'S GREAT QUESTION TO MOSES

Immediately I dropped to my knees, shaking. Even by peering intently and trying as I might, I still could not see who was speaking to me. Finally I managed a stuttered reply, "H-h-here I am."

"Don't come any closer, Moses!" the voice warned me. "Take off your sandals. You are standing on holy ground. Do you know who it is who is speaking to you, Moses? I am the God of your Fathers: the God of Abraham, Isaac, and Jacob."

Terrified, I scrambled to grab my woolen scarf and pull it tightly across my eyes. Surely if I dared to look at my Fathers's God, I would die. Even standing there in his awesome presence, I trembled all over. Still I hung on expectantly to listen for any word he might speak to me:

> "Moses, I have been watching the misery of my people in Egypt. I have heard them cry and groan because of their harsh treatment at the hands of the Egyptian slave drivers. I am deeply touched by their plight and concerned about their suffering. So I have come down to rescue them from the hand of the Egyptians. I will lead them out of Egypt and bring them into a good and ample land, a land flowing with milk and honey. So, Moses, go now! I am sending you to Pharaoh to bring my people, the people of Israel, out of slavery in the land of Egypt."
>
> (Exodus 3:7–10)

Hearing his voice, I gasped. What was that he was saying? Did he indeed say something about sending *me*?? I felt buoyed by exhilaration. But at the same time, I felt drowned by overwhelming fears. Stunned, I could hardly breathe. So many questions, so many crucial questions swirled within me!

How could I be sure, first of all, that I'd really even heard the voice? But then, I reasoned, hearing the voice was probably no more amazing than seeing the bush that was not being consumed by the flames. And what about the message? Did it sound authentic? Hm. How was I qualified to know? Well, I guess that voice didn't seem too much different than the ones my Fathers had received from their God. I admit that I bounced back and forth in my wondering. But I finally concluded: why *shouldn't* their God choose to speak again?

But these questions weren't even the tougher ones. What perplexed me most was this: If the God of my Fathers chose to speak, why would he choose to speak to *me*? To someone else, perhaps. But I'm just an aging shepherd living out here in the desert among Midianites, not even among my own people.

Decades had passed since my Hebrew mother, in one last act of hope, placed her baby into a pitch-lined basket along the bull rushes of the Nile River. Years passed since I had grown up as the son of Pharaoh's daughter in the opulent courts of Egypt. Years had passed since, in anger, I had slain the harsh Egyptian taskmaster who was mistreating one of the Hebrew slaves. Years had passed since, as a hunted murderer, I had fled to Midian where Jethro gave me his own daughter Zipporah in marriage to bear me sons.

Now I wondered with even more incredulity, why would God ever call such an unlikely creature like "Moses" for such a crucial rescue mission?

And just suppose that I did accept this unbelievable assignment. How could an aging shepherd like me possibly expect to be taken seriously by the great Pharaoh of Egypt? Or, even by my own Hebrew people for that matter!

"Oh, God, who am I?" I asked. "Who am I that I should go to Pharaoh and deliver the Israelites out of slavery in his land?"

In my wildest dreams, I couldn't possibly see myself going to see Pharaoh. I'd be the last person he'd listen to—an insignificant old shepherd, so unwelcome in Egypt, just another hated Hebrew.

You see, Egypt had finally freed itself from domination by the foreign Hyksos people. Now Egypt's new Pharaoh, fearing that other foreigners living inside the country might likewise rebel and throw out his dynasty, was now facing a tough problem with the Hebrews presently living along the eastern delta region of the Nile. Indeed, the original seventy direct offspring of Jacob (the alien Israelites who had found refuge in Egypt during the famine of Joseph's day 400 years before) had now multiplied into tens of thousands.

Quickly identifying these Israelites to be his greatest threat, Pharaoh was now determined to secure his rule by breaking their backs. So he decided to conscript all of these Hebrews as slaves. He can surely utilize their labor to build massive pyramids and the glorious treasure cities of Pithos and Raamses. Further, Pharaoh can easily place harsh Egyptian taskmasters over them to oppress them without mercy, thereby hopefully reducing their numbers over time. (Alas, this second cruel strategy failed.) So Pharaoh then used a second method to wipe out these unwanted Hebrew foreigners forever. He ordered all Egyptians to kill at birth, all first-born Hebrew baby boys.

GOD'S GREAT QUESTION TO MOSES

That's why my own mother desperately tried to hide me from such a fate. For several months my mother secretly kept me, little Moses, quiet and safe before she reluctantly had to let me go. The good news is that the daughter of Pharaoh himself found me in that woven basket in the reeds of the Nile. And apparently I was "adorable enough as an infant" that the Princess adopted me.

That's why I came to grow up in the opulent courts of Egypt, learning how to read and write, how to plan and strategize, how to rule, how to administer and lead people. I assumed that someday I (this alien Hebrew) might even grow up to hold a position of great power and responsibility in Egypt.

Ah, but those dreams of mine had faded so long ago. By now, I was just a simple shepherd. How could I possibly lead the helpless Hebrews through the barren wilderness to Promised Land.

Now I burst out laughing these years later. I couldn't imagine myself striding prominently into the magnificent palace of Egypt, wearing my smelly shepherd's garb when I came to confront Pharaoh. What a picture of opposites! His palace, with its gigantic friezes and hieroglyphic paintings, had become the world center of arts and learning. With its clever magicians and sorcerers, Pharaoh's court served as the hub of Egypt's full blown worship of all the gods derived from nature.

This sophisticated, hard-hearted Pharaoh would surely never let his Hebrew slaves go without a fight. Any such battle over the slaves would surely be fierce and "to the death." And if needed, wouldn't Pharaoh ultimately pit all of the nature gods of Egypt against the God of the Hebrews. And where would that leave *me*? Why, I'd be caught right in the middle. Squeezed. Perhaps even crushed. Isn't that precisely what my Father's God was asking of me? I, Moses, would become the intermediary between God's cosmic power struggle with the mighty ruler of Egypt. Certainly that was a task for which I felt grossly unprepared and painfully unsuited.

No, my accepting such a gigantic task was ridiculous. Impossible. Go to powerful Pharaoh in a shepherd's sandals and smelly garb? Not on your life! I knew enough not to try that. I couldn't even imagine it.

And yet, I surely could feel an incredible surge of excitement pulsing through me as I pondered such an impossible assignment. Me, a Shepherd-Deliverer? What wonderful irony! I wondered and wondered about it. What a delightful temptation. It's was almost "too good an opportunity to miss."

What a grand adventure! If only I still had the courage.

Reading my troubled mind, the God of my Fathers stepped in to reassure me: "Oh, don't worry, Moses. I will be with you. And this shall be a sign unto you—when you have brought my people out of Egypt, you shall indeed worship God again on this very mountain!"

∼

"I will be with you!" What a promise! And it should have been enough.

Looking back, I realize how vitally important was God's assurance that he would be with me. Much later I would realize that this is all we ever really need to know in life. But at that time, I was far more wrapped up in the mind-boggling logistics of how to liberate such a vast flock of now-enslaved people and get them successfully out of Egypt. What a humongous assignment!

Oh, but even if I supposed that Pharaoh would listen to me, I then faced another giant obstacle. How could I possibly assume that the Israelites would ever listen to me?

You see, my fellow Hebrews in Egypt scarcely knew me anymore. I had little contact with them during my early days, except for brief visits with Miriam and Aaron. For forty years now, I'd seen no one. I'd been completely hidden away, out in the endless deserts of Midian. So, if my people ever saw me again, would they even know me? Might they perhaps shrink from me, remembering that I was once a murderer? Yes, I had some real reasons for deeply fearing my own people's reactions, both their reactions to me and then to my strange message from our God. That's a "double whammy," as you folks say today.

Realistically, acceptance of me by my fellow Israelites seemed like such a knotty problem that I thought I should alert the Almighty.

> "Now Lord," I argued, "just suppose that I do go to the Israelites. And suppose that I also assure them that 'the God of your Fathers' has sent me. Do you honestly think they will believe me? And what if they ask me about your power, about your name? By this I mean that they will undoubtedly wonder whether the God of our Fathers is indeed still related to us and is indeed willing to be active on our behalf *today*, not just in the old days of Abraham, Isaac, and Jacob. So, if they ask me for your name, what shall I tell them?"

Before I could breathe my final word, God answered me: "You want to know my name, Moses? *'I AM WHO I AM.'* That's what you tell the Israelites, Yes indeed, *'I AM WHO I AM* has sent me!'"

GOD'S GREAT QUESTION TO MOSES

Wow! What a sacred moment. To me, "I AM" had revealed his own name. And by doing this, my God was making clear that he is indeed entering into a special relationship with me. So I took time to hallow his blessed name. And I pondered it tenderly in my heart:

"I AM." Simple. Direct. Unequivocal. There was no hesitation, no hint of not-having-quite-arrived, no exaggeration. "I AM." Positive. Assured. Self-validating. He is alive and well, and not to be questioned. "I AM." Current. Continuous. There was no apology, no explanation, no contextualizing. "I AM." Complete. Self-contained. Secure. There was no sense of needing unless he chose to need; not needing freed him to choose to become vulnerable at will. "I AM." Unique. Other. Transcendent. Although I was made in his image, I could see his image only as through a glass darkly. "I AM." Self-knowing. Unsuited to human adjectives. Existing apart from definition. What he is, he is; what he chooses to be, he will be. His name is above every name—"I AM!"

What incredible self-disclosure. What a God. And he's *my* God!

Most important to me, I now knew that my God was now ready to act on behalf of his beleaguered people here in Egypt. As my Fathers discovered before me, no longer would he be transcendent only (a God who remained above and beyond us.) "I am with you!" was his solemn oath. And this extravagant promise to me, to us, should have been enough.

But as yet, I still wasn't quite sure of my decision. So I decided to press I AM: "Just suppose, however, that the wise elders of Israel don't believe me or don't want to listen to me? Suppose they tell me, 'The God of our Fathers didn't really appear to you.' What shall I do then?

I AM understood my fear and gave me two signs, two miracles. First, he caused the staff in my hand to turn into a serpent when I threw it to the ground and revert to a staff when I picked up the serpent by the tail. Then he also caused my hand to become leprous whenever I placed it inside my cloak and revert to normal the next time I put it in again. "If they don't believe the first sign", he said with a slight chuckle, "they might believe the second! And, in case they aren't impressed with either, just take a pottery jug, dip it into the Nile to fill it with water, then immediately pour out the 'clear water,' then show that it has turned to blood. That should be persuasive enough!"

I was certainly convinced. But what about the elders of Israel? And what about mighty Pharaoh? Surely they would believe these! And yet . . . ?

During the silences, I kept on pondering. Every time I thought of Pharaoh, my stomach tied itself in knots. Every time I thought about the elders and the multitudes of Hebrew people, my head grew dizzy.

Still, up to now, my behavior had been rather normal, even admirable under the circumstances. But now absolute panic began to spread over me like a creeping chill, refusing to release me from its fiendish grip. In my mind, I began to shrink in size into the smallest possible human being I could imagine. I felt impotent. Painfully human. Utterly useless!

And then, when I could contain my frustration no longer, I poured out to I AM my paralyzing fear, a fear of not being adequate for his service.

So I began to pray:

"Oh God," I began, "perhaps you've noticed as I've been conversing with you that I d-d-don't speak very well. I never have, ever since birth. I'm not eloquent. I s-s-stutter and s-s-s-stammer. I t-t-trip over my tongue. My words don't glide smoothly."

    S
      I
        L
          E
            N
              C
                E

He paused—to give me time to ponder what I had said. And then his answer shot back at me with the force of an arrow hitting the target at dead center. His voice carried both sternness and reassurance. And, shaking his head, he questioned me with the skill of a consummate teacher:

"MOSES, MOSES, WHO MADE YOUR MOUTH?"

I was stopped dead in my tracks! Absolutely stunned back to reality once again! How painfully obvious! How could I have overlooked it? Who indeed had made my mouth? Was it not my Creator? Was it not this very God who was pressing now me into his service? Surely the God who made me knew all about me, even my inadequacies.

I felt embarrassed. Foolish. How could I have been so stupid? How could I have been so fearful? How could I have focused so completely on myself and not on him?

"Besides, Moses," God continued, "I myself will be with your voice, and I will teach you what to say."

Me adequate for service? No, that wasn't the issue, he was telling me. My God was adequate. That is the issue. And I was finally beginning to glimpse this truth more clearly.

At last I could feel my deepest fears subsiding. I could feel the festering boil of fear inside me begin to release its poison. Already I was receiving his healing, his divine shalom. How strange, I reflected, that I had been wounded and now healed by the same probing question.

By now, I should have felt content. But I didn't. Not yet.

While my mind had at least partially grasped the profound truth implied in I AM's question to me, my feelings had not yet caught up with my understanding. So I blurted out something to I AM that I've always wished I could take back: "Oh God, send *someone else* to be your prophet! Send someone else to deliver Israel. Please! P-l-e-a-s-e!"

For the first time in our conversation, I suddenly heard him breathe out his anger against me. My pathetic outburst had proved that I was still more focused on my own lack of adequacy than on the adequacy of my God. I had offended the Almighty by choosing not to believe, not to trust him.

Amazingly, even then he didn't turn away from me. Nor did he let me resign my assignment. Instead, while still taking into account my deep feelings of inadequacy, this God of love created another way for me to be his prophet.

"What about your brother, Aaron?" I AM asked me. "He can speak well. In fact, he's already on his way here to meet you. You shall speak to him and give him the right words to proclaim. It will be as if he were your mouth and as if you were 'God' to him. So get ready! Pick up your staff with which you will be able to perform miraculous signs—signs for the Hebrews as well as for Pharaoh. Now, go! Go down, Moses, way down in Egypt land and tell old Pharaoh, 'Let my people go!'"

This time I did not argue. Finally assured that my not being "adequate" for his service would not handicap him, I did exactly as the God of my Fathers—*my* God—told me. My dear brother Aaron went with me. And so did I AM!

∼

As they rightly say, the rest is His-story!

It's really too bad that you already know all that happened. Otherwise, I'd spin yarns that would amaze and astound you. But I'll give you a hint.

Before Pharaoh would let my people go, I AM had to send ten terrible plagues upon Egypt. Water turned to blood. Plagues of frogs, gnats, and flies inundated the land. Cattle died. Boils covered man and beast. Hail destroyed crops, and locusts devoured whatever remained. Darkness hung over the land like a thick, impenetrable blanket.

Then—in one final blow—came the most heart-stopping plague of all. Throughout Egypt all of the firstborn sons of the land, and the firstborn of the cattle as well, were swept away in one dark night of mourning. All of the families in Egypt wept that night. All but the Hebrew families.

That's because I AM instructed us Hebrews to spread the blood of a lamb without spot or blemish over the doorposts of our homes so that the angel of death would see it and "pass over" our firstborn. And when we heard the wails rise from the households of Egypt, we stood in awe and gratitude that I AM had indeed graciously spared us.

In this great demonstration of power over the nature gods of Egypt, the God of our Fathers showed himself to be more than adequate. He triumphed gloriously! Pharaoh and the Egyptians witnessed it. So did I. And it should have been enough.

∼

But this struggling flock of Hebrews was just beginning to learn about the awesome adequacy of the great God who had chosen us to be his people.

Still basking in the joy of God's delivering us from bondage in Egypt, we Hebrews faced our first crucial test of faith in the Wilderness. Trapped between Pharaoh's approaching Egyptian army and the Sea of Reeds, we had absolutely nowhere to turn. Then, just when our too-fragile hope ran out, our terrified people experienced a miracle we could never forget. We saw our God pile up the waters of the Sea so that we could pass through on dry ground. And at the very moment we reached safety, the impatient waves let loose their fury, destroying all of Pharaoh's chariots.

At first we stood numb. Mute. Stunned. Then whoops of joy burst forth from our lips. Our elation swelled. With jubilant songs, we celebrated God's power and loving-kindness in parting the Sea to save us.

As we sang together in worship, I watched the little flock that God had chosen begin to place its faith in the mighty one who proclaims: "I AM the Lord your God who brought you up out of the land of Egypt, out of the house of bondage." And for as long as I had breath, I kept urging my fellow

Israelites to speak often about this day, to teach this saving truth diligently to their children and to their children's children.

If I hadn't comprehended before, I now was certainly beginning to realize that, although I, Moses, acted the part of "The Shepherd-Deliverer," it was really I AM who was our Shepherd-Deliverer. He simply worked his will through an ordinary human being like me. Incredible! And this revelation explained why my own "adequacy" for service never was the issue. Our God was adequate. That is what set his people apart from the other nations. That is what we needed to understand and cherish.

Already we had experienced I AM as our Shepherd Deliverer. Now in the Wilderness, we began to understand him as our Good Shepherd as well.

This Shepherd-Deliverer continued to go with us, just as he promised, in a pillar of cloud by day and a pillar of fire by night. Like a Good Shepherd, he cared for us. He miraculously made the bitter waters sweet at Marah. He fed us until we had our fill of manna and quail. He brought forth cool streams from the rock in the desert. He caused our clothes to remain new and our sandals firm all during our long forty-year wilderness journey. He even protected us from our enemies. In all ways, he remained faithful to the covenant promise he made with his people at Mount Sinai:

> "You have seen what I did on your behalf in Egypt, how I carried you out on eagles' wings and brought you to myself. Now if you obey me completely and keep my covenant, then out of all nations you will be my own treasured possession. Although all the entire earth is mine, you will be special to me—a kingdom of priests and a nation set apart as holy unto me."
>
> (Exodus 19:4–6)

On that day at the foot of Mount Sinai, the place of my own "burning bush," became a burning bush for all God's people. In response to the God of the Covenant, the entire flock gratefully responded: "We will do everything our God has told us to do!"

At our declaration of relationship, we rejoiced wildly. With I AM, the powerful and gracious Shepherd-Deliverer with us, what could ever go wrong?

∽

But sheep have a way of wandering astray, you know. And we Hebrews certainly were wandering men and women.

Soon it became woefully apparent that we did not always respond to God's love by obeying his instructions for our welfare. Many times we failed miserably to live up to our part of the Covenant. Often we simply grumbled like spoiled children; some even longed for the leeks and garlic of Egypt.

Free at last from Egyptian bondage, our emerging nation didn't know how to behave in this environment of freedom. Like willful adolescents asserting our selfhood, we struggled to express our independence. Acting rightly toward God and toward each other was an art we still desperately needed to learn.

So, with infinite patience and perseverance, I AM began to parent us. To my surprise and joy, he allowed *me* to be part of the important process of molding the people of God.

Three months after he delivered us from Pharaoh's armies, God led us to the mountain of Sinai, back where, as a wandering shepherd long ago, I had first met I AM. Now once again I AM called me to ascend that mountain. There, exactly as he had promised long ago, I again worshiped him. And there, I now received his own Law—his Ten Commandments—for his people.

In this Law, and in the instructions that followed, I AM taught us how to worship him as the God above every god. But knowing from the outset that we would fall into sin which would separate us from him, he offered a way, by offering up sacrifices, so we could become restored to full fellowship again.

He also taught us how to behave in right ways with our family, our friend, our neighbor, even our enemy. He taught us that right relationships with others are linked inextricably to our relationship with God. Both relationships must be clean and healthy for God's blessing.

As leader, my task was to instruct the people in this Law, to urge them to obey, and to lead the way in following it. If only I could have helped my people understand from the beginning that these gracious commands would bring us God's shalom—peace, joy, wholeness, life at its fullest!

But as you know, I had my hands full with our stiff-necked people. Sadly, the shadow of the Serpent fell on us many times. Worship of the golden calf. Rebellion in the ranks. Constant murmurings. Plagues of serpents and leprosy as punishment for our sins. Refusing to trust God and to enter the Promised Land because our spies feared the giants there.

Fortunately, Miriam and Aaron helped me shepherd the people. But increasingly I found that I was the one who spoke with boldness to the flock.

I was the one who organized them for work and worship. I was the one who arbitrated their disputes, and, when that became too burdensome, I was the one who appointed judges to hear their cases. I was the one who interceded with an angry God on behalf of his disobedient and fickle people.

And I say this with all meekness, because I was beginning to grasp the process by which I AM works in history—by using little people like me who respond to his call.

As I performed whatever he asked of me, I quickly discovered that "being adequate for service" simply means to be "available for his use." Available for use! Available to do what he tells us. Nothing more! He will do the rest!

We simply accept his call by offering ourselves as his servants, as empty vessels for his use. At times we may not see many results. At other times we become amazed onlookers at God glorious deeds among us.

Adequate? Many times I've thought back to the day when a stuttering eighty-year-old shepherd pleaded with God to send someone else. Surely I couldn't possibly do what he was asking of me. Surely, I thought, I couldn't be the Shepherd-Deliverer of my people. Oh, my! What a crucial role in history I would have left unfilled. And what indescribable joy I would have missed.

But I was "adequate" only because *he* was adequate.

∼

After forty years of wandering in the Wilderness, at last the flock of God stood poised at the entrance of the Promised Land. Of the adults who had come out of Egypt, only Caleb, Joshua and I remained. But only Caleb and Joshua would enter Canaan. I would not lead the people in, nor would I be allowed to enter the territory over the Jordan.

Disappointed? Yes. But I understood. I had failed to acknowledge God's holy power before the people when I brought water out of the rock at Meribah. When I got the news, I pondered the possibility of arguing with God to let me go into the land. But then I remembered his powerful question to me when I had objected once before: "Moses, who made your mouth?" I knew that my life and times were in his hands. So I accepted his decision. I knew that the real Shepherd-Deliverer would continue to go forward with his people, through dear Joshua. And I felt content that the focus of the people would rest on I AM, not on Moses.

At age one hundred twenty, my body was still fit and my eyesight clear. I climbed to the top of Mount Nebo. There I AM graciously showed me the entire land which he had promised to his little flock. It was absolutely perfect.

Looking wistfully at the Land of Promise, I indulged the prerogatives of an old man by spending time remembering. I finally concluded that I had led quite a life! If you had asked me about my life before age eighty, I'd probably have said something like this:

"I was an abandoned child. I grew up as an adopted orphan in a single parent family. My playmates taunted me by labeling me a foreigner. When I finished my education and was just ready for an important job in the government, I lost my temper and slew an Egyptian. When word spread that I was a murderer, I fled for my life to Midian. There I tended someone else's flock of sheep for forty years on the back side of the desert. What a wasted life! What a miserable life!"

I laughed at my gloomy description. It was little wonder that I had originally questioned my "adequacy" at the burning bush. As I recalled how hard I had tried to avoid God's leadership call, I now thanked God for his sharp question which shocked me back to reality. God had indeed made my mouth! And he was all that I, indeed we, had needed.

Looking back over those eighty years, I could see God's hand all along. I also marveled at the abundant skills with which God had been gifting me throughout the bizarre turns of my early life. Education in Egypt. Reading, writing, administration, leadership. Even my forty uneventful years in Midian were not wasted. Who would ever have thought that leading sheep is not all that different than leading a flock of wandering people? Then suddenly at age eighty, all of my life somehow became useful to I AM.

What was my most powerful, most lasting memory of this long life? I thought back to that day when, as a discouraged leader of faithless people worshiping the golden calf, I had pleaded with God to let me see the dazzling light of his presence. How audacious I was. I was really telling God, "I want to know you much more fully."

And on that dark day, the great I AM graciously answered his tired servant's request, in words and deeds forever emblazoned upon my heart:

> "I will make all my splendor pass before you and in your presence
> I will pronounce my sacred name. 'I AM' the Lord, and I will show
> compassion and pity on those I choose.

> I will not let you see my face, because no one can see me and remain alive, but there is a place at my side where you can stand upon a rock. When the dazzling light of my presence passes by, I will put you in an opening of the rock and cover you with my hand until I have passed by. Then I will take my hand away, and you will see my back but not my face."
>
> (Exodus 33:19–33)

At his side! A place upon the Rock—for me! So many times during my painful forty years in the Wilderness, this amazing promise comforted me. Now as I lay down to die on Mount Nebo, I could feel once again the closeness of his side where the rock was safe, warm, secure.

And when at last my eyes opened, I had indeed entered the Promised Land—even before my people entered Canaan. But this Promised Land was far more glorious than anything I had seen from Mount Nebo. This Promised Land was filled forever with the dazzling presence of God himself. There on the Throne reigned the Lamb, our Shepherd-Deliverer, slain as an eternal sacrifice for my sins from before the foundation of the world. And this I AM—my Good Shepherd, my Shepherd-Deliverer—would be "with me" for all eternity!

∽

Oh my! If I had my life to live over again, I wouldn't worry nearly as much about the dark threads woven through the tapestry of my life. These somber tones only await the gold of his presence to create a masterpiece, even at age eighty. Nor would I worry as much about my "wasted" years. As the prophet many centuries later would utter from the mouth of God: "I will restore the years!" And I certainly wouldn't worry as much about my own "adequacy." By the end of my life I had fully experienced the all-powerful God who is more than adequate to act on our behalf.

Dear Moses of Today, I pause to remember that the issues that plagued me may not be the same ones you struggle with. After all, you live after Advent. You have the advantage of having witnessed for yourself the coming of the Christ as the eternal Shepherd-Deliverer of his flock, a flock that includes you. You've witnessed his matchless power and grace as he came to dwell among you. You have seen the Rock in full view.

But, even with the fuller revelation of God in Jesus Christ, I suspect that the issue of "response" to the great I AM remains much the same for you as it was for me. And perhaps that's one reason why my story has been passed down from generation to generation.

So, I encourage you to keep looking for burning bushes! Keep turning aside to see. Keep listening. Keep saying "Yes!" to God. Keep on heading toward the Promised Land. And, of course, be sure to remember who made your mouth! Then all of your life will overflow with God's beautiful surprise, and calls to serve him with joy—sometimes in ways you've never even dreamed.

When you may be tempted to feel inadequate for the tasks to which God calls you, may our God bear you up on eagles' wings so that you will experience even more fully the promise of his everlasting Covenant with you in Jesus Christ: "Lo, I AM with *you* always!"

V.

GOD'S GREAT QUESTION TO JOSHUA

"WHAT ARE YOU DOING WITH YOUR FACE DOWN IN THE DUST?"
A question of balance
JOSHUA 7 AND 8

TRUMPETS BLASTED. TRAMPING CEASED. A cacophony of shouts rose from the people. Foundations cracked. Fortified walls began to crumble. With a frightening thud, once-invincible Jericho came crashing to the ground!

All around us, we felt the earth shudder and shake. Shockwave followed shockwave, so great was the impact.

Dust gusted outward as Jericho's stone walls and shattered dwellings collapsed. Then the dust began to swirl upward in giant columns toward the heavens. With dust plugging their nostrils and clogging their mouths, our men rushed headlong into the chaos. At Yahweh's command, we destroyed everything in that city—all except Rahab and her family who huddled near the window draped by a scarlet cord.

All of Jericho's bounty, her gold and silver, her articles of bronze and iron, we retrieved for the Lord's Treasury, and then we destroyed ("devoted"to Yahweh) the entire city, just as he had commanded. Amid tumults of wild rejoicing, we put fallen Jericho to the torch. As we watched flames engulf the rubble, we gratefully sacrificed all of Jericho for a burnt offering to the Lord.

Our eyes widened with wonder at God's great power. Who but Yahweh could have devised such a battle plan?

Mighty Jericho had fallen. What incontrovertible proof that Yahweh still dwelt with us, just as he had during all the days of Moses! With absolute certainty, we celebrated this conquest as the first fruit of his promise to our Fathers that he would give us the entire land of Canaan for our inheritance.

What a victory! God was surely with us!

Buoyed by Yahweh's triumph at Jericho, I sent a couple of advance men straight from the battlefield to scout out the area near Ai. While I assumed that Yahweh would again command the victory at Ai, I knew that my responsibility was to make sure we had done our part in reconnaissance. So I instructed two of my best soldiers: "Go up and spy out the whole region of Ai, Bethel, and Beth-Aven."

They quickly brought back a report. "You need not send many men to Ai to take it," they told me, "particularly since your men are weary from today's battle. There's certainly no need for the whole army. Perhaps send two or three thousand. That should be enough. Only a few men dwell in Ai. Victory there will be easy for us."

So I sent them off with 3,000 of our finest troops to capture Ai.

Meanwhile back at the camp, everyone's lips celebrated our shattering victory at Jericho. "And the walls came tumblin' down" became the theme of many a spontaneous song. Eyes sparkled. Women danced. Children bustled through chores with fresh vigor. Hebrew pride swelled. Here and there the most unlikely old Israelites burst into impromptu psalms of gratitude.

Throughout the whole assembly of the people, the air was bursting with excitement, relief, and gratitude.

I couldn't recall seeing such unrestrained joy in forty years. Not since that glorious day when we were fleeing from bondage in Egypt. Not since that glorious day when Yahweh had miraculously parted the Sea of Reeds, rescuing us at the final moment from the pursuing Egyptian armies. Now had come another glorious day for the children of Israel. Now another day to be remembered. Now, once again, jubilation reigned!

And the, at the height of our ecstasy, came unexpected and terrifying news.

Breathless and forlorn, our soldiers straggled back into camp. Their shell-shocked faces reflected utter surprise and confusion. They gasped a tale of being completely overpowered and routed by the few men of Ai. "They swarmed over us at the very gates of the city," they moaned. "All we could do was to flee for our lives. They pursued us savagely the way to the rock quarries of Shebarim. And there, they slew many of our number."

As the remaining soldiers made their way back to their campsites, I heard one family begin to weep, then another. Thirty-six men did not return that night. Their bodies lay lifeless near the rock-pile of Shebarim, pierced through by the spears of Canaan.

Deathly quiet stole over the entire camp, a quiet punctuated only by uncontrollable sobbing.

Just the unthinkable idea that heathen people had defeated the flock of Yahweh caused my heart to melt and become as water. What a strange turn of events, I reflected. Hadn't Rahab confided to us just days before the battle of Jericho that everyone in Canaan was "melting in fear because of the Israelites and their powerful God?" My, how the tables had turned.

Throughout the dark night, I couldn't catch any sleep.

With the first rays of morning light, I rent my clothes in humility before Yahweh. I sprinkled dust over my head. All the elders followed my example. In utter agony and confusion, I prostrated myself before the Ark of the Lord. Surely, I thought, Yahweh would meet me there.

∽

With my face sunk down in the dust, I continued to lie prostrate on the ground throughout the entire day. Grief overwhelmed me. Fear gripped me. I felt baffled. Stunned. Paralyzed. I could not talk to anyone, not even to the other elders. I could not think straight. I could not even voice my prayers. I waited there alone in dreadful silence.

What had gone wrong? What could possibly have gone wrong?

In the loneliness of silence of the dust, a host of terrifying questions and pictures paraded across my mind.

I thought back to a memorable day, almost 40 years ago now, when Moses had commissioned twelve of us to go up into Canaan to spy out this land. Caleb and I looked from the mountain top and saw all of the Promised Land, from the Negev desert to Lebanon, from the Euphrates to the Great Sea. What a place! A land flowing with milk and honey. When we returned to Moses, we detailed our report carefully. Caleb and I described vineyards and abundance. We described great cities surrounded by thick stone walls. We described giants living there, descendants of Anak. Even so, we urged Moses to go up immediately to possess the land, because surely Yahweh would be with us, just as he had promised.

Now a cruelly unwelcome thought hit me. Perhaps Caleb and I had been wrong. We had been outnumbered in our report by ten to two. Perhaps we too should have been cautious. Perhaps the others had been right all along.

And yet...

And yet, hadn't Yahweh been with us at Jericho? What else could possibly explain our glorious triumph? Was not this victory his sign that we would soon conquer all Canaan?

Hadn't Yahweh promised this land long ago to our forefathers? Hadn't he reaffirmed his promise to us under Moses? When he gave us his Covenant, what had he told us?

> "I will take you as my own people, and I will be your God. Then you will know that I am the LORD your God who brought you out from under the yoke of the Egyptians. And I will bring you to the land I swore with uplifted hand to give to Abraham, to Isaac, and to Jacob. I will give it to you as a possession. I am the LORD."
>
> (Exodus 6:6–8, emphasis added)

No, the promise of Yahweh couldn't have been clearer. This land would surely be our inheritance. So what had gone wrong?

Confused, I continued to ponder. Perhaps I was the wrong leader for the people. Was that possible?

As I recalled, I'd never really sought to be the leader of my people. Moses, my friend, had been our leader. I was more than content to follow him. I felt honored as a young man just to be his trusted aide. I had journeyed with him to Mount Sinai where he received the Commandments from the Lord. I had descended the mountain with him to confront the tragedy of the idolatrous golden calf. I had even been entrusted by him with the safety of the Tent of Meeting—the special place where God himself talked with Moses in the Wilderness.

Then I remembered the day when the unwelcome news came that God would not allow Moses to enter the Promised Land with us. How did Moses respond? Always the good leader, Moses had asked Yahweh that day to appoint a new leader. And I, Joshua, was chosen. Until the day I died, I could never forget that moment.

On that day of commissioning, Moses and I stood before the Lord at the Tent of Meeting. There Yahweh commissioned *me* to lead his people into Canaan, the land he had promised us. Moses laid his hands on me in front of the entire congregation of Israel. In doing this, he laid on me full authority to command the people after his death, asking Eleazar the priest to receive God's decisions for me by inquiring of the sacred stones, the Urim and Thummim.

I shook my head. No, I wasn't the wrong leader. There could be no doubt that Yahweh had installed *me* as leader of this fledgling little nation that he had chosen for his own.

Maybe the problem was my military strategy.

I laughed. This troublesome thought didn't seem to fit me. Oh, I'd certainly had my military victories. When Moses needed someone to lead the Israelites into battle against the Amalekites, for example, he had chosen me. We encountered a tough battle and emerged victorious. But all along, I was aware that it was Yahweh who displayed his mighty power that day. And although I had led the troops well and fought well, I had no doubt at all that it was Yahweh who was our successful Commander.

In a symbolic act, Moses had even changed my name from "Oshea" ("Salvation") to "Joshua," meaning "Jehovah is Salvation." ("Joshua" is the Hebrew equivalent of the name 'Jesus", the one who would later save his people from their sins.) So, wherever I went and whatever I did, I bore a name that constantly reminded me that YAHWEH (Jehovah) is the one who brings military success, not leaders like me.

By now mid-day had long passed. Still there was no word from the Lord. Still, I faithfully remained there on the ground with my face buried in the dust. I grew more and more impatient. I grew more and more isolated from those I led. I grew more and more frantic.

I cast about for answers. And I found none. Anger began to well up within me. Hadn't Yahweh himself told me: "Joshua, be strong and of good courage, for I will be with you. I will never leave you nor forsake you. I will give you every part of the land on which you set your foot. No one will be able to stand up against you all the days of your life."

Gradually I convinced myself that Yahweh had been grossly unfair to us. And to me personally. He had promised. And he had failed to keep his promise. It was a terrifying thought! And if this terrifying thought were true, then what hope was there for me—or for this little nation as yet with no name of its own, as yet with no land of its own?

I had run out of possible explanations. I had run out of possible comforts. I had nowhere left to turn.

Steady, "Unflappable Joshua." "Old Faithful." That's what people called me behind my back, and they meant the titles most kindly. Sometimes I had questioned whether I weren't by nature too even-tempered, too boring. But no longer. I certainly wasn't steady now. I was clearly knocked off-balance. What on earth was happening to me? Why was I feeling so enraged? Why so desperately confused?

Only my intense anger held back bitter tears of despair.

Finally I could stand the dreadful mystery no longer. I could stand the silence no longer. I could stand the impasse no longer. If Yahweh would not speak to me, I vowed to speak to him.

Carefully I clothed my words with politeness and reverence. But with the straightness of an arrow, I took deadly aim with my verbal thoughts in order to penetrate the very heart of Yahweh. In utter hopelessness and frustration, I unleashed my thinly disguised attack as I prayed to him:

> "Ah, Sovereign Lord, why did you ever bring this people across the Jordan if you were just going to deliver us into the hands of the Amorites to destroy us? We were better off in the Wilderness. Why have you done this to us? If only we had been content to stay on the other side of the Jordan!"

"The Jordan!" I heard myself say. Just that word prompted a stream of memories within me. Wasn't it just days ago when the priests had entered the Jordan River with the Ark of the Covenant? And hadn't the waters piled up in a heap for our people to pass through, even though the river was at its flood stage during the harvest season? Of course at the time I had thought that Yahweh was the one who made this miracle possible. But now I began to question everything. Perhaps it wasn't a miracle after all. Perhaps some movement of earth upstream near Zarethan had simply coincided with this sacred moment instead. Ah, who could know?

I returned to my blistering accusation of Yahweh:

> "Oh Lord, how can I make sense of the fact that Israel has been routed by its enemies? You told us that we could know you were with us when we saw that you vanquished our enemies. And now what? Can you imagine what will happen to us when the Canaanites and the other people of the country hear about this? Why, we'll be doomed. They will surround us and wipe out our name from the face of the earth. And then what? What will you do then to protect the honor of your great name?"

Anger! Doubt. Fear. Ingratitude. Impatience. My words betrayed all this and more. In my outburst, I bared myself to him completely, heresy and all.

Still there was no answer.

As shadows disappeared, I knew the sun was setting. Night approached. But in the copper streaked dusk, I remained prostrate before Yahweh, with my face in the miserable dust.

Then came the crucial moment of my life. Without warning, from out of nowhere, the voice of Yahweh seemed to envelope me.

"JOSHUA, JOSHUA, WHAT ARE YOU DOING WITH YOUR FACE DOWN IN THE DUST?"

What was I doing here in the dust? Praying. Well, more or less praying. Didn't he understand that? Despite my harsh questions to Yahweh, hadn't my prostrate position for an entire day demonstrated to him my deep reverence and respect?

"You ask me, 'What am I doing?' I'll tell you what I am doing. I am calling on you, Lord, to save your people. I am pleading with you to do exactly as you promised!" Well, at least those were my thoughts. Fortunately my mouth remained shut. And, fortunately, I was too stunned to speak.

"JOSHUA, STAND UP! WHAT ARE YOU DOING WITH YOUR FACE DOWN IN THE DUST? JOSHUA, STAND UP!"

Stand up? Why didn't he want me down on the ground? Didn't he want my worship? Wasn't he pleased with my humility? How else could I show my reverence for him? I didn't understand. Who would dare to stand up before the Almighty?

I couldn't help recalling how, just days ago on the way to Jericho, I had encountered a being called the Commander of the Lord's Army. When I finally comprehended who he was, I had bowed low to him in reverence. In some ways, this was my "burning bush" experience. Realizing I stood on holy ground that day I, like Moses before me, had removed my sandals. My response of falling to the ground before the Lord's messenger had been appropriate and acceptable then. Why not now? Why not now?

"JOSHUA, STAND UP!"

As Yahweh continued to speak to me, I would gradually begin to understand the difference—a difference that made "all the difference." Just faintly, I would begin to glimpse the import of his searching question to me as I lay buried in the dust, I would begin to see that I had overlooked one terrible possibility which made my behavior quite inappropriate.

> "Joshua, stand up! Israel has sinned! They have violated my covenant and disobeyed my commands. Against my instructions, they have taken some of the 'devoted things' that belong to me. They have stolen and lied. You will discover that they have put the devoted items with their own possessions.
>
> "That is why Israel cannot stand against its enemies. They have to turn their backs and run because they have condemned themselves to destruction by their disobedient actions. I will not be with you anymore until you destroy whatever among you is causing your own destruction.
>
> So go now, Joshua. Go, consecrate the people."
>
> (Joshua 7:10-12)

As Yahweh spoke, I began to understand that I had overlooked one terrible possibility: sin. The possibility of our sin hadn't even occurred to me. I had blamed everything on Yahweh. Not only was that a foolish and insolent attack, I had thereby failed to see the truth and so I failed to do what was necessary to correct the situation.

Yahweh was incredibly gracious. Immediately he gave me specific instructions of what needed to be done. Task after task he listed for me. Yahweh had important work for me to do. In the morning, we would uncover together the sin which had destroyed us, the sin which was the root of our trouble.

At last I could feel my equilibrium return. At last I was ready to get up from the dust. At last, I could feel myself beginning to relax.

Once again, Yahweh and I were talking. Having now begun again toward new beginnings, I stretched out on the mat in my tent. And that night I slept soundly.

⁓

With the first rays of light, I arose. I threw over me my rough woven tunic. Fully committed to my list of tasks, I rushed to confer with Eleazar, the priest who would help me in the Lord's work today. It was Eleazar's job to consult the marked stones he wore in the ephod over his heart. These sacred lots would surely reveal who among us was guilty.

I called for the children of Israel to gather together and present themselves.

Just last night I had brought them the verdict of Yahweh. So, I told them: "Brothers, sisters, I bring you sad news. One among us has done a disgraceful thing. He has broken the Covenant of our God. He has disobeyed and taken things from Jericho which were 'devoted to Yahweh.' Instead, he has taken them for himself. Therefore, whoever among us is caught with the 'devoted things' that belong to God shall be burned with fire, along with all that belongs to him."

So, now they stood massed before me in solemnity, each tribe grouped separately. Stretched as far as the eye could see, the people all looked much the same to me. My brothers and sisters. Fellow warriors. Longtime friends who had struggled alongside me through the inhospitable desert.

But today I knew that at least one was different. And I didn't know who. This was my second task, to discover which one it might be.

One by one, I called each tribe before me. Judah was singled out by the lot of the sacred stones. Then I signaled for each clan of Judah. The clan of Zerah was chosen. Then the Zerahites came forward by families. And Zimri (Zabdi) was taken. Again and again the lot was cast. Finally I knew the man—Achan, son of Carmi, the son of Zimri, the son of Zerah, of the tribe of Judah.

Achan stepped forward and stood before me, trembling.

My heart stopped. Why Achan? I knew he was a good man, a good husband, a good father. What a shame! What had happened to this dear Hebrew man to cause such disaster?

"Achan, my son," I began sorrowfully "before Almighty Yahweh, I implore you to tell the truth. Conceal nothing. Uncover the terrible deed you are hiding. Tell me what you have done."

Achan confessed everything. Although Yahweh had instructed us to destroy Jericho and all its contents, Achan had spotted a beautiful Babylonian robe in the rubble. He suddenly coveted it so much that he felt powerless to resist. So he grabbed the robe, along with some silver and gold as well. He showed us where he had hidden them underneath his tent.

We all felt terribly pained for Achan and his family. But Yahweh had been very clear. "I will not be with you as long as you tolerate disobedience. I will not be with you until you put away whatever among you is causing your destruction." So we put it all to the torch, just as we had at Jericho. To this day, Achan and his rubble is called the Valley of Achor—"disaster".

As soon as the sin of Achan was removed, the Lord turned from his fierce anger.

Now, once again, the Lord spoke to me: "Joshua, son of Nun, be afraid no longer. Be discouraged no longer. Take your whole army. Go up and attack Ai, but be sure to set an ambush beforehand behind the city. For I have delivered into your hands the king and his people, his city and his land."

So I did as Yahweh commanded. I chose our best fighting men and sent them by night to take up positions behind Ai and Bethel. They would wait there until I gave them the signal.

Early the next morning, I led the remaining troops toward the northern gates of Ai. When the king saw us approaching, he and all his men rushed out of the city to attack us. Just as we planned, we teased them outside the city walls. Just as we had done before, we turned tail and fled toward the desert. And they kept on pursuing us. We lured all of them away from Ai. Not a man was left behind to guard the city with its gates flung open wide.

As the enemy came after us, they were not aware of our ambush. Then, at the crucial moment, I raised my javelin toward Ai, as Yahweh had commanded. At this signal, our advance troops arose from their positions and rushed forward to capture the city. They encountered no resistance at all. As Yahweh commanded, they quickly grabbed the plunder and livestock before they set the city aflame.

To their horror, the soldiers of Ai and Bethel looked back and could see nothing but smoke as their city burned to the ground. They became completely demoralized. We continued to attack our enemy, both from the front and from the rear. We squeezed most of them between us. And until we hunted down every enemy soldier on the plain or into the desert where they fled, I continued to stretch forth my hand holding the javelin just as Yahweh had commanded me.

Finally, nothing remained but a heap of ruins.

Compared with Jericho, Ai was a quiet victory. But it was an even more important battle for our people. We had avenged our initial defeat. And we had brought back vast plunder, as Yahweh instructed. But more important, we had learned some painful lessons there.

When we came back late to our camp, I was bone weary. Quite a day for even a seemingly young soldier, I mused. Still, I was not ready for sleep. My mind was too full. Full of gratitude. And full of emerging thoughts about Yahweh's probing question to me yesterday when I lay there in the dust.

Gradually the issue was growing a bit clearer for me.

I could see that Yahweh was a God who wanted my utmost devotion, respect and humility. Otherwise, why would he have instructed me to build altars to memorialize the crossing of the Jordan River? Indeed he wanted my absolute worship. This I had always understood.

But now I began to see that Yahweh and I were also in relationship! "I will be your God." Yes, that was surely part of it (and by far the more important part.) Yet there was more: "And *you* shall be my people." That was the second part, the other side of the equation. And this crucial component is what I had overlooked after the first defeat at Ai when I spent the entire day with my face down in the dust.

Although I hadn't seen it at the time, what a "to do" list I had been avoiding that day. I certainly hadn't meant to shirk my duty to Yahweh. But in my excessive piety, I could see that I had failed to do some crucial work for him.

"Go, consecrate the people, for Israel has sinned."
"Destroy among you what is destroying you."
"Go up and attack Ai."
"Set an ambush."
"Hold out your javelin."

Yet how could I, the leader of all Israel, do these crucial things when, important as worship is, I was still hiding face-down in the dust in my extreme piety? I now knew that I could never again doubt that Yahweh would do his part, as he promised. But now I also knew that this was only one side of the agreement. I too must be available to do my part, a part that fully depends on me to clear the way for his divine activity. "You shall be my people. You shall do what I expect my people to do." So I had overlooked an extremely important part that, as the people's leader, only I could play in the Covenant relationship with Yahweh.

I nodded quietly to myself. Into my blackest night, light was finally shining through.

Perhaps I can simply put it this way: For the people of God, there is a time to *let* things happen, and there is a time to *make* things happen. Yes, there is a vitally important time for me to prostrate myself with my face in the dust before the Lord. But, just as surely, there is an equally important time for me to "stand up" and get us all working on what only we can do. It's a question of careful balance, isn't it?

At last I could see my mistake all too clearly. In a subtle and devout way, I had missed the basic meaning of "worship." I had forgotten that the meaning of "worship" is quite literally "service." And so I had excluded my service as a valid and important part of my worship. Yahweh, in his great love, couldn't allow that. And I'm grateful he could not.

With my renewed vision for the link between worship and service, the link between right-believing and right-acting, I was now ready to build the altar for Yahweh at Mount Ebal, as Moses had instructed me long ago. There all Israel, all of the men, the women, the children, and the aliens living among us, would join me in renewing our commitment to the Covenant and to the God of the Covenant.

This great moment was dramatic! Half of our people stood in front of Mount Gerizim. Half stood in front of Mount Ebal. And in the valley between these two groups, we positioned the Ark of the Covenant. All of us riveted our eyes on it. And we waited in silence.

In front of this vast assembly, I read aloud the whole Law of Moses. I omitted nothing. I read all of the blessings and curses that Moses had already given to the twelve tribes as they prepared to enter the Land of Promise. I also read Yahweh's instructions to us about right living, his commandments about our "behavior" as part of our "worship," those commandments about loving our neighbor as part of our loving God. (To us who know the Lord, all of life is sacred; nothing is secular; and nothing is outside his concern and domain.) So, with all my heart, I prayed that we might remember what we had learned. If only we could keep our balance. If only we could continue to see our "worship" and our "service" as inextricably linked together. Then surely we would enter the glorious promised "rest" of this Promised Land.

What a unique, special moment this was for me!

Perhaps I was a foolish old man, but I really wished I could have shared this moment with Moses. I hoped that somehow my old friend was watching. I thought he'd be pleased. But I knew with even greater certainty that Yahweh was watching and smiling. And so was I!

~

Joshua of Today, I hope that our painful defeat at Ai (or rather, my painful defeat in the dust) may be helpful to you on life's long journey.

I pray that whenever you seek the will of God, you will find it. I'm sure that at times you will find it, as I did, with your face sunk deep down in the dust. But at other times, perhaps you too will find it as Yahweh prods you to your feet to do whatever he tells you—or to do what you already know needs to be done, so that you can move forward in fellowship with him.

My wish for you is simple to say and difficult to do. May you always keep searching for God's poise in your life, that delicate point of balance between all of the various perils of life. Balance between the perils of a piety that is inactive, and of a frantic activity that is not well-rooted in spiritual soil. Balance between your words and your deeds. Balance between your creedal profession and your everyday practice. Balance between God's activity and your activity. May you keep remembering that 'faith without works' is almost as dead as works without faith. So, may you keep searching for that holistic understanding of human life played out under God's sovereign hand—an understanding that brings everything back into balance and that results in God's ultimate "well-done!"

As you too face the difficulties of life, Joshua of Today, may Yahweh also bless *your* lying down (even in the dust!) and *your* rising up (to help someone) from this day forward and forevermore!

VI.

GOD'S GREAT QUESTION TO ELIJAH

"WHAT ARE YOU DOING HERE?"

A question of assurance

1 KINGS 17–19; 2 KINGS 2

"Elijah was a man of passions, just like you and me." That's how the writer of James described me in the New Testament.

"A man of *passions*?" Oh, yes! Many passions. Grand passions. Passions that were poles apart.

Since the book of James was referring to my grand moment of courage on Mount Carmel, I will begin my story there. But let me forewarn you that this glorious day set off a terrifying hornet's nest inside of me. And my hope is that, as James suggests, you will be able to glimpse your own struggles amid my warring passions.

∽

Jehovah found me, a Tishbite, living beyond the Jordan River, near Gilead. There he commissioned me to be his prophet, to deliver his message to Israel's wicked King Ahab.

So I quickly pulled a hairy garment over my towering frame, secured my wide, leather belt, and set forth immediately for the palace. With unfeigned boldness I strode into the King's presence. And as if breathing forth fire, I pronounced the terrible words of God's impending judgment on the ten northern tribes of the divided Kingdom, saying:

"In the name of the Lord, the living God of Israel whom I serve, I tell you that there will be neither dew nor rain for the next several years, King Ahab—until I speak again!"

And it was so.

So, for three years the azure skies above the Northern Kingdom barred entry to all clouds. For three years the earth cracked in agony. For three years parched lips looked in vain for water to soothe their dryness. For three years the specter of death haunted Israel as her punishment for worshiping foreign gods.

Now, after three years of dust, of famine, of thirst, Jehovah was sending me back to confront King Ahab and all of his people. The time for a showdown had come.

At stake, I knew, was the faith of our people. In the balance hung the future religion of Israel. This would be a to-the-death contest of power between the deities competing for allegiance. Which one would really win the hearts of the people? The foreign gods of Ahab and Jezebel? Or Jehovah, God of Israel?

In front of the altars on Mount Carmel throngs of expectant people crowded together. The Israelites. King Ahab. And the pagan priests. 450 priests of Baal, and 400 priests of Asherah supported by wicked Queen Jezebel.

My voice thundered as I addressed the people. I wanted to make abundantly sure that they understood how crucial this moment was. Whatever they would decide this day could determine the very survival of Jehovah as the God of Israel. In words echoing those of Moses and Joshua, I pleaded with the children of Israel to make a choice, and to choose carefully which deity they would serve:

"How long will you continue to limp between two opinions? You keep hopping back and forth between worshiping Baal and worshiping Jehovah. The time has come to decide. If Jehovah is God, then worship him; but if Baal is god, then serve him!

I am the only prophet of Jehovah still left. And there are 450 prophets of Baal.

So, bring two bulls. Let the prophets of Baal take one, kill it, cut it in pieces, and put it on the wood. Then leave it there. Don't light the fire. I will do the same with the other bull. Let the prophets of Baal pray to their god, and I will pray to Jehovah.

And the God who answers by sending fire—he is God!"

Unless my God answered by fire, I knew that my life was over. I'd surely be killed on the spot. But what a way to dramatize the crucial issue for the people. By my all-or-nothing choice, I was enacting a parable before them. I wanted them to see how much my confidence rested in the power of Jehovah. Even my name, "Elijah" bore my very message today: "Jehovah is God!"

I made sure that no one could believe that any trickery was involved on either side. So I gave Baal's priests their choice of bulls. Then I allowed them to build their own pyre for the sacrifice and to call first upon their gods. And it was so.

With a burst of frantic activity, the pagan priests began their imploring.

All around me, I watched eyes grow wider. Beads of perspiration dotted priestly brows. Bodies strained forward. Men jostled each other for a clearer view. A hush fell over Mount Carmel. Troubled faces told the story. The people were still "limping between two opinions."

This was the painfully serious side of a struggle.

But as the minutes yawned into hours, I began to see the utter absurdity of this struggle too. I'm a big, burly, outdoorsman who deals with what's "real," what I can touch and feel. And to me, none of the pagan priests' frenzy made any sense to me whatsoever.

Imagine the idiocy of grown men calling upon gods which they themselves make out of wood and stone. How can they possibly expect these man-made gods to answer? Just picture it. Creatures made in the image of God gashing themselves with spears and razors in order to gain the attention of gods made in their own image. How sad! If Queen Jezebel had been born an Israelite rather than a foreign princess from Phoenecia, I wondered, would she would have been so willing to support all these ridiculous gyrations in the name of religion?

Meanwhile, the more the priests of Baal ranted and raved in their deafening ecstasy, the more dreadful became the contrasting silence of their gods. It was pathetic. Laughable. Ludicrous. Absurd.

Finally I decided that the farce had gone on long enough for the priests and people to become uncomfortable. So I began to tease. Then to taunt. I felt just a twinge of conscience, but I convinced myself that my measured jests would help to unmask the heathen gods before the people. So about

GOD'S GREAT QUESTION TO ELIJAH

noontime, in order to enliven the contest, I offered my tongue-in-cheek suggestions:

"You priests! Why don't you try praying harder to this god of yours? Maybe he's lost in a delightful day-dream. Or (who knows?) perhaps he's gone off to relieve himself in the bushes. And of course, he could have taken off on a long journey without advising you.

Oh, I know. He's probably fallen asleep. Old gods need lots of naps, you know. And they get quite deaf. So, try screaming louder. And try shaking him. Surely that will awaken him."

Annoyed by my insults, they ranted and raved even more furiously until mid-afternoon, gashing themselves, until the blood flowed. Still, no answer came. So they began to dance to the beat of their chants. Still no word. Still no message from their gods.

As I watched these pagan priests among us, I began to see just how utterly faithless our people had become. And I began to marvel that Jehovah had been patient with us for so many years.

How long had this blasphemy gone on? It seemed as if we had been "whoring after other gods" almost as far back as the Covenant itself. Our forefathers had worshiped the golden calf in the Wilderness. But that was nothing compared with what we were doing now. When Solomon's kingdom finally split apart about a century ago, hadn't King Jeroboam once again erected two huge Golden Calves for us to worship at Dan and at Bethel? Hadn't he told us in the Northern Kingdom, "*Here* are your gods who brought you out of Egypt?" Incredible! And to make it worse, what a string of evil kings had followed Jeroboam, each one committing "more evil in the Lord's eyes than had his fathers before him."

Now the Northern Kingdom had yet another wicked leader, King Ahab. Not only had he continued the "high places" and the "sacred groves" of his ancestors, but he increased Israel's sins. He built a Temple to Baal in Samaria, an altar where he encouraged Israel to offer sacrifices to the pagan god. Then when Ahab married a foreign princess who worshiped Asherah, he adopted Jezebel's god as well.

What faithlessness! And over so many years. It's no wonder that Jehovah was angry. No wonder he was sending such severe punishment. No wonder that he wanted his people to return to him.

This was the moment of decision. If the people of Israel were ever to return to Jehovah, it must be now. Right now—at the very height of their pagan priests' chants.

So I stepped forward. And I called all the people to come close. As they gathered around me, I could see their curiosity being transformed into expectancy.

In silence, I began to repair the old altar of Jehovah which Israel had let fall into disrepair. As a living parable, I took twelve uncut stones, one for each of the twelve tribes of Jacob. Oh, what memories this would evoke in the people's hearts. With these twelve stones, I formed a sacred altar where, once again, I could offer the appointed sacrifice for sin, as Jehovah had commanded us long ago.

Around this pillar of stones, I dug a trench large enough to hold gallons of water. Upon the stones, I placed some wood. And when I had cut the bull into pieces, I laid it atop the kindling.

"Fill four jugs with water and pour it over the offering and the wood," I commanded. And they did. "Do it again." I insisted. And they did. "Just once more," I ordered. And it was so.

I paused in silence.

All of us could hear the steady drip-drip-drip of the water as it filtered down from the drenched sacrifice and began to fill up the trench.

And then—just at the appointed hour of Israel's evening sacrifice—I approached the sacred altar of Jehovah, and I prayed loudly enough for all to hear:

> "O Jehovah, God of Abraham, Isaac, and Jacob, prove now that you are the God of Israel and that I, your servant, have done all these things at your command. Answer me, O Lord, so that this people shall know that you, Jehovah, are God and that you are bringing them to yourself once again as your people."

I remained with my head bowed. Around me I could hear quiet gasps. Filled with awe, some dropped to their knees. Others raised their faces toward heaven. Their many hopes, and fears, heightened the expectation.

Then I waited for my God.

And suddenly from on high, Jehovah rained down fire! Fire that completely consumed the sacrifice. Fire that destroyed the wood and the stones. Fire that scorched the ground. Fire that reduced the water in the trench to a mere vapor.

Just as our God had breathed fire from heaven long ago in the Wilderness to initiate our whole system of sacrifices, so he breathed fire from heaven now to restore it. His fire was surely a sign that he was ready once again to receive offerings for sin from his people. Jehovah was willing to restore his fellowship with his people if only his people would "set themselves apart" by their exclusive worship of him.

When the people saw what had happened, they flung themselves to the ground in contrition, crying out in loud voices, "Jehovah is God! Jehovah alone is our God!" Finally Israel had stopped limping between two opinions. Israel had finally chosen Jehovah once again. Jehovah's fire had ignited flames inside hearts that had grown cold.

As the people danced and shouted for joy, I turned to King Ahab and said, "I can already hear the sound of rain approaching. Now go. You can now eat as much as you wish, in confidence that the harvest will indeed come this year."

While Ahab ate, I climbed to the top of Mount Carmel. There I bowed in prayer, asking the Almighty to send rain he had promised, to redeem the parched land. Seven times I sent my servant to search the sea for a sign. On the seventh time, he returned breathlessly, saying, "I can see a cloud, but it's still no bigger than a man's hand."

As soon as I heard his words, I hurried to send a warning to King Ahab. "The rain we so desperately need is fast approaching. You must board your chariot immediately lest its wheels become mired in mud on the way back down the mountain to the plain of Jezreel."

Black clouds gathered quickly. The sky darkened. A strange wind began to blow. And then, after three long years, the rain began to fall once again in Israel. A welcome gift from the God of the heavens. At first, just drops. Then faster and faster. What a welcome sound, the sound of abundant rain!

I was beginning to get drenched. So I tucked my singed garment into my leather belt, and I began to run as hard as I could down the mountain. Empowered by the wind of the Spirit, I somehow overtook Ahab and arrived back home in the valley even before the King's chariot.

Jehovah had shown his mighty power on Mount Carmel. Jehovah had won the hearts of the people. And once again, Jehovah was enthroned as the God of Israel.

What a day! What a day! WHAT A DAY!

∽

And what a difference a day makes.

By daybreak the next morning, I found myself running again. This time I was running in frantic terror. I was speeding southward down the muddy road from Jezreel to Beersheba. Like a man possessed, I was now fleeing for my life.

Why? Oh, I forgot to tell you. After Jehovah's glorious triumph at Mount Carmel, the people and I banded together. Before nightfall, we destroyed all the false prophets of Baal and Asherah. And you can't possibly imagine how this angered Queen Jezebel! So she had vowed to kill me before this day was over.

I roused my servant and bid him come with me. We traveled by the quickest route down to the southernmost part of Judah. But before long, I became exhausted. Confused. Afraid.

What was happening inside me? I couldn't explain it. Just yesterday I had witnessed the power of the Almighty on Mount Carmel. And today here I was running away in sheer terror. I felt so powerless. So impotent. So panicked. Now it was the "courageous" Elijah, rather than the people of Israel, who was "limping between two opinions."

When we finally reached Beersheba, I left my servant there. I journeyed on alone for a full day further into the bleak Wilderness.

Finally spent, I slumped down under the shade of a broom tree. Bone weary. Lonely. Hungry. Thirsty. Totally depleted in mind and body. And I prayed: "Jehovah, this is Elijah. I've had enough! I can't possibly stand any more! Take my life from me. It's of absolutely no use to me anymore."

Having delivered my troubled spirit into his sovereign hands, I fell into a deep, deep sleep. After a while, an angel touched my shoulder, saying,: "Arise! Eat!" I looked around. Near where I had laid my head, I found a fresh loaf of bread and some water. I ate and drank. Then I slipped back into merciful slumber.

Once again the angel awakened me. "Wake up! Eat, or the long journey ahead will be too much for you."

"The long journey ahead?" What long journey? Where was "ahead?" Where was I going? I really didn't know.

I realized that I had become so fearful and disoriented that I hadn't even been able to think. So I had run instead. Driven by terror. Driven by despair.

Where was I now? At the edge of the Wilderness of Sinai. My impulsive dash southward suddenly made sense to me. Some divine, or primal, instinct had been leading me all along. And now I knew where I had been heading. Consciously or subconsciously, I was heading toward Mount Sinai. I was heading toward the mountain of Jehovah.

GOD'S GREAT QUESTION TO ELIJAH

But I still didn't understand why.

Every step I took during my forty-day journey, I could picture the children of Israel as they wandered through this same desolate land for forty long years. And this caused me to think of Moses. Dear Moses! What a brother! Surely Moses would understand what I was going through now. Alas, what a shame it was that I couldn't talk with Moses now, face to face.

But in the secret of my own heart, I was beginning to envision something far better than talking with Moses. There *was* someone with whom I could talk face to face, and that was Jehovah, God of Moses, who dwelt on the sacred mountain.

But even as I celebrated this emerging dream, a terrifying thought hit me. If I ever got to the holy mountain, how would I dare talk face to face with Jehovah, I wondered? Just the prospect of such an encounter brought me chills. Jehovah was too powerful, too "other", too transcendent. How could a puny mortal man like me ever converse with such a mighty God, the God who had rained down fire from heaven on Mount Carmel?

Day after day, I pondered what I could say to him. At last I finally framed my thoughts into words. And I memorized them, line by line:

"Jehovah, Almighty God, I have always served you zealously. But the people of Israel have broken your covenant. They have torn down your altars and killed all your prophets. Now, behold, I am the only one left, and they are trying to kill me too."

Quite a speech! Magnificent in self-pity. Arrogant in self-serving. Elevated in self-importance. Selective in memory. I'd quite forgotten that Obadiah had hidden one hundred prophets of Jehovah in caves to save them from the massacre of Ahab and Jezebel. And I was rather ignorant. I really had no reason to believe I was "the only one left."

But for now, this was all I could think to say. So I kept repeating it over and over. In the awesome presence of Jehovah, I didn't want to panic and forget my message.

After forty days, I finally reached the holy mountain. Wanting to be refreshed when I met my God, I climbed up to a safe place on the rock and dropped off to sleep in a cave.

Some time later, I don't know when, Jehovah awakened me. And as he approached me, he uttered a most strange and unexpected question:

"ELIJAH! ELIJAH, WHAT ARE YOU DOING HERE?"

Now, I wish you could fully appreciate how I felt at this moment. For forty days and forty nights I had dreamed of this glorious encounter. *My* encounter! My encounter with the great God of Israel. In my imagination, I had simply assumed that this meeting would be fully as dramatic as the day on Mount Carmel. But it wasn't. Not at all! Not at all!

Jehovah's words shocked me. They were so terribly common. So very usual. So like common chatter in the marketplace. So terribly human. So unlike a God. It was if he were to say to you today, "Hi there! Whatcha doin' here?" His words sounded so ordinary that it was downright extraordinary.

But whether I was startled by him or not, and whether I was offended by him or not, I had to give him an answer. So my numb lips obediently began to mouth the words I had already committed well to memory:

> "Jehovah, Almighty God, I have always served you zealously. But the people of Israel have broken your covenant. They have torn down your altars and killed all your prophets. Now, behold, I am the only one left, and they're trying to kill me too."

Oh, I presume that Jehovah was listening to me. But he surprised me by not responding to my prepared statement. Instead, he said very simply: "Go to the top of this mountain, Elijah, and stand upon the rock in my presence." And it was so.

There, Jehovah himself passed by me in all of his magnificent splendor. As he passed, the mountain shook with a fierce wind. Rocks shattered. Mountains split apart. Boulders crashed around me. I looked for my God. But the God I was looking for was not in the whirlwind.

Again the earth shook—this time with a violent earthquake. With all my energy, I struggled just to keep my balance. I wondered whether the mountain could endure, much less whether I could possibly survive. Once more I looked for Jehovah. But the God I was looking for was not in the earthquake.

After the earthquake came a blazing fire. With awe and wonder, I recalled how Moses had once met his God at the burning bush on this mountain. So I again looked for Jehovah. But the God I was looking for was not in the fire.

Finally, after the wind, after the earthquake, after the fire, came one hushed whisper! One solitary, hushed whisper. And it came—to *me*!

And what did he whisper? I'm not sure, but I have a strong hunch. I believe that Jehovah was pronouncing before me his sacred name, just as he had to Moses years ago. And why do I think this? Because by the time I was wondering what he had said to me, I had already hidden my face deep in my cloak. In the instant of that holy whisper, I had instinctively shown my deepest reverence.

With my face still covered, I came and stood once again at the entrance of the mountain cave. And guess what happened. Once again Jehovah asked me the same strange question as before, in the same ordinary way:

"ELIJAH! ELIJAH, WHAT ARE YOU DOING HERE?"

I still didn't know what to say. By now I realized that I hadn't quite answered his question the first time. Yet I could think of no other answer. So I began my now-familiar speech again:

"Jehovah, Almighty God, I have always served you zealously, and now they are trying to kill me too."

But by the time I finished my recital, a strange peace had somehow worked its way throughout my battered body and soul. I could feel a transforming difference inside. I was becoming alive again. I was becoming whole again. What could explain it? His soft whisper? Yes, but more than that.

I struggled to piece together all that had been happening to me since that one great day.

Back there on Mount Carmel, I realized, I had witnessed the transcendent God. I had seen him stoop down from heaven that day to show himself in a mighty triumph of power. But on the very next morning when Jezebel threatened to kill me, I had fled in terror. Why? Because I was afraid and I was in trouble. And now I was discovering that when you're afraid and in trouble, there's nothing lonelier than having only a transcendent God. The God I knew on Carmel had gone back "home" somewhere. And now where could I turn for my own solace? The God of the Mount surely existed "way above and beyond" the everyday reach of an ordinary person like me.

But then, I argued with myself, hadn't God been "with me" in some sense during the three years of drought? Hadn't he sent ravens to feed me? Hadn't he commanded the widow of Zarephath to give me bread and water? Surely, the grace of Jehovah was the only thing that could persuade a scavenger bird to release its prey, or a poor widow to give up her last meal. So why wasn't all that assurance enough? Because, I argued, those evidences of his grace came when I was serving as the prophet of Jehovah. Back then, I was his mouthpiece. Back then, I was "on duty" for my God.

But alas, that holy ministry was now complete. Once the rain began to fall on Israel, surely my importance to Jehovah had ended. Or had it? *Or had it?*

All along I had never doubted that God was real and that God was "there" in some sense. Yet in the cauldron of my own life, the burning question increasingly became: But is Jehovah also there for *me*? That's what I desperately needed to know. That's why I had come to Mount Sinai. I had come here because I had to find out for myself if the transcendent God would really draw near to *me* amid the troubles and trials of my own miserable existence!

Now at last I had my answer. I had found his assurance!

Just as Jehovah had rained down fire on Mount Carmel, he had sent the wind, the earthquake, and the fire here too. But here on Mount Sinai, the transcendent God had added something more. He had given me important evidences of his divine grace to me as a person. He called me by my name! He called out to me in a question borrowed from the most familiar, the most ordinary jargon of human existence—he used the language of a friend! And then He spoke into my ear in a hushed whisper, his incredible surprise of intimacy! What gracious touches of shalom to a disintegrating man.

Here at Mount Sinai, he had indeed come—just to meet *me*!

"**What are you doing here?**" "Whatcha doin' here?" Thanks to God's great question, I finally was able to see, and embrace, two truths together. Jehovah is indeed the transcendent God of power who had parted the Red Sea for Moses and who had rained fire from heaven on Mount Carmel. But as surely, Jehovah is also an immanent God who cares enough to reassure even a frightened "hero" of yesterday by stooping down to whisper into his ear.

What a day!

∼

Finally there came another day, the day of my departure from this world. Once again there was a journey. For companionship I took with me Elisha, the prophet upon whom I already had cast my mantle. When we reached Gilgal, I said to him: "Elisha, stay here. Jehovah is sending me to Bethel." But faithful Elisha insisted on traveling with me, on to Bethel, and then on to Jericho.

Again at Jericho, I tried to send him back. But he would not. I gathered that somehow he sensed that Jehovah was coming for me this day.

At last we approached the mighty Jordan River. I folded up my cloak and struck the waters. They parted. We two walked over on dry ground.

Now I became increasingly aware that we were nearing Mount Nebo, the place where Moses had departed. After conferring a double portion of my spirit on Elisha for his ministry, I felt an urge to turn around one last time to glimpse the Land of Promise just once more. "I looked over Jordan. And what did I see, comin' for to carry me home? A band of angels comin' after me! Comin' for to carry me home!"

What a sight! Who would have guessed it? I couldn't believe my eyes!

In a flaming chariot, the King of Kings swooped low to gather me up to be with him. Oh, if only King Ahab could see *my* chariot. But, alas, he had made another choice and lay wasted. Then once more came a divine whirlwind, much as I had experienced on Mount Sinai. I could feel myself being lifted up from the earth. Jehovah was taking me home.

"Oh, my lord master! I can see the chariots and horses of Israel!" exclaimed Elisha.

As I heard him cry out, I wondered if that was all he saw. In all of the excitement, would Elisha also see the rich symbolism? He'd never have a clearer picture. Jehovah's own chariots of fire had descended from heaven to earth, to bring a mortal man to be with him forever. A transcendent God? Oh, yes! And an immanent God? Amazingly, he was that too!

What a day!

∽

At the time of my Translation into glory, I had no idea that I was yet to experience yet another dramatic day. Once again I would appear upon the earth. Once again I would be on a mountain. This time, on the Mount of Transfiguration.

Jesus, God's Messiah, had come to this mountain that day together with three of his disciples, Peter, James and John, to pray with his Father. He wanted to prepare himself for dying on the cross just days ahead of him, and to talk with his disciples about his impending "exodus" from this world. Suddenly as the disciples looked at him, Jesus's face began to shine with an unearthly glow and his garments became dazzling white. In brilliant incandescence, the Christ became transfigured before their eyes.

And standing alongside the Messiah that day, two figures appeared who were also bathed in light. One was Moses. And I was the other.

When then the clouds of heaven opened, we all heard the voice of Jehovah declare: "This is Jesus, my beloved Son, with whom I am well pleased. Hear ye him!"

Struck with awe, Jesus' disciples flung themselves down and lay prostrate on the ground in awe. When they dared to look up again, Moses and I had vanished from their sight. Jesus alone remained.

At this moment, I heard Simon Peter ("not knowing what he was saying", as the text records) suddenly blurt out: "Lord, if you wish, I'd be glad to build three Tabernacles here—one for you, one for Elijah, and one for Moses."

I should be flattered. But dear Peter had missed the point by a mile. Three tabernacles were hardly appropriate. Only one! And yet behind Peter's blundering impulse lurked a profound truth. Peter was, of course, referring to the annual Jewish Feast of Tabernacles, commemorating the Israelites' forty-year Wilderness wandering when the invisible God dwelled ("tabernacled") among them in the Tent of Meeting. And now, I wondered if perhaps Peter hadn't subconsciously glimpsed something even more incredible. Right here in their very midst, this same God was again "tabernacling" among them. Somehow God had emptied himself into a visible human body for all to see, in the person of his Son, Jesus Christ. Peter's mountaintop companion, John, would later write of witnessing Jesus's incarnation: "The eternal Word became flesh and dwelled (tabernacled) among us. And we saw his glory for ourselves, the glory as of the only begotten Son of the Father, the epitome of grace and truth."

In this brief vignette on the Mount of Transfiguration, I glimpsed God's transcendence and God's immanence linked together forever—in the God-Man, Jesus Christ.

I had witnessed the dawn of a glorious new day.

~

My dear Elijah of Today, I have a prayer for you. I pray that with one hand you will always hold tightly to the truth that Jehovah, the Almighty God of power, exists above and beyond anything we can possibly imagine. And with the other hand, always hold tightly to the truth that this same Jehovah cares about you amid all the pains and doubts of your human existence.

Sooner or later the troubles of life are likely to buffet you so mercilessly that you will be tempted to let go with one hand or the other. But I beg you not to give in to those unwise passions.

If you let go of the almightiness of God, you will ultimately be left with despair. (Who can abide a loving God whose has no power?) And if you let go of the God who cares about you, you will ultimately be left with despair. (Who can abide a powerful God who has no love?) But a God of awesome power linked together with a God who cares deeply about you personally—that's the Christian gospel of the God-Man, Jesus Christ. And this good news provides us hope that endures amid all of life's struggles, amid all of our days.

So, then, with full assurance of faith, may you draw near to the Almighty God, as he also draws near to you!

VII.

GOD'S GREAT QUESTION TO JONAH

"DO YOU HAVE A RIGHT TO BE ANGRY?"

A question of mercy

JONAH 1–4

SELDOM HAVE SO MANY people enjoyed making fun of a prophet and his strange tale. "A whale of a fish story," some have called it. And I can understand how intellectual sophisticates of the scientific age would prefer to concentrate on a "whale hotel" with its "water-logged" guest than on the troublesome life story of a real prophet named Jonah.

Others have simply termed me the "Reluctant Prophet." I'm a bit embarrassed by that description. Oh, I agree that I was certainly reluctant. But that's too simplistic. From my vantage point now, I realize that I'm hardly worthy even to be called a "prophet" of the Lord, the Covenant God. But then, that's just one of the many things which I know now that I wish I'd known back then.

～

I grew up as a typical Hebrew boy in a Galilean village called Gath-Hepher, between Cana and Nazareth. Our land in the north of Palestine was part of the heritage bequeathed forever to the tribe of Zebulun. As the son of Amittai, I worshiped regularly in the synagogue. Three times a day I prayed toward the Holy Temple on Mount Zion. Night and day I meditated on the Law of God.

Every Sabbath I enjoyed listening to the elders read aloud the Sacred Writings showing how God had led our Fathers in the past. I celebrated that I was an offspring of Abraham, of Isaac, of Jacob. They reminded me that I too was a child of the Promise. This was my greatest joy. And this joy was worth living for. Even dying for.

Being one of "The Chosen"—this became a large part of my identity. Being "chosen" linked me with the all-powerful God of the ages who had faithfully hovered over people, led them out of captivity in Egypt, shepherded them through the Wilderness, ushered them into the Promised Land. "I will be your God," he had promised us. "Just be careful to obey everything I have told you. Destroy all the heathen inhabitants of the land of Canaan. Tear down the heathen altars. Do not marry heathen women. Then I will remain with you." At least, that's the way I heard his message to us.

How glad I was that I didn't have to endure the fate of those not chosen by God, those uncouth Syrians to the north or the half-breed Samaritans to the south. And, thank God, we were so far separated from the godless Assyrians to the east. For that, I often expressed gratitude to God.

From time to time, traveling merchants came through our village. I heard them spin yarn after yarn about the opulent wonders of the capital of Assyria, depraved Nineveh. Stories of unthinkable wealth. Gold. Silver. Vast treasures plundered from vanquished peoples. Stories of awesome military power. Swift chariots. Fleet cavalry. Flashing swords and sharpened spears. Stories of lavish, riotous living. Orgies in the royal palace. Slave girls. Rampant prostitution. sorcerers and witchcraft.

Back then, I couldn't admit even to myself how utterly fascinated I was by such a city. And so Nineveh became the symbol of all that repulsed me. Nineveh! I'd spit whenever I heard the word. "Godless Nineveh! Someday, may God judge you as harshly as you deserve!" As I grew older, this became one of my most earnest prayers.

∼

"Jonah! Jonah!"

The voice called me from nowhere. It was startling, yes. But more than that. The voice drew me irresistibly toward it. Could this voice belong to the God of my Fathers? Was that possible? But what could he want from this young peasant from Zebulun?

Scarcely had I time to ponder when the voice continued its message.

"Jonah ! Jonah!" I have something I want you to do for me. This was indeed God's voice, I was sure. "Jonah, I want you to be my prophet."

His prophet? A prophet of the Lord, the Covenant God of Israel? Was he giving *me* the privilege of taking his own words and speaking them forth?

Maybe you'd have to be a deeply religious Hebrew lad to comprehend just how much those words meant to me. I recalled the powerful prophets of old, like Samuel and Nathan. And I remembered more recent ones, like Elijah and Elisha.

To be his prophet meant that I would be the intermediary between the Covenant God and his people, perhaps even to the king. It wouldn't be easy, I knew that. Prophets led tough lives. Often they were lonely. Often misunderstood. Often persecuted. Often fleeing the wrath of kings and princes. Often proclaiming to their own people a message of doom they didn't even want to believe, much less speak forth. Oh, no!

I began to tremble. Almost before I knew what I was saying I blurted out, "Oh God, you're not asking me to proclaim devastation on my own people, are you?"

"No, not at all," said the voice, "much more important than that."

I relaxed and smiled. "Perhaps he will give me a message of blessing," I pondered. "Perhaps a message to the king. And perhaps the king will be so pleased that he will richly reward me." A myriad of such glorious thoughts raced through me at such speed that I couldn't possibly describe them.

"Oh Lord, I am your humble servant," I responded. "Just speak your word and I will do it. I will go anywhere. I will say anything. I will do whatever you ask."

In the awkward silence that followed, I began to ponder what I had offered. Was that really what I'd be willing to do? I felt a bit uneasy inside. Was it anticipation? Or dread?

"Jonah, son of Amittai: Go to that great city and preach against it, because its wickedness has come up before me."

"But Lord," I protested, "You said I didn't have to prophesy doom against my own people."

"No, Jonah. Not to your own people. I want you to go farther. The circle of my love, you see, is much larger than you can imagine. I am commissioning you to be my prophet to the wicked capital of Israel's great enemy. I am sending you to Nineveh!"

"Nineveh?" I hoped that my squeaky high-pitched tone hadn't revealed my absolute incredulity. "Nineveh!" he replied. And then, absolute silence.

~

All night long I wrestled with my mandate. No nightmare could top this. How could God do this to me? How could he call me to be his mouthpiece, and then send me to outcasts, to those who were Not Chosen—to godless sinners who even dared to taunt our God? At best it was a bad plan.

Oh, I could certainly understand God's desire to bring destruction on Nineveh. But why give them a warning first? They had already declared themselves to be the sworn enemies of the Promise. To "warn" such conscience-less infidels was to show utter weakness. That was not worthy of a righteous God! Surely the people of Nineveh would laugh haughtily in his face. No, God hadn't given the plan enough thought. And I couldn't be party to such a mockery.

And furthermore, consider what would happen to *me* if the people of Nineveh chose to repent? Had he bothered to think of that? If they chanced to repent, I wouldn't even be acclaimed a true prophet, because the impending doom I proclaimed wouldn't come to pass. So, after all my pain and struggles to warn infidels, I'd simply be "hung out to dry." And any good prophet from Israel was properly entitled to much more respect than that. No, I couldn't accept such a proposal.

I tried to reason with the God I couldn't see. Silence. I pleaded. Silence. Finally I screamed at him to reconsider his ill-advised plan, for the sake of his own good Name—and mine. But all I heard was absolute, unmovable silence! Well, I'd given him a chance to change his mind.

Before the first rays of light, I had packed. With a wistful glance at the sleepy town of Gath-Hepher, I decided to turn my back on Nineveh and follow instead the dusty road down to Joppa.

Joppa's glistening harbor was replete with tall ships from exotic ports. I recognized some of them. Tyre and Sidon in Phoenicia. Salamis in Kittim (now called Cyprus). And "Tarshish"?

Somewhere I'd heard of Tarshish. Wasn't that another name for "Spain" at the farthest point of the Great Sea? Or was Tarshish in North Africa? Or near India? No matter! It was far away—from Nineveh—and from God.

It would be a lengthy and dangerous voyage to Tarshish. But the wooden vessel seemed sturdy enough, with voluminous sails and oiled riggings weathered by many a violent Mediterranean storm. "Yes, Tarshish. I'll go unnoticed there. And what about Nineveh? Whatever! Let Nineveh perish without a prophet's warning."

Proud of my decision, I hurried to board the vessel that creaked and moaned with each gentle lapping swell.

I quickly observed what a filthy, scurvy crew they were. Foreigners, most likely Phoenicians. Wretched pagans. Vile. Uncouth. "Not likely to honor the prophet of the Lord," I concluded. So I scurried below, found refuge alone in the miserable quarters of the smelly hold, and fell asleep at long last.

~

I was startled from my sleep by violent shaking at my shoulder. Someone was yelling at me. The entire vessel heaved and belched. Wood split and crashed against metal. I could hear frightened sailors wail frantically in an unknown tongue.

Struggling to pry open my eyes, I came face to face with terror. Giant beams cracked. Pottery jugs smashed against the wooden planks. Whirled around by incredible force, I slammed against the door and landed bleeding against the stairway. My stomach turned. My head swirled dizzily with each jolt of the ship. I felt sick.

The sailor who had awakened me pleaded urgently. "We have done everything we can. Pray to your god, Sir, if you have one!"

I was pained by his lack of understanding. I explained to the godless man that I was a devout Hebrew, a worshiper of the God of the Covenant, and that I was running away from him rather than deliver his message of impending destruction to heathen people of Nineveh. My spirit swelled with pride.

Instead of receiving this pagan sailor's respect and gratitude, however, I experienced his rage. "What have you done? It must be because of *you* that these seas churn, threatening our lives too." He turned heel and rushed back up on deck.

Drawing lots, the crew desperately tried to make sure that I was indeed the one who had angered the god of the seas. What should they do? Since they had already jettisoned the cargo, I finally mustered my courage and offered for them to throw me overboard to calm the raging sea.

To my amazement, these heathens responded with fear. Immediately they began praying to the only gods they knew, asking for forgiveness for what they were about to do. Then, having unburdened their tortured souls, they unceremoniously hurled me, prophet of the Covenant God, into the sea.

Through pelting rain and gale-force winds I plunged headlong into the freezing waters. Like a man suddenly possessed, I desperately sought to stay afloat. Why I struggled, I don't know. At that point I wanted nothing more than to disappear forever from the face of the earth. Angry waves landed their powerful punches. Seaweed tangled and choked me. Frantically, I gasped for breath. Water poured through my mouth and nose. Overpowered and overwhelmed, I began to sink.

While the seas churned wildly, inside I was churning even more. Deep within me, that is where the real drama was being played. So much flashed upon my memory. I recalled my pleasant youth in Galilee. The warmth of our family fellowship. Eating olives, pomegranates, and roast lamb together. Strolling through grain fields at harvest time. Prostrating myself toward the glorious Holy Hill.

From the depths of my being, some primal instinct kept compelling me to continue fighting to hold onto life. But hard as I fought, I sank deeper. Down. Down. D-o-w-n. Finally everything turned black and deathly still.

With all my meager power, I began to cough. As I struggled to expel the inhaled water, I managed to replace it with short gasps of air. Absolutely convulsed by this frantic heaving that engaged my entire body, I finally fell in an exhausted heap to the very bottom. Totally limp, with my will vanquished, I lay motionless.

∽

I have no idea how long I remained there. Perhaps days. And then I awoke. Eyes smarting. Muscles cramped and aching. All I could see was pitch blackness. Where was I? Sheol, I surmised. Sheol, the silent world of the dead from which I could never return.

Dejected, I hid my face in my outstretch hands. And then this touch caused me to think. I could still feel my hands and my head. In fact, my entire body. Would that be true if I were really in Sheol? I wasn't sure.

But if not in Sheol, where was I? I laughed aloud at a funny thought: perhaps a big fish had swallowed me and was allowing me to reside in its hospitable belly. What a wonderfully impossible scene! And yet to a true believer, a Hebrew, nothing was ever impossible. Still? Ah, no matter. Wherever I was, I felt safe.

Just the thought of Sheol brought to my consciousness the comforting, yet incisive, words of the Psalmist which I had memorized line by line in my youth. Words about the Covenant God. Words perhaps even more appropriate here than when first uttered:

> "Where could I go to escape from you? Where could I get away
> from your presence? If I went up to heaven, you would be there
> If I lay down in the world of the dead, you would there to help
> me; down in the world of the dead, you are there to help me."
>
> (Psalm 139:7, 8)

How gracious is the gift of remembering. Especially when we remember the God who created us and who continues to love us, no matter how far we flee from his sight.

Suddenly I had only one desire. If only I could prostrate myself once more to pray to the God of my Fathers—to turn toward Mount Zion—to seek his presence in the Holy Temple once again!

Days had passed since I had prayed, since the day I'd heard the voice. Now I stretched out fully, face down. How familiar and how good it felt. I began to position myself toward the Holy Temple, recalling the special promises given to God's 'Chosen People' at its dedication. If only I could turn toward him there, perhaps he would still hear me.

But alas, where was his Holy Temple? In the blackness I couldn't even imagine in what direction I might find it. I was beginning to feel "lost."

Again, briefly, I recalled my strange idea that I could be inside a giant fish in the depths of the ocean, about as far away as one could possibly descend from the Holy Temple on Mount Zion. I wondered if God were able to see me right now. And if so, what would he see? Just a puny, trembling little prophet groping around inside the pitch-darkness of a "whale's belly?" Now that's funny! How absolutely ironic. And how very sad.

Well, whatever!

In the midst of my growing frustration about where I was and where the Holy Hill was, I finally reached a comforting conclusion. Could it be that that the more important thing was, not which direction the Temple happened to be, but for me to be willing simply to turn around from where I was fleeing. Surely if I turned around with all my heart and soul and mind and strength, wouldn't the God of the Covenant himself find me?

Infused with pure awe and wonder, I poured out my soul before him, holding nothing back. What security I felt in his presence! My words tumbled out without effort. Words partly mine, partly borrowed from the

GOD'S GREAT QUESTION TO JONAH

Psalms. Mingled together, they became my own hymn of gratitude, of remembering his presence . . . of hope in his saving promise, and of my own renewed promise to my God:

> "In my distress I called to the LORD
> and he answered me.
> From the depths of Sheol, I called for help.
> and you listened to my cry.
> You hurled me into the deep,
> into the very heart of the seas,
> and the currents swirled about me;
> all your waves and breakers
> swept over me.
> I said, 'I have been banished
> from your sight;
> yet I will look again
> toward your holy temple'.
> The engulfing waters threatened me,
> the deep surrounded me;
> seaweed was wrapped around my head.
> To the roots of the mountains I sank down;
> the earth beneath me barred me in forever
> But you brought my life up from the pit,
> O LORD my God.
> "When my life was ebbing away,
> I remembered you, LORD,
> and my prayer rose to you,
> to your holy temple.
> "Those who cling to worthless idols
> forfeit the grace that could be theirs.
> But I, with a song of thanksgiving,
> will sacrifice to you.
> What I have vowed, I will make good.
> Salvation comes from the LORD."
>
> (Jonah 2:2–9)

With these words of God's saving grace on my lips, I felt convulsing begin in the walls all around me, much like a woman experiencing childbirth. (I laughed in amusement.) But then, with one giant forward motion, I was thrust headlong onto a sandy beach.

Drenched. Tattered. Covered with vomit. But safe at last—and strangely renewed.

Israel's God, my God, had indeed heard me. Even in the depths, his grace had reached me.

"Jonah!" For the second time, that voice called in familiar tones. "Jonah, go to the great city and proclaim the message that I gave you." My heart leaped for joy. A second life! And now a second chance!

I rose up immediately, empowered with fresh vigor. And this unkempt- but-repentant prophet of the Lord journeyed on his way once more. This time, to Nineveh.

~

My ministry went quite well in Nineveh. It was a larger city than I imagined. Built initially by Nimrod, grandson of Cain, the once small village had by now mushroomed into a place where hundreds of thousands of people lived. Even the inner city walls measured nearly eight miles in circumference. It took me three days just to walk through it.

As soon as I had finished my first day's journey into Nineveh, I proclaimed the Lord's message: "Forty more days until Nineveh will be destroyed!" I cried loudly and with as much persuasion as I could muster.

As I spoke, I became aware that something more powerful than my "words" was affecting the people. I couldn't explain their overwhelming response. From the greatest to the least, countless men and women believed. They donned sackcloth to show their repentance. They even declared a fast.

What surprised me most was that my message of doom spread so rapidly. It didn't take long before even the King of Nineveh heard the news. He immediately rose from his throne, removed his royal robes, covered himself with sackcloth, and sat down repentant in the dust.

Then the King proclaimed to all Nineveh:

> "Do not let any man or beast, herd or flock, taste anything; do not let them eat or drink. But let man and beast be covered with sackcloth. Let everyone urgently call on God. Let them give up their evil ways and their violence. Who knows? God may yet relent

and with compassion turn from his fierce anger so that we will not perish."

(Jonah 3:7–9)

I couldn't believe that such godless barbarians would ever listen to such a message. Why should they care about the God of the Hebrews? Whatever! Living in such luxury and depravity, they surely wouldn't stay repentant for long. Just blindly following a religious fad right now, I reasoned. Curs! Pagan dogs! Let them play at their religion. We'll see!

Nor did these evil people pay the slightest attention to the one who had brought the message. Surely I wasn't invisible, was I? Perhaps they chose to ignore me because I was a 'foreigner.' Tempted to be hurt by their indifference, I kept reminding myself that *I* was the Chosen one, not these godless Gentiles.

As for me, I felt satisfied. My work bore all the marks of success. Never had so many people been so touched by the message of a prophet of the Lord. After he had given me another chance to do his work, I had fulfilled my mission to the letter. I had completed my work in proclaiming Nineveh's destruction. Now God would faithfully do his.

As I left Nineveh, I shook the dust of my sandals against the capital of wicked Assyria, Israel's deadly enemy.

What a difficult and long journey it had been since I left Gath-Hepher! Depleted, I made myself comfortable on a hill outside of Nineveh. A perfect vantage point. I would wait there for the Lord to mete out his inevitable justice on Nineveh.

∽

Forty days passed. And forty nights. Nothing happened. Nothing at all. I couldn't believe it. And yet I *could*.

My anger burned. Then smoldered. Then broke loose. In a fit of violent rage and righteousness indignation, I confronted the Almighty in searing tones:

"Lord, didn't I tell you? Back there in Galilee, that's exactly what I said that you would do. That's why I fled. And it was a good decision.

"What kind of a God are you? You talk to us about justice. Yet what do I see in you? You're full of grace and compassion. You're slow to anger. You abound in love. You relent from sending calamity. How does that square with your demands for justice?"

Just as my words had come easily when I lay prostrate in the belly of the fish, so they spewed forth easily now as I shook my fist in his face. Unabashed honesty, I called it.

I climaxed my soul-cleansing lecture with one "to-the-death" challenge. "Now Lord—in light of your choice to spare Nineveh and to 'hang me out to dry'—just take away my life from me. It's far better for me to die than to live any longer," I sighed angrily to underscore my point.

He didn't respond. Whatever! I was sure he'd heard.

So I sat down confidently. I waited for the Lord to change his mind.

On the hill east of Nineveh, I constructed a simple lattice-work shelter to shade me. A little vine with expansive leaves immediately sprang up and grew rapidly over the shelter to ease my discomfort. "Well, this is about the first *good* thing that has happened to me," I huffed.

But by morning, wouldn't you know it, some ne'er-do-well worm had chewed the root of the tender plant. Already the valiant little vine was withering. I felt sad, mostly for myself. But I also felt sorry for the courageously struggling plant, struck down in the innocence of budding life. How unjust! How merciless!

Then a fierce, scorching wind tore through my lattice. The blazing sun raised blisters on my balding head. I grew quite faint. I felt absolutely miserable.

With my blood boiling, I informed the Lord even more urgently that I would most certainly prefer to die than to live.

Well, that got his attention. And his full voice followed quickly:

"JONAH, DO YOU REALLY HAVE A RIGHT TO BE ANGRY?"

What a crazy question, I thought. I brushed it off with a glancing blow: "You bet! I'm angry enough to die."

"Oh Jonah, how can I teach you?" came our Lord's sorrowful reply. "It was *I* who brought the storm, you know. Only my gentle hand knew how much that fragile boat could suffer before the winds would batter it to pieces. But you did not understand how safe you are with me.

"It was *I* who brought the fish to shelter you, even when you had fled as far as you could go from my presence. But you did not understand that no one is beyond the open arms of my love, Jonah, not even sputtering 'Chosen' Prophets' and not even the 'foreigners' of Nineveh.

"Then I returned you safely to land. I even gave you a second chance to be my prophet. But you did not understand that to be my prophet is to receive a gift that must be completely poured out, all used up. I did not call you to give me advice or to evaluate my message, only to speak forth my own words as I gave them to you.

"And now, Jonah," he continued, "I provided the plant to bring you comfort. Then I was the one who sent a worm to destroy the plant. I hoped that you could grasp my parable. For one brief moment I sensed some tenderness and compassion in you, Jonah. But so quickly your tenderness and compassion withered." Yahweh sounded so sad, as if he no longer knew how to bridge the growing gulf between us.

"Jonah, don't you see? If you were concerned about this little plant that grew up yesterday and is gone today, can you not comprehend how much I care for the people of Nineveh, people whom I created, just as I created you? Yes, I have truly 'chosen you,' just as I have 'chosen the Hebrew people.' But my vast love allows me to choose whomever I will. You see, "I am who I am," and I will show mercy on whom I will show mercy. Can you comprehend that?

"And Jonah, suppose you don't share my concern for the 'godless foreign men and women' of Nineveh. But what about the others there? Should I not at least spare the 120 thousand little children and the animals? After all, what sin have *they* committed against me? Why should I punish them? They don't even know their right hand from their left. How could I serve my justice by destroying the innocent? Is it not 'God-like' for me to exercise my own loving-kindness and tender mercy? Aren't these the very terms you use to describe the Covenant God? And especially when my justice is satisfied by their repentance, should I not show them my mercy, just as I have shown it to *you*, Jonah?

"What kind of a God am I, you ask? The Hebrew God of the Covenant, yes. But just as surely the God of all Creation. To the children of the Promise, I have chosen to entrust my message of salvation. I longed for you to share the love you found in me with others—even with Israel's enemies—so that they too may come to know that **I AM GOD** over all the earth.

"NOW, DEAR JONAH, DO YOU STILL BELIEVE YOU HAVE A RIGHT TO BE ANGRY?"

∼

I wish I could tell you that his wonderfully unmasking question turned me around immediately. Alas, it took a long time for his great question to penetrate my many layers of self-pity, self-righteousness, and self-hate.

For a while I continued to loathe the Assyrians even more than I loathed myself. In the meantime, God's question kept on doing its quiet work. I kept talking with him. And he patiently began revealing to me my arrogant xenophobia, my smug "Chosen-ness," my desire to keep my own God exclusive to me, or perhaps to "us." Revealing my very rigid "letter of the law" piety. Revealing my unbending pride. Revealing my passionate desire to receive God's mercy while not wanting to grant his mercy to anyone else. Revealing my narcissism that blinded me from seeing the miserable plight of others who don't yet know the God that I know.

Now my greatest regret is that there are so many things I wish I had known all along:

I wish I had known that no one is beyond God's loving care, not reluctant prophets, nor "foreigners" to our religious establishments. How all-encompassing is the wide circle of his great love. How dare I limit it?

I wish I had known the real meaning of "mercy" and "compassion," words that I recited with ardor but without much understanding. In Gath-Hepher, I knew about God. But on the hill east of Nineveh, I finally met him!

I wish that I had known that he will never really 'hang me out to dry.' Not in my failure. *Nor* in my success. He is the God who spoke to me, and chose to speak to me again. He is the God who sent me, and sent me once again. He is the God who provided the winds and storms and shelter. He is the God who patiently confronted a pouting prophet who had foolishly squandered his perspective. He is the God who caused my ministry to triumph, even when I felt like a failure, even when I deserved to fail, and even when I wanted to be a failure.

I wish that I had known that the way to my fulfillment is to rejoice in those things that rejoice the heart of God. So my ministry became a "hard thing," instead of the inestimable joy that could have just as easily been mine.

I wish I would have known what a glorious opportunity I may have missed. Of all the ancient prophets, I alone was called to bring the message of our Lord far beyond our Promised Land. Perhaps I could have become the Old Testament equivalent of the Apostle Paul who was sent to all the Gentiles of Macedonia. But I failed to understand either God's mercy or his urgent vision for people that I somehow couldn't see. Alas, I was too blind, too angry, too unmerciful!

But despite all my lacks, "*our* ministry" was successful beyond anything I could possibly imagine. Simply because of him. Because of his great compassion. Because of his mercy. Because the godless people of Nineveh were far too important to him to allow me to get in the way of their precious salvation.

∼

The written story of Jonah breaks off at this point. I don't want to spoil the holy tension that this Scripture plants within you. But I really need to confess to you that I finally saw things God's way, partly in this lifetime, more completely in the presence of God himself. I finally came to understand how much God loves me—*and* how much he loves others too—even those whom I may despise. And finally I glimpsed the great mercy he had so graciously shown to *me*.

I also began to see how much mercy God had showered on the ministry of a very reluctant, pouting prophet. Imagine! Centuries after this, the Son of Man would graciously use my life to illustrate his own mercy poured out in sacrificial death:

> "For as Jonah was three days in the belly of a huge fish, so the Son of Man will be three days and three nights in the heart of the earth."
>
> (Matthew 12:40)

And then this Jesus, the God-Man, showed me that he can even bring holy fruit out of an unholy ministry. In perhaps his greatest act of mercy, he gave me a lavish inheritance of brothers and sisters in the faith from Nineveh—"foreign" believers that he found more acceptable to him than some of my own "Chosen" people—believers I will finally stand alongside at the last day:

> "The men of Nineveh will stand up at the judgment with this wicked generation and condemn it, for they repented at the preaching of Jonah, and now one greater than Jonah is here."
>
> (Matthew 12:41)

My story, unfinished in the Old Testament, finally came to glorious completion in the New Testament, as the Christ One finally came who is in every way "greater than Jonah." It is in *him* that we see what real mercy looks like!

I continue to be amazed at God's merciful grace. Grace that listened to all of my foolish lectures. Grace that in wisdom ignored them. Grace that insistently decreed divine blessing for all, for everyone, no matter how hard I fought against it.

Jonah of Today: I hope that my larger-than-life story encourages you. May it help to guide you in your own struggle to share gladly God's abundant love with others. And may his grace, mercy and peace be with you always, wherever he may send you!

VIII.

GOD'S GREAT QUESTION TO EZEKIEL

"SON OF MAN, CAN THESE DRY BONES EVER LIVE AGAIN?"

A question of renewal

EZEKIEL 37:1–14

BONES! NOTHING BUT DRY bones! Everywhere I looked, as far as the eye could see, the parched valley lay strewn with human bones—dry bones!

Face to face with such utter devastation, I was completely stunned. I could not feel. I could not think.

Yahweh brought me here to this valley. By the breath of his Spirit, he lifted me up high so that I could survey more carefully this grim scene of death. Bone after bone. Unconnected. Scattered. Stripped bare of sinew and flesh. Bleached white by the unrelenting sun. Totally devoid of life. Humanity departed. Useful no more. Dry, dry bones!

"Son of Man," the Sovereign Lord said to me as he explained his parable: "These bones are the whole house of Israel. They keep saying, "We are all dried up. We have no more nation. We have no more life. We have no more future. We have no more hope."

By now I had already served for several years as the "mouthpiece" of Yahweh to his erring people, uttering no words of my own. But here in this valley of dry bones, for the first time he suddenly turned to me and asked me a question, a question to which he fully expected me to give him an answer:

"SON OF MAN, CAN THESE DRY BONES EVER LIVE AGAIN?"

A straightforward question. But I could find no straightforward answer. My mouth fell strangely silent. I could feel turmoil spread throughout my entire being as I now struggled to respond.

∽

As I pondered his question, I realized that I understood all too well this valley of the dry bones.

When I was about twenty five years old (597 B.C.), my family and I were among the thousands in the Southern Kingdom who were captured by the Babylonians, ripped loose from the Promised Land, then driven far away into exile. Our once-powerful army smashed. Our king dragged off by King Nebuchadnezzar. Our people scattered. Our hope shriveled.

We dispossessed refugees entered the strange country of Babylon feeling absolutely sick at heart. There we raised our voices day and night to the God we had known back in our own land.

Our deep pain and sorrow is recorded for you in the Psalms:

> "By the rivers of Babylon we sat and wept
> when we remembered Zion.
> There on the poplars
> we hung our harps,
> for there our captors asked us for songs,
> our tormentors demanded songs of joy;
> they said, 'Sing us one of the songs of Zion!'
> How can we sing the songs of the Lord
> while in a foreign land?
> If I forget you, O Jerusalem,
> may my right hand forget its skill.
> May my tongue cling to the roof of my mouth
> if I do not remember you,
> if I do not consider Jerusalem
> my highest joy."
>
> (Psalm 137:1–6)

Almost two hundred years before, we Judeans had watched the Northern Kingdom fall, its capital of Samaria captured, its people scattered to the four winds. Assyria mingled many of the Jews among its own people. Now we Jews hardly knew where to find our old brothers and sisters. In fact, that's how they in fact became the ten "lost tribes" of Israel.

By comparison, we captives from Judah were surely more fortunate. Our captors allowed clumps of us Jews to settle together in ghettos within various cities throughout Babylon. Here we could still remain reasonably separate and distinct from those around us. But even this comparative 'blessing' could not comfort us. And so our laments rose to heaven:

> "All the splendor has departed
> from the Daughter of Zion.
> Her princes are like deer
> that find no pasture;
> in weakness they have fled
> before the pursuer . . .
>
> 'Is it nothing to you, all you who pass by?
> Look around and see.
> Is any suffering like my suffering
> that was inflicted on me,
> that the LORD brought on me
> in the day of his fierce anger?'"
>
> (Lamentations 1:6, 12)

Through our tears, we struggled hard to make the best of our captivity. But never far from our thoughts were the Holy Hill of Jerusalem and the rich soil of Judah. With a sadness too profound for words, I settled down with other exiles on the banks of the Kebar River in Babylon, far from my homeland of Ephraim.

Why were we here? How could this possibly happen to us?

Raised by my family toward the priesthood, I may have tended to think more about Yahweh more than did others. Yet for all of us, this was a time of deep and painful soul searching. Not since Joshua faced defeat at Ai, not since the Northern Kingdom fell to Assyria, had we faced these same nagging questions.

Why had Yahweh allowed a godless nation to defile our holy land and carry us off to captivity? Hadn't he indeed promised to be *with us*? Was it even possible that Yahweh was impotent before the gods of Babylon? (What a troubling thought, but we had to ask it.) And where was Yahweh now?

Did he still care about us in our miserable exile? Or had he banished us from his sight forever? Was Yahweh perhaps the God of the land of Israel only? Or should we still seek to worship him in this strange land, so far from his Holy Temple?

Dry bones! Yes, we certainly were. Scattered, dry bones! As I pondered the question of Yahweh, I first had to acknowledge this morbid fact. As his people, we were indeed getting all dried up. Worthless. As good as dead.

"CAN THESE DRY, DRY BONES EVER LIVE AGAIN?"

Like many other exiles, I am sure there was a time when I would have answered: "No, the people of Judah and Israel can never be renewed."

But for a very special reason, I now could no longer answer that way. Not since the fifth day, of the fourth month, of the fifth year of our exile. Such an important date I would celebrate forever. That was the day when the Sovereign Lord allowed me to see him for myself. That was the day when I heard his prophetic call to me. That was the day when I viewed his incredible power and glory. That was the day when my old narrow understanding of Sovereign Lord suddenly burst its seams!

I'd like to try to describe for you what I saw on that glorious day. But how can one possibly put it in human language without sounding terribly bizarre? So I beg you to be patient with me and to set free your imagination. What I viewed that day was utterly unlike anything I'd ever seen before.

In that sacred moment, I glimpsed what looked like lights exploding in the air. Burning embers. Molten metal. Radiance more brilliant than the sun. Wild flashes of lightening. Blazing torches suddenly erupting into streaks of purest white light. Refracted colors bursting forth into deep rainbows. Storm clouds shielding an intense brightness that would blind mortal men.

Oh, and I heard sounds, so intense and clear. Sounds like the rushing of mighty waters. Sounds like a vast tramping army. Sounds like rolling thunder. Sounds like the voice of God himself.

At the center of these flashing lights, I saw four creatures that appeared to be like men. Yet each of them had four faces and four wings. "Cherubim," was my guess. These four beings moved together, wherever they willed, huge wheels attached to their flaming bodies. But unlike the huge chariot wheels of Babylon's armies, their wheels were "wheels within wheels" that allowed these new beings to change course without having to make a turn. And each whirring wheel was rimmed with eyes all around it.

GOD'S GREAT QUESTION TO EZEKIEL

I couldn't believe what I was seeing. Awesome and majestic! Transfixing! Magnetic! Utterly inexpressible in human terms.

Above this supernatural display of light and sound and motion in the firmament, there rose a glorious throne made of sapphire. Seated on the throne was what looked like a man, a man made of shining bronze. Fire girded his waist. From every part of him radiated dazzling lights, like many rainbows building one upon another.

No one had to explain this to me. I knew this surely could only be the presence of the Lord.

Immediately I fell face-downward to the ground. I dared not utter a word before him. I simply felt for myself the awesome power of our God.

Only then did I hear his voice speaking to me. "Mortal Man, stand up! I want to talk to you."

While he was still speaking, I could feel the breath of the Spirit enter me and lift me to my feet. Otherwise, I'm not sure I could have moved at all.

Face to face with me now, the Sovereign Lord issued his call to me:

> "Son of Man, I am sending you to be my prophet to the all the people of Israel. Just as their ancestors did before them, they have rebelled against me. They do not listen to me. So I am sending you to speak my words to them. Oh, they will not hear you either, as they have not heard me. But you must be the faithful watchman who will warn them of impending destruction. Then, whether they listen or not, they will surely know, Son of Man, that a prophet has been among them."

"Son of Man!" Through the years, I heard him call me by that name perhaps ninety times or so. You could also translate it as "Mortal Man" or "Offspring of Adam" or "Son of Dust." All well describe the Hebrew name he called me.

At times I wished that he would call me by my own name, "Ezekiel—God is strong." But he never did. He preferred to use the more generic title for me, "Son of Man." Somehow it always recalled for me how God named the first man "Adam—generic human being." So, each time that God used the term "Son of Man," I felt confronted anew with my own smallness, my humanness, my frailty. Each time I was struck afresh by the absolute power and sovereign-ty of the Lord. He was my "*Thou*." I simply bowed before him.

And lest I might ever be tempted to believe that I, Ezekiel, was important in myself, Yahweh offered an object lesson, a lesson both to me and to the people. In part to underline his great power in comparison with mortal men, Yahweh paralyzed me during much of my ministry. And he made me mute—that is, until he gave me *his* words. Then he suddenly empowered me to speak them forth with great force, a force I could never have mustered on my own.

What a Sovereign Lord I saw that day! A God of incomprehensible glory and grace. A God who could still speak powerfully, even to a mortal man, even to a mortal man presently exiled in far-off Babylon. And no one who had ever glimpsed the awesome presence of Yahweh that day could ever possibly believe that he didn't have the power to bring back life again—even to our dry old bones.

"SON OF MAN, CAN THESE DRY BONES EVER LIVE AGAIN?"

Now I knew that I couldn't say "no" to God's great question. That answer would violate everything I knew about the omnipotence of Yahweh. I knew our Lord was Sovereign over his creation. I knew he had more than enough power to do whatever he chose to do with us.

But on the other hand, could I answer "yes?" This was by far the tougher question.

∽

If I answered "**yes**, these dry bones *can* live again," I would come perilously close to affronting the full righteousness of the God who had commanded us to be his holy people, his "set apart" people.

You see, our history as the nation of Israel stretched back to the time when we first met and worshiped Yahweh as our God of the Covenant at Mount Sinai. "I will be your God and you shall be my people. Only be careful to do all that I have commanded you." This is what he had impressed upon us.

Through all the years since then, our Sovereign Lord had kept his promise to us with absolute faithfulness. But time and again we stiff-necked people had failed him. We had sinned. We had fallen short of God's glory. We had become unclean, both in our actions and in our thoughts. We had refused to set ourselves apart as holy unto the Lord. Like dumb sheep, we had ignored our tender Shepherd. We continued to go astray.

Oh, once in a while we acknowledged our shortcomings. But even then we seldom took our sins with deadly seriousness. Surely a loving God, the

God who covenanted with Abraham, would overlook our failures, wouldn't he? That is, this is the way we reasoned until disaster struck us. And still we couldn't believe that our God would really punish his own little flock.

But one day I clearly saw for myself the magnitude of our people's sins. On this day the Spirit whisked me off to Jerusalem. And what he showed me in one short glance caused me to realize that Yahweh had every reason in the world to destroy us, his faithless people.

Here are just some of the horrors I saw in our Holy Temple:

At the north gate of the Temple, I saw a pagan idol standing, awaiting its ardent Jewish worshipers. Then, near the entrance to the Temple's courtyard, I saw paintings of things we always detested—crawling creatures like lizards, unclean animals, even pictures of idols. And something even more unbelievable. Seventy elders of Judah were there, each with a censer dispensing fragrant incense before these idolatrous pictures. Can you imagine such blasphemy? Right there in the Holy Temple of Yahweh.

And that's not all!

I even saw our Hebrew women sitting at the gate of our Temple weeping for "Tammuz," the fertility god of Babylon who was reported to have died and, along with him, the ability of these wives to bear children, or so they believed.

And then came another shock. Between the sacred altar and the portico stood twenty-five of our most religious men with their backs turned away from God's holy altar. Instead of worshiping the Most High God, they were stretching forth their arms to worship the rising sun.

We had become a people addicted to our idols! We had surely forgotten our first love with our Covenant God.

How could all this idolatry have grown to such pagan proportions? Even as I wondered, I could feel my heart breaking inside of me. I kept shaking my head in disbelief. Where had we gone wrong?

My thoughts took me back to the days of old when our forefathers conquered Canaan. In this new land they had found "high places" and heathen altars. Oh how I regretted that they had never completely torn them down, as Yahweh had commanded. Surely that's why we had found it easy to mingle our religious beliefs with those of the pagan Canaanites. Surely the root of our problem was our failure to worship exclusively our Sovereign Lord.

Then, once we had lost sight of Sovereign Lord, what enormous religious confusion developed! We began to view our worship as experience, rather than as affirmation of our historic faith. Every worship experience, therefore, needed to be heightened, sensationalized, pushed to the extreme. And soon the "experience" became more important than worshiping our God. Even sex, pressed to the extreme of religious prostitution before the pagan gods, had become a sacred rite for many. Tragically, some Israelites even sacrificed their own children to Molech at the strange fires of heathen altars.

I shook my head. If only we had done as Sovereign Lord had charged us. If only we had destroyed all the "high places" of heathen worship. If only we had remained faithful to him alone. But we hadn't. We had caused all this.

Now I was beginning to see our nation, the "Chosen People," from Sovereign Lord's point of view. For hundreds of years Yahweh had struggled with his people as they kept on running after foreign gods. Finally, he had too much of our idolatry and he had deliberately turned his back on us, first in the Northern Kingdom, and now on us in Judah. And in one last symbolic act, he even removed his presence from our Temple, his dwelling place among us. Suddenly before my eyes, all I could see were the stark contrasts, the utter whiteness and the utter blackness. Sovereign Lord, and puny man! His dazzling purity, and our gross uncleanness. His light inexpressible, and the darkness of our sin. His comforting presence among us, and his terrifying departure from our midst.

In light of such incompatability, God gave me these dreadful words of prophecy to speak to my people:

> "Therefore, this is what the Sovereign Lord says 'I myself am against you, Jerusalem, and I will inflict punishment on you in the sight of the nations. Because of your detestable idols, I will do to you what I have never done before and never will again. I will inflict punishment on you and will scatter all your survivors to the winds. Because you have defiled my sanctuary, I will withdraw my favor; I will not look on you with pity or spare you.
>
> I will destroy your high places. Your altars will be demolished and your incense altars smashed; and I will slay your people in front of your idols. I will lay the dead bodies of the Israelites in front of their idols, and I will scatter your **bones** around your altars. Then you will know that I am the Lord.'"
>
> (Ezekiel 6:3–4)

With these terrible words, Yahweh made clear the judgment that he would mete out against our unrighteousness. In response to the faithlessness of his people, God himself had decreed our destruction. Sure words.

Final words. Unambiguous words. Words of banishment, of exile. Words of separation between us and our God.

And when the destruction of Jerusalem finally came, this was the final destruction of our hope as well. From then on, we began to rot in a foreign land. We became the "living dead." We became much like the grim scene of death I saw before me in the dusty valley—nothing left but dry, dry bones!

"MORTAL MAN, CAN THESE DRY BONES EVER LIVE AGAIN?"

Certainly I couldn't answer "yes." That would deny the very words the Sovereign Lord had given me to proclaim. Words of death. Death to the faithless, to the unclean. Death to all those who worshiped idols, to those who profaned the Sabbath. Death even to his own Covenant people, Israel and Judah.

So, I couldn't answer "yes." And I couldn't answer "no." What, then, could I say? What was left to me as an alternative? Surely there must be one. I still felt absolutely torn apart, perplexed to the core. So I still fumbled to find an answer to God's great question.

For one final time, I struggled through the arguments again. I couldn't say "no" because that would violate the power of God. But I also couldn't say "yes" because that would violate his perfect righteousness and justice.

So, what had I overlooked? Suddenly one thought hit me.

I had overlooked one possibility—the one possibility that Yahweh would once again display his loving-kindness. He had already severely punished his people by scattering them as prisoners in foreign lands. This was right and just. On the other hand, God had told us that this punishment wasn't what he had wanted most:

> "I take no pleasure in the death of the wicked but
> rather that they turn from their ways and live. Turn!
> Turn from your evil ways. Why will you choose to
> die, O house of Israel?"
>
> (Ezekiel 33:11)

Already he had already given me comforting words of hope for our people stuck in a strange land. Words of quiet, determined tenderness. Words of amazing grace to a rebellious people deserving of exile and even deserving of death in the valley of dry bones. And what was his message to us? While casting down our own faithless shepherds, Yahweh now assured us, saying:

> I myself will search for my sheep. I myself will rescue my people from all the places where they were scattered on that dark day. I myself will bring them back again from the nations and settle them in their own land. I myself will be the shepherd of my sheep and cause them to lie down in peace once more. I will be their God, and my Servant David shall be Prince among my people ...
>
> I will sprinkle clean water on you. I will cleanse you from your detestable worship of idols. I will put a new heart and a new spirit within you. I will take away from you your hardened heart of stone and give you a heart of flesh. Then, once again you will live in the land I gave to your forefathers; you will be my people, and I will be your God. When the ruined cities of Israel are refilled with my own little flock again, then you will know that I AM the Lord!
>
> (Ezekiel 34:11—36:38, paraphrased)

What words of hope! Hope we could never bring to ourselves. Hope from above. Hope from the Sovereign Lord. He was ready to act on our behalf.

With such a God-given promise, I finally felt ready to give answer to the profound question asked me by my Sovereign Lord. In my response, I vowed to avoid the arrogance of presumption yet still protect his righteousness and holiness. And I was desperately counting on his mercy.

"SON OF DUST, CAN THESE DRY BONES EVER LIVE AGAIN?"

At last I replied to him, simply, in the only way left to me: "Oh Sovereign Lord, Only YOU know! Only YOU know!"

He alone retained that choice. He alone could speak the Word. He alone could breathe his Spirit again into lifeless mortal men whom he had created from the dust. He alone he could bring dry bones to life once again Only *he*!

∼

"Well then," said Sovereign Lord as he stretched his arm toward the valley of dry bones, "you must again open your mouth, Son of Dust. Raise your voice! Prophesy to these bones. Tell them: 'Listen to the word of the Lord!'" Once more I looked down at the scattered bones. So pathetic. So hopeless.

GOD'S GREAT QUESTION TO EZEKIEL

So distant from the other members of the body. So emptied of the image of their Creator.

Then, just as I had already given forth the word of the Lord so many times at his command, I opened my mouth once more. And again I spoke forth the word of Yahweh.

To my astonishment, even as I was speaking I could hear strange sounds—like something rattling. I glanced around to discover what would cause such a rumble. It appeared to be the sound of bones rubbing against each other. First one, then another. They began to touch. They began to connect. And even as I watched, they began to find their proper place next to each other. And then they joined together. Soon entire skeletons began to form the shape of men and women, right there before my eyes.

I now watched these bones take onto themselves sinew and muscle. Skeletons began to stir and to stretch tall. Finally skin crept over the bones, covering their exposed flesh once again.

But then something unthinkable happened. This amazing process of reconstruction suddenly stopped. This creative act refused to continue. I gasped in horror because, even though these bodies had somehow become complete, there appeared as yet to be no breath no breath in the dusty forms.

I looked anxiously at Sovereign Lord. I felt helpless. Although I was his prophet, he had given me no more words to speak. And still these forms lacked life. I saw their desperate need. But I had no other avenues open to me. While my hopes soared, I could do nothing. The choice was his. I simply waited for my God.

"Mortal Man," he said to me, "the time has indeed come for renewal. Speak to the wind. Tell the wind that the Sovereign Lord commands it to come from the four corners of the earth. Tell the wind to breathe life once again into these bodies and renew them. Speak *my* word, Son of Dust!"

I couldn't possibly miss his point because of his underlining repetition. Several times in this short command Yahweh used the word "ruach." In Hebrew, "ruach" can mean several things, "wind" or "spirit" or "breath." When I heard Yahweh unfold his play on words, I think I appreciated the way he spoke almost as much as what he gave me to say. "Ruach, ruach, ruach!"

What a message! At last! A good word. A word of hope. A word pregnant with full life. "*Ruach!*"

So I prophesied the word of Sovereign Lord with great joy. And the word he gave me to speak did not return unto him void but accomplished its purpose. Through the wind, the spirit, came to breathe life into bodies that once were only dry bones in a dusty valley. Now, one by one, they stood upright again. Full of life. Full of breath. Full of energy. The mighty army of the Lord once again.

Before my eyes, I saw the Word become flesh! Before my eyes, I saw the Word breathe life.

Now here before me stood the remnant of Israel. Revived. Renewed. Resurrected. Restored. No longer dry bones. No longer scattered. No longer useless. Re-created by the Sovereign Lord whose word had created them in the first place. Filled anew with the presence of their Lord. Human beings, once again bearing the living breath of their Creator!

In that sacred moment, I could feel a strong wind blowing. I wasn't sure what had brought it. I wasn't sure where it was going. But somehow, at the word of Yahweh, this wind had done his bidding. And what ensued was life.

Then the vision gradually faded. Gone from my view was the valley of the dry bones. From the Almighty showers of blessing rained down on our dusty land, just as he had promised.

～

This revival, this parable, in the valley of the dry bones was only the beginnings of Yahweh's promise of renewal—to Israel, and to people of all time as well.

It wouldn't be very long before our exiles would return from the foreign nations where they had been scattered. No longer would God's people be divided between North and South; they would become one nation again. They would revive their sacred worship at the Temple of the Lord. And soon Yahweh would again reveal his power by punishing the unbelieving nations that had taunted the God of Israel.

And so we would see many of these gracious prophesies fulfilled.

But of all the prophecies Sovereign Lord gave me, I was aware that some pertained to the future. Especially one promise. God spoke with such love and tenderness about "one shepherd over my flock" that I came to understand how unique this great leader would be. Even though I wished that he would come soon, I suspected it still might be centuries before this Good Shepherd from the house of David would appear.

Then I saw even farther, to the end of history. In the vision he gave me, I glimpsed (as the Apostle John would many centuries later) an even more awesome day to come. I saw a Temple fully restored, with the glory of the Lord present once again. This Temple stood in the midst of a holy city, planted in a holy land. From this city streamed water. No longer "water" that was simply showers of blessing, but a mighty river—the river of life. Trees lined its banks, trees laden with fruit for food, trees yielding leaves for healing. And this city's name? "The Lord is there!"

To the remnant of Israel, this came as new revelation. Because the Covenant Lord had promised to remain "with us," we could now begin to picture an even more glorious time—perhaps in the far distant future—when we dry bones who had just begun to experience his renewing power in our lives would someday dwell together, fully transformed, in a more perfect land. And at last we would be "with Him."

What a Sovereign Lord! Relentless and purposeful through the darkest days of our history. Always pointing us forward toward an eternal destiny. Powerful. Righteous. Gracious. Willing to speak his word and send forth his breath to renew, to re-create, his "Sons of Dust." A God whose might and mercy are always available to redeem and revive us, even when we are only dry bones in a dusty valley!

∽

This, then, is my story—a story of strange visions and parables acted out, a story which I only partially understood myself at the time.

But the key to my understanding came when I saw the Sovereign Lord for myself. I saw his power, and I saw his righteousness. And I saw his gracious favor reaching out toward all those who turn again toward him. Only then could I struggle to answer his question, *a question directed to those in any age who have lost all hope of renewal:*

"SON OF MAN, CAN THESE DRY BONES EVER LIVE AGAIN?"

And so, Ezekiel of Today, my great hope for you is that, whenever you feel like dry bones in the dusty valley, you too will not lose hope. Even if you find yourself rotting in some far-off land, be assured that your God has not forgotten you, that he has not turned his back on you! Whenever you turn to look at him in all of his holiness, then your renewal is possible. Then, it only awaits his "word" and his "breath" and his "spirit!"

How to experience this renewal from God? From our own history you can see that it's not something automatic. Not something you and I can drum up. Not something we can earn. We can only "prepare a way for the Lord." We can only turn away from our distracting preoccupation with things other than God himself. We can only wait for the word from our Lord. We can only wait for his breath to enter our lifeless forms once again. The initiative and the timing always belong to him, you see. Why? Because he is God!

But as you wait for your renewal, keep looking expectantly toward the one Shepherd who indeed did come, just as Sovereign Lord promised. This Shepherd, the Christ, assures us that, "They who hunger and thirst after righteousness shall be filled." To those of us whose hearts are eagerly fixed on him, he offers his full renewal. And his saints through the ages testify that they have discovered his promise to be true.

May the Sovereign Lord who raised from the dead our Lord Jesus, that great Shepherd of the sheep, through the eternal Covenant, cause you to be perfectly refreshed, revived, and *restored* so that you may do what is right and well-pleasing in his sight!

IX.

GOD'S GREAT QUESTION TO JOB

"WHERE WERE YOU WHEN I MADE THE EARTH OUT OF NOTHING?

A question of perspective

JOB 1–42

ALL ALONE, I SAT amid the smoldering ashes. Until now, I had always associated ashes with repentance. But now these ashes began to imply something different: Death! "Dust to dust. Ashes to ashes."

Everything I had was now gone, like a fleeting breath, like a brief candle snuffed out. All around me lay ashes, ashes like the refuse spit out by some voracious carnivore. Ashes, the dusty reminder of my agonizing loss.

Stunned. Grief-stricken. Empty. Words would not come. Nor could I cry. My sadness transcended description and shamed normal flowing tears into paralyzed submission. What had gone wrong? And *why*? No worthy explanation came to mind. For the first time, I was encountering the darkness of the seemingly absurd. And I felt so alone.

Until this day of crisis at mid-life, my years in the land of Uz rivaled the Paradise of Eden's Garden. Mine was a life of shalom, life as God meant it to be. I was wealthy. Yes, that was part of my joy, largely because we regarded wealth as a sign of God's favor and presence among us. I owned 7,000 sheep, 3,000 camels, 500 yoke of oxen, and 500 donkeys. I had servants to care for all that I possessed.

And God had blessed me with a perfect family: seven fine sons and three daughters. I guided them carefully while also giving them room to grow. They all had their own homes, and on birthdays they took turns providing food and drinks for their celebrations. At the conclusion of their times together, I always sent for them to have them purified. Early in the next morning, I offered up to God a burnt offering as a sacrifice for each of them, just in case they might somehow have sinned and cursed God in their hearts.

Despite all my wealth, my greatest joy was my relationship with the Almighty. He was my way, my truth, my life. I couldn't imagine existence without him. I lived my days believing that he observed everything I did and said. (Although I wouldn't be able to say this about myself, my biographer wrote that I was "blameless and upright, one who feared God and shunned evil," a statement the author attributed to God himself. He also said that I, Job, was "the greatest man among the peoples of the East.") All I know is that I did revere the Lord with my whole being.

Then one day, without the slightest warning, all my blissful joy came to an end. Utter calamity befell me.

During one of my children's birthday celebrations, my servant ran breathlessly to me with bad news. "While the oxen and donkeys were grazing nearby, the Sabeans attacked, killed your servants, and carried away all the animals. Only I, your servant, have escaped to tell you."

While he was still speaking, another came. "Fire fell from heaven", he told me. "It burned up all the sheep and servants. Only I am left to bring you the news."

While he was still speaking, one more messenger came. "Behold, master, three raiding parties of Chaldeans swooped down, slaughtered your servants, and carried off your camels. If I alone had not been spared, there would be no one to tell you this sad news."

And while this servant was still speaking, yet another messenger came with terrible words that cut me to the heart. "It's your own sons and daughters, sir," he began. "While they were celebrating together, a mighty wind swirled in from the desert, attacked the house from all four corners, and collapsed the dwelling down upon the heads of your offspring. Behold, Sir, beneath the rubble lie your children. All are dead. None survived. Only I have escaped to tell you."

I sat in silence. Eyes staring outward. Shivering inwardly. I could do nothing. I could say nothing. Nothing could possibly make a difference

GOD'S GREAT QUESTION TO JOB

now. All of my goods were gone. All of the children I cherished were gone. So I continued to sit, mute and motionless, until I could begin to make some sense out of the senseless.

A blur of feelings and thoughts possessed me. Warm memories. Disbelief. Anger. Sadness. Confusion. Dread. Helplessness. Never had I felt so much like "a child of the dust." And this thought suddenly reminded me of my Creator. Surely my God had not deserted me. I was still created in his image, wasn't I? And these musings began to bring me the perspective I needed so badly in the midst of my calamity.

Somewhere in this process, I began to move again. I arose. I tore my robe as a symbol of grief and mourning. I shaved my head as a sign of humility before the Almighty.

And then I did something that, in retrospect, I'm surprised that I did so easily at that moment of grief. I fell to the ground, and on my knees, I again worshiped God with all my heart. Despite the devastating rape of my whole being that I was experiencing so painfully, I held nothing back from my Creator.

Raising my eyes toward heaven, I praised my Father. "Oh God, you have given to me everything that I have ever enjoyed. You could give them to me because they are yours to give. And only you have a right to take them away again. So, with a heart clear toward my Maker, I can still say, 'Blessed be the name of the Lord!'"

Everything I had was gone—except my God! And somehow my relationship with him was just enough to sustain me.

But as yet, I didn't realize that a worse day or more was looming.

Once more I sat upon the ash heap. From the crown of my head to the calluses of my feet, sores attacked my body. I writhed in anguish. I couldn't sleep, I couldn't eat, I couldn't think. Scabs and puss were only the external signs of the pains and poisons within. I no longer felt like a human being. All I could do was to scrape my festering wounds with broken pottery pieces I found on the ash heap.

My wife watched me suffer, knowing that she couldn't help. She was still suffering too. At last, she couldn't stand it any longer. "Why don't you put an end to all this misery?" she asked me. "Why are you holding onto life by maintaining your integrity with God? Get it over with! Curse God—and die."

Even in my pain, I knew that she wasn't speaking sensibly. So I shocked her back to reality: "My dear, you are speaking like a foolish woman, like one who doesn't know right from wrong. So I ask you: Shall we praise God when things are going well and then withhold our praise when life is not the way we wish it to be? Shall we accept good as from God's hand and not, at the same time, accept what to us seems evil? Shall we really worship God for what we expect to receive back from him?"

Oh, I was preaching good theology. But inside, I felt the sting of her argument. Little did I know then what a war was starting inside of me, a war in which my wife was only the first of many to play "devil's advocate" with my arguments as I tried to make sense out of my unwelcome struggle.

Outwardly my faith shined as gold; I did not particularly sin with my lips. But as I continued to scrape my boils, inwardly I began to hold my golden faith in precarious tension with my growing fears and doubts—until more powerful assailants challenged me further.

∽

Like a spark that ignites a prairie fire, news of my misfortunes spread throughout the world of my acquaintances. Soon everyone had heard that Job's great fortunes had been reduced to ashes.

Now, there are many things that you can't see from an ash heap, but I discovered that you can scan the horizon eagerly for the approach of friends. From far off, I saw them coming. Three esteemed colleagues, friends of mine, agreed together to come and console me, Eliphaz the Temanite, Bildad the Shuhite, and Zophar the Naamanthite. I was touched that they would come to be with me in my hour of overwhelming need.

I managed to struggle to my feet to wave to them in the distance. But nothing I did attracted their attention. Didn't they see me? Couldn't they imagine that this sagging frame of a man with blackened skin was the once-great ruler whom they had seen dispensing wisdom and justice at the city gates? How the mighty had fallen! How great was my misery! How great was the surprise of my friends!

When they finally grasped who I was, they slumped down to the ground beside me. My friends simply mirrored my pain on their empathetic faces. For seven days we bore the sorrow together, not knowing how to express our grief. For seven days they said nothing. For seven days I said nothing. Silence reigned. Then no longer could I stand the silence, the pain, the loneliness, the mystery of my unexplainable suffering.

When I finally opened my mouth, out rushed words revealing the depth of my despair and misery. "May the day of my birth be expunged forever from the calendar of history! Oh that God had never parted the darkness or hovered over the chaos of creation to bring light and life! I wish I had never been born! Why could I not have been aborted before birth or have been stillborn; then I would now be resting in bliss with kings and magistrates gone on to Sheol before me."

Gradually I also began to voice my anger and wonderings. "Why does God give light to those in misery—just so that they can see their misery more clearly? Why does God continue to grant life to the soul suffering bitter reversals—just so that he can suffer longer? Where indeed has God's protective hedge about me gone? Now it feels as if he has turned the tables, even hedged me in so that I cannot escape my pain. And why? Even my name, Job, means 'Where is [my] Father?' My God, my God, why hast thou forsaken me? What I feared most has come upon me. Suddenly God's Shalom has vanished!"

There was so much that I didn't understand, so much that I longed to know. But at last I dared to voice my complaints, the legitimate outcries of a "son of dust!"

But can you see what was happening to me? I was now questioning honestly. I was trying to make sense out of my predicament. I was attempting to resolve why God had allowed evil to touch an innocent life like mine. In this process, I was beginning to think, to feel, to grope, to integrate, to imagine. And aren't these the very forces that cause us to grow, especially when we voice them to the Almighty, even when we really don't know where our Father is?

∼

When I ended my complaint, my three friends rose to their feet in unison, as if by some hidden signal. My old friend, Eliphaz, the eldest and wisest, began to speak gently, the first of three rounds of questioning by my friends.

"Dear Job, will you allow an old friend to venture a word with you?" Eliphaz asked. I nodded. "Perhaps I can help by reminding you of the wise counsel you have given to others in times of trouble. Should not your piety be your confidence, and your blameless ways your hope? Think! When have you ever seen the innocent perish? I certainly haven't. Of course, we can't be presumptuous; if God charges his angels with error, how much more mortal men who live in houses of clay. But if I were in your shoes, I would appeal my case to God: I would lay my cause before him. He saves the needy, gives hope, and shuts the mouth of injustice. Happy is the man whom God corrects; so do not despise the discipline of the Almighty. He wounds, but he also heals. We three have examined these truths and find them so."

Eliphaz had started out graciously enough, but it soon became clear that he had not fully accepted my assertion of innocence. I was surprised, and then offended. "A despairing man should have the devotion of his friends, even if he forsakes the fear of the Almighty," I told him. "Show me where I have been wrong. Would I lie to you? Please reconsider, my pious friend, for my integrity is at stake."

And then I turned toward God himself. "My days are swiftly coming to an end—without hope. Remember, O God, that my life is but a breath." But then, instead of marveling that God had created man as the "crown of creation," I cried out: "What is man that you make so much of him, that you examine him every morning and test him every night? Even if I have sinned, why do the small sins of a little man like me affect you? And if my sins somehow offend you, why don't you just pardon me? Pretty soon, Lord, I will lie back down in the dust. Then it will be too late. Then you will look in vain for me but you won't find me." (I was assuming, of course, that God would have to settle all accounts justly within this lifetime, within *my* lifetime.)

Bildad broke into the conversation. "Your words are nothing more than wind, Job! Does God ever pervert justice? *If* you are indeed pure and righteous, even now he will rouse himself on your behalf and restore you. Then your glorious beginnings will seem humble in comparison with your prosperous future. So if I were you, I'd look more closely at traditional theology, at the wisdom of our fathers. Their wisdom teaches us that the destiny of all who forget God is like the plant ripped from its spot near the source of water; its life withers away. But of course, since God never rejects a blameless man, he may yet restore laughter to your lips and clothe your enemies in shame."

I heard abundant sarcasm in his voice!

"Ah, Bildad", I replied, "you are trying to prove too much. How on earth can a mortal man be righteous before God? Look at God's wisdom. Look at his mighty deeds. Look at his power. Even if I were thoroughly 'righteous', what standing would that give me to dispute with the Almighty? How could I answer him? Despite my innocence, I could only plead for mercy. If only there were someone to arbitrate between us, to lay a hand on his shoulder and mine, to bridge somehow the dark chasm now between us! O Lord, remember that you once molded me like clay when you created me. Will you now turn me back to dust again? Lord, be merciful. At least turn your judgment away from me so that I can have a moment's joy before I die!"

Enter Zophar into the verbal melee. "Isn't someone ever going to silence you? Job, you stubbornly insist on your innocence. Absolute nonsense! Otherwise, why are you suffering? Oh, how I wish that God would speak up and attack your famous 'wisdom'. For I am sure that God has even forgotten to repay you for some of your sin. Still, if you put away your sin, you will surely put away your trouble, you will be secure again, and you will re-gain your hope. But if you're wicked, your hope will become but a dying gasp."

At this point, I became angry. "Doubtless you three are the only wise of the earth and wisdom will die with you," I charged. "But your maxims are proverbs of ashes and your defenses of God are fashioned of dust. You're simply remaking God in your own image. How do *you* know what is right and what is just? To God alone belong wisdom and power. Though he may well slay me, I will continue to hope in him alone. I plead for only two things: May he stop his torment of me . . . and may he summon me so that I may answer his charges!"

Then I poured out my soul, a torrent of deeply felt thoughts at random, more to God than to anyone:

> "Man born of woman is of few days and full of trouble. He springs up like a flower and withers away, but like a fleeting shadow, he does not endure . . . For a tree, at least there is hope; if a tree it is cut down, it will sprout again . . . But man dies and is laid low; he breathes his last and is no more . . .
>
> "If only you would conceal me in the grave until your anger is passed! Set a time, and then remember me. *If a man dies, will he live again?* . . . All the days of my hard service, I will wait for my renewal to come! . . . You will call and I will answer you . . . Surely then you will count my . . . steps [and] you will cover over my sin."
>
> (Job 14:1–17, emphasis added)

This theme of the "tree cut down" and "sprouting again" fired my imagination. Unfortunately, at the time, I could not push beyond the barrier of my own misery and impending death. While I sensed my hope beyond Sheol was very real, my hope was far too fragile. So, in agony, I retreated to deep despair:

"But as a mountain erodes and crumbles, and as a rock is moved from its place, as water wears away stones and torrents wash away the soil, but you destroy man's hope. You overpower him once and for all, and he is gone... He feels the pain of his own aching body and mourns only for himself!"

(Job 14:18–22)

From my first ray of hope that began to reach out, what a statement of despair! And yet, what a fitting conclusion this is to the first round of my struggle to reunite my fractured soul.

Although I couldn't see it then, I had made a good beginning. After months of paralyzing confusion on my ash heap, I was finally voicing my concerns. I held on tightly to my belief that I was suffering unjustly, but I still couldn't figure out why a just God would allow my misery. "If God is God, he is not good," I concluded; "and if he is good, he is not God!" Obviously these options pulled me in totally opposing directions.

I really could affirm much of what my three "friends" said. But my problem was this: my theology didn't stretch far enough to embrace my growing knowledge of reality. I couldn't get past the one undeniable truth - I, a righteous man, was suffering!

Now, watch my friends begin to squirm as they saw me start to push out the boundaries of my understanding—and watch me begin to squirm amid the twists and tangles of my search for wisdom, and for God, my Father.

~

Eliphaz spoke: "Your words are like the hot east wind, Job, because sin prompts your mouth. Why do you think you are the only one who is wise? Have you listened in on God's council? No! But the wisdom of gray-haired men through the ages is on our side."

"Listen to me," Eliphaz continued. "I will explain [to you] the truth of the ages. The wicked suffers torment all of his days because he dares to shake his fist at God. But before he dies he shall be paid in full; his branches will not flourish but shall become barren, stripped bare of all the fruit that true righteousness instead could have brought him."

Old Eliphaz was confirming my worst fears. First he had not accepted my innocence. And now he was dashing my emerging hope that if God didn't make things right in this lifetime, perhaps there was something more beyond the grave. So I lashed out at my friends, calling them "miserable comforters." Their hostility cut me deeply, almost as much as the surprising silence from the God whom I had worshiped for so long.

By then I was learning that when even friends turn against you, we still have a solace in our heavenly Father. So I turned to God and said:

"O earth, do not cover my blood. Don't try to obscure the reality of my suffering. May my cry never be laid to rest. May truth and justice never ignore me.

"But even now, my witness is in heaven; my advocate is on high. Pouring out tears on my behalf, he pleads with God for me as a man, pleads for his friend! Perhaps my God will be the one to put up a pledge of security to redeem me, since all my kinsmen have deserted me."

"Come on, all of you," I cried to my miserable kinsmen. "Try again to understand. In the midst of utter darkness, you re-define 'darkness' and call it 'light.' But think! If the only home I can hope for is the grave where decay is my father and the worm is my mother, where, then, is my hope?" I knew there had to be a better answer, a more complete understanding, a way to bring back together the twin truths of "God's goodness" and "his God-ness"—truths pried so far apart by these painful circumstances that I had never before endured.

Bildad: "Job, why do you keep trying to re-define truth? Just face the obvious fact that you've done evil, and evil will 'get you.'" So, your roots will dry up, your branches will wither, and the earth will be purged of your memory. You won't even have descendants to remember you!" Oh, what a cruel reminder of my children's death not many months ago!

"Oh Bildad," I responded, "how long will you try to crush me? The truth is that God has wronged me. He has stripped me bare of honor; he has removed the crown from my head; and now he uproots my hope like a tree." (As you see, I was still assuming that a "regally righteous man" would be surrounded with plenty; I didn't yet see that the Almighty might possibly call the "crown of creation" to suffer.)

Anyway, my own words made me feel sorry for myself all over again. Where were my friends and kinsmen? Where were my servants? Even my own wife was offended by my stinking breath. Little children ridiculed me. Such a great reversal surely couldn't just be ignored or sloughed off. No, such a calamity deserved to be engraved in stone so that no one could ever forget such unjust and enormous suffering!

In tension with my suffering, however, another truth was beginning to emerge. I was beginning to sense something I had never known before.

Surely there was a Redeemer, *my* Redeemer, who lives. And surely someday he would stand upon this dusty earth. And somehow, even if my flesh were destroyed, I would still see him. I would see him with my own eyes. I would see him on my side. And in some small part of my soul, this strange new and hopeful truth found settled refuge.

And suddenly I realized that if this were true, and I was convinced it was, then my friends were in grave danger of God's judgment on *them*. "Fear the wrath of the Almighty's sword," I warned them, probably partly in anger, partly in love.

Zophar completed the second cycle of conversation by rehashing his argument that "from of old, ever since man was placed on earth, the wicked have perished. And so it's the *children* of the wicked who must make amends for the wicked man whom God has struck down." I thought of my seven sons and three daughters lying in the grave, also struck down in innocence, and I resented simplistic Zophar for his dogmatic theology, a theology without reality, and without mercy.

I could no longer stand his argument that "it has been true from the beginning that the wicked suffer during their lifetime and come to a terrible end!" Balderdash! That's not what I had seen. And if Zophar dared to be honest, he knew it wasn't true too! Often the wicked continue to prosper, grow old, and increase in power. Homes secure. Children around them. They show no evidence of God's wrath upon them. Then they go down to the grave in peace. Had I really watched the lamp of the wicked regularly snuffed out? No!

And as for the argument that God stores up his wrath at the father's wickedness and then inflicts punishment upon the sons, what a distortion of truth. No, the record must be set straight. Each individual must pay for his own sin; each man and woman must be accountable before God. I was accountable for my own sins. And that's precisely why I was arguing now.

No, these old understandings about God's justice didn't fit the truths of life as I was experiencing them. So I could do one of two things: I could throw out the old truths about God, or I could re-examine my understanding of them. But I could no longer go on in the same old way. I needed a breakthrough!

By the end of round two, I had really come a long way. The Job who once saw himself primarily as a "child of dust" was beginning to grasp hold again of his other side—as "crown of creation." I still couldn't put all this into words. But increasingly I was drawing back into a relationship with my Creator, my Father whom I most sought. The arguments of my fair-weather friends were becoming repetitious, a fact which signaled their lack of power. From my ash heap, I was now pounding noisily on the gates of Heaven. I fully expected an answer. If not now, then surely beyond the grave somehow—maybe—I hoped. Oh, I really didn't know!

∼

By now all of us were getting tired of the impasse. Eliphaz, the gentle mystic, lectured me again, informing me that I couldn't possibly be of much interest to the Almighty, and, further, that my suffering must mean I was simply claiming to be righteous but that my sins were indeed endless." And if I hadn't committed sins, I must have omitted to do justice. Bildad agreed that surely a mortal like Job, "who is but a maggot and a worm," couldn't possibly have much standing before Almighty God. Ugh!

Alas, how readily those enjoying lives of ease react with contempt toward those enduring misfortune!

"What glorious insights you all have shared with one who is broken in spirit," I shouted at my three friends. And—while I still hoped in God—I wasn't sure that he was really listening to me either. So I verbalized my thoughts as they came, and released them into thin air:

> "If only I knew where to find the Almighty! But I go to the east, to the west, to the north, to the south, and I cannot see him. *But he knows* where I am and the way I have lived. When he has tested me, I will come forth as gold, for I have followed his ways and esteemed him.
>
> "I long to state my case before him, but, alas, who can oppose him? He stands so far above us and does what he pleases. And so I am terrified of him."

Like my friends, I truly believed that God does dispense justice in the end. But I couldn't accept their assertion that God always dispenses his justice quickly or with any clear pattern.

You see, if my friends were right that God stamped out wickedness as soon as it surfaced, then why was the world still so full of obvious injustice and evil? But it was. All one had to do was to observe the robbers who terrorize widows, or the fatherless children who are snatched from their mother's breasts, or the righteous poor who are raped and maimed and trampled all their lives by all sorts of evil people.

No, my friends couldn't see the void in their simplistic wisdom. They had failed to explain why an innocent man like me was suffering unjustly. And since the facts didn't fit their theory, they had only one way out of their air-tight doctrine. They concluded that I must have sinned.

"As surely as God lives," I continued, "I will never admit that you are in the right. Until the day I die, I will never deny my integrity; I can never deny what I know to be true. I will hold steadfastly to my belief that I have acted rightly before my God. Only in him can I possibly find any hope."

Such affirmation felt so good and right. But even this affirmation left me face to face with the mystery of my own suffering. "Where is my Father?" I couldn't let go of my miserable plight until I knew what was happening, and most importantly, why.

> "But alas, where can a son of dust find wisdom? Where can an 'adam' find the dwelling of understanding? It cannot be bought; its' value is far beyond price.
>
> "Yet the almighty knows the way to find wisdom; he knows where it dwells. For he sees everything; he has tried and tested wisdom. And then he instructs dusty man, 'Fear God. That is the beginning of wisdom. Shun evil. That is the beginning of understanding!'"

My, what an affirmation I expressed of God's sovereignty over wisdom and over Creation! I meant it! I *knew* it was true!

And just this little bit of light breaking into my darkness allowed me to begin to accept my unexplainable suffering. Finally I could look it squarely in the eye. Only then could I consign to the dust all of my life's dead glory. Only then I could move on to express the pain of my present, such a stark contrast with my former life of Shalom:

"But now younger men than I am mock me. I have become a byword among them. They detest me, they keep their distance, they spit upon me. Now that God has unstrung my bow and afflicted me, they throw off all restraint."

Just because I was suffering, people thought I must have done evil. So they had driven me out of our former community. Even my three "friends" had turned their consolations into a quarrelsome attack. All of this hurt me deeply.

But what hurt even more was that the Almighty was silent. Totally silent! And when God is silent, where can a son of dust find hope? Where, oh where was my Father?

"I cry to you, O God, but you do not answer; I stand before you, but you just stare at me. Strangely, you turn on me, you attack me, you snatch me up and drive me before the wind, you toss me about in a storm! But I do not understand why.

Have I not wept for the troubled? Have I not grieved for the poor, knowing that the same God who made them also made me? Yet when I hoped for good, evil came. And when I looked for light darkness came! Don't I have a right to expect something more from a just God? Does he not watch me and weigh my actions?"

Again I affirmed my innocence from sins which would explain the depth of my suffering. I even vowed a seven-fold oath of my integrity, where I called down terrible destruction upon me if I were not speaking the truth. To whom was I speaking? To my God, I hoped!

> "Oh, I wish I had someone to hear me! Finally I've signed my defense. Now let the Almighty answer me! May he write down all the charges against me. Then I'll fold up the accusation and wear it on my head as a crown. Then I'll approach him like a prince. I will give an account of my life."

With these words of challenge, I stopped speaking. "It is finished!" I, Job, would await the answer of my God. With one hand I held on tightly to myself as "son of dust" and with the other hand to myself as "crown of creation." I was getting eager to see what would happen next.

∽

What happened was a terrible letdown, a miserable interruption in the flow of the grand drama which I had expected to follow my golden silence.

Enter young Elihu, sputtering. Elihu was a little man, a pompous man, a man whose name means, "He is God" (which adds greatly to the irony).

All during my conversation with my friends, I had watched Elihu on the sidelines shift anxiously from one foot to another. I had heard him gasp at my audacious words, and I knew he was losing his battle to keep silent. Now that the three elders had ceased to speak, Elihu became absolutely enraged because his three friends hadn't knocked me completely flat. Now he seized his chance. In silence, he strode across the ashes toward me as if he were performing on a giant stage:

> "The Spirit of God has made me, and the breath of God gives me life," he informed me. (I gathered that he was trying to convince

me to give his words the full weight of Scripture.) And then in a surprise move, he called me to account to Him, as if he could measure me against some golden yardstick: "Answer me, Job, if you can. Prepare yourself, and confront me."

Oh, no! Not again. But I endured his many words.

Although I heard nothing new in his soliloquy, I felt that he summarized the others' points rather well. And periodically, he couldn't resist throwing in a vicious barb, like: "Oh that Job might be tested to the utmost for answering like a wicked man!" Ouch! Why hadn't he left his magnificent golden yardstick at home in his own closet?

And Elihu had another common problem. You can see it in his statement: "Bear with me a little longer and I will show you that there is more to be said on God's behalf." I stifled a chuckle. Would the Almighty need a pontifical little man like Elihu to defend him? And then, having already implied his intimate personal knowledge of God, Elihu concluded that: "the Almighty is beyond our reach." I stifled chuckle number two. Poor Elihu couldn't see the incongruity of his own back to back statements.

Although I agreed with much of what Elihu said (albeit pompous, shallow and judgmental), I admit to heaving a huge sigh of relief when the little windbag's speeches began to wind down.

Actually I couldn't really tell whether Elihu had finished. So, what caused him to stop? Oh, it was glorious! Long-winded Elihu ("He is God") was unceremoniously interrupted by a powerful whirlwind—and by God himself!

~

In the midst of this heavenly whirlwind, I could hardly breathe. Swirls of ashes rushed in every direction. Against gale forces, I struggled to remain upright. And when the wind had finally died down, an amazing thing had taken place. I looked all around me. But I looked in vain for my old ash heap. It had vanished. It was completely gone. Swept away by the breath of God!

Like many worshipers before (or after) me—Moses, Elijah, Ezekiel—I didn't need to be told that I was in the presence of the Lord. I just *knew*. Now I knew where my Father was. He was right here!

Then Grace spoke. My Father, the loving God of the Covenant, stooped down from his Throne to answer his little dusty creature named Job. Out of the storm, out of the primordial chaos of creation, out of a whirlwind foreshadowing the final judgment, my God called out—to me!

At last I could put my case before the Almighty. At last I could question him about the mystery of suffering. At last I could find wisdom. At last I could be vindicated.

Ah, but it didn't happen just the way I wished.

It was my God who took the initiative, not I. *He* spoke to *me*. And I trembled in his awesome presence:

> "Who is this that darkens my counsel with words without knowledge?
> Brace yourself like a man;
> I will question you,
> and you shall answer me."
>
> (Job 38:2, 3)

I gasped. I wasn't at all prepared for such an encounter. Why had I been so darned brash? Why had I even demanded a hearing? Why had I dared think I could ever stand before him?

And then, without letting me squeeze in a word, the Almighty let fly question after unanswerable question, wave upon wave, overwhelming me into insignificance. And then came his crushing question:

"WHERE WERE YOU WHEN I MADE THE WORLD OUT OF NOTHING?"

> Tell me, if you understand. Surely you know!
>   Who shut up the sea behind doors
>   when I said, 'So far you may come and no farther'?
> Have you ever given orders to the morning,
>   or shown the dawn its place?
> Have you journeyed to the springs of the sea?
> Have the gates of death been shown to you?
> Have you comprehended the vast expanses of the earth?
> Tell me if you know all this.
> What is the way to the abode of light?
> And where does darkness reside?
> Can you take them to their places?
> Do you know the paths to their dwellings?
> Surely you know, for you were already born!

> You have lived so many years!
> Who endowed the heart with wisdom
> or gave understanding to the mind?"
>
> (Job 38:2–36, selected.)

Oh, my aching head! I became dizzy with the enormity of the questions he was asking me. I could scarcely catch my breath. It was as if my Father were quizzing me from a list cataloguing all the world's mysteries that man couldn't possibly understand. I felt completely inundated. After wave upon wave of the most beautiful and awesome questions I had ever heard, the Lord turned to me and concluded with these frightening words:

> "Now, will the one who contends with the Almighty
> correct him? Let him who accuses God answer him."
>
> (Job 40:1)

And oh, what a big mouth I had. "*Accuse God?*" I guess that's what I had been doing. I had been trying to vindicate myself at God's expense. But I hadn't meant any harm. I had only been trying to figure things out. Still, grieved that I had overstepped my proper relationship to my Creator, I finally answered him:

> "I am unworthy—how can I reply to you?
> I put my hand over my mouth.
> I spoke once, but I have no answer—
> twice, but I will say no more."
>
> (Job 40:2)

In humble acquiescence, I bowed before him. I felt pleased with my answer. Unfortunately the Lord wasn't. He saw that my acquiescence did not necessarily imply my agreement. In fact, I really had not answered my Lord's question.

And so, the God of the whirlwind took a large breath and began his second round of questioning me:

> "Job, brace yourself like a mighty man of valor;
> I will question you, and you shall answer me.
> Are you ready to discredit my justice?
> Do you want to condemn me to justify yourself?
> Do you have a right arm like God's?"

Then he said the oddest thing: "Consider Behemoth, which I made along with you." (I'm not sure what you call Behemoth today—perhaps the hippopotamus or the elephant?) But I heard God describe with such delight how he fashioned Behemoth as a proud, powerful, invulnerable creature. Invulnerable—except before God, his maker. And he described Leviathan. Once again I could hear the obvious affection with which he had created the beast—and again, very vulnerable before him.

"Consider Behemoth!" Yes, the God who creates us is allowed to fashion whatever he wishes. But if a haughty Behemoth thinks he's beyond the reach of the Almighty, he's oh-so mistaken. Just as God had described himself as stamping out the world with a cookie cutter ("like clay under a seal"), he clearly conveyed to me his absolute freedom to create what he chooses, with whatever quirks and warts, and with whatever paradoxes he decides to encapsulate in it. The truth is: "This is my *Father's* world!"

Everything that God has created now pleasures him, serves him well, remains vulnerable before him. Even a mighty man of valor, even a "son of dust," like me. Even a hurting man, the "crown of God's creation," like me. All things are in his ultimate control. Nothing frustrates his purposes! "And though this world with devils filled should threaten to undo us, we will not fear, for God has willed his truth to triumph through us."

"WHERE WERE YOU WHEN I MADE THE EARTH OUT OF NOTHING?"

"I wasn't there." I had to admit it. I didn't know how he did it. I didn't comprehend how he held everything together. I knew very surely that I couldn't have done it. But he knew everything. So, he could do everything. And only he, then, could hold everything in ultimate harmony.

Suddenly, I began to realize how shallow and how wrong had been my perspective. I had centered my thoughts far too much on Job. (I suppose that's an almost universal reaction to our suffering.) But in subtle ways, I suppose that I had somehow misplaced my affection. Much as I had tried to avoid it, in over-reacting to my unjust suffering I could see that, unknowingly, I had shifted my focus from heaven to earth. Instead of seeing the majestic firmament, instead of seeing the gracious Covenant God, I had, understandably, but unfortunately, concentrated far too much on my own damn ash heap.

Now my perspective began to shift. I still had received no more insight about the reason for my undeserved suffering. I had not called God to account, as I had once wished. I had not even given account of myself, as I had once wished. But I gained something much better. At last I found my Father! In his presence, I could no longer see the ash heap. I could only see his glory. And, best of all, he was with me!

Now I didn't seem to care as much about "Why." Now I cared about "Who." "O God, my God, what is [mere] man that thou visitest him? What incredible love! What unfathomable grace!"

In the presence of my Father, I found that I longed only for his mercy, only for the gift of his grace. Apart from this understanding, wouldn't I be worshiping my God for some selfish gain? And such a concept was not worthy of God—nor of humankind. From this point on, I would continue my desire to worship him, regardless of what happens. I would worship him simply because it is the best and "rightest" thing to do. Nothing, nothing else!

All my questions, all my wonderings, all my demands for knowledge, I now would gladly leave them to "mystery!"

Although the reasons for my suffering would remain a mystery, I now knew that God could always "sanctify to me my deepest distress." And little did I guess that such a cosmic perspective would set the stage for the coming one day of the "Suffering Messiah" as my mediator, my advocate, my redeemer.

While I had believed that "the words of Job are ended," I was wrong. I still had to give answer to my Father. Until now, I had only shut my mouth before him—a small but good beginning. Now I must do much more. I must throw myself in wonder and gratitude on his gracious mercy:

> "O Lord, I know that you can do all things;
> > no plan of yours can be thwarted.
> Surely I spoke of things I did not understand,
> > things too wonderful for me to know.
> My ears had heard of you
> > but now my eyes have seen you.
> Therefore I despise myself
> > and repent in dust and ashes."
>
> (Job 42:2, 3, 5, 6)

"*Dust and Ashes!*" No longer did they represent death and loss. Once again, they represented repentance. Once again, they represented the natural response of a worshiping creature bowed before his wise Creator. What shalom! With my perspective renewed, I felt fully restored.

∽

And then came my great surprise.

It was as if the ashes from the heap where I had sat for so long were somehow reconstituted to their original state. My friends and kinsmen returned with presents. But even more. The Lord doubled the number of all my flocks. And he blessed me with seven more boys and three girls. Incredible!

And so, from my Father's hand, I took my life back again. But I did not take it back in the same old way. It wasn't something that I "deserved." I knew that. Yet my God was pleased that I had remained "upright and blameless" before him. And in an act of pure felicity, my Father had chosen to restore my fortunes and make me a better steward of all he had entrusted to me.

And was the restoration of my fortune necessary? Yes, no (mostly no), and maybe.

Yes, I had passed the testing; there was no further reason to deny me what I had accumulated and managed well.

No, we all learned that a righteous person can indeed suffer, that wealth and calm seas do not necessarily imply God's favor, and that poverty is not necessarily a more blessed state before God. And most important, whether we are wealthy or poor, we certainly cannot deserve God's favor.

Maybe! If we remember God's speech about Behemoth and Leviathan, we can affirm that God loves everything and everyone he has created. He loves to bless us even more than we love to be blessed. Maybe in testing me he decided that he could trust me to worship him, to love him, to serve him "for no hope of gain," "no thought of prosperity." But, alas, I've said far too much, for *everything* God did for me was purely from his grace! He just wished to do it!

∽

Job of Today, I thank you for suffering along with me. You are indeed a true "friend." Perhaps you struggle too.

My prayer is that you will confront your faith honestly before God. Either the Christian faith is a statement about reality which is true, or it isn't. And if your faith collides violently with the truth of life as you experience it, you have to be honest about that. Then, take your doubts, your frustrations, your questions to God-Friend. He can handle them. He can handle you, even in your times of darkness. Perhaps he will show you—as he showed my friends and me—that the truth as you've understood may not be his truth. And in this process, painful as it is, perhaps you will come to find and embrace your Father whom you were seeking all along.

In your times of prosperity as well as in your sufferings of the soul, Job of Today, may you always turn to God! And in doing this, may you be assured in your deepest being that he, the God-Friend who did indeed "make the earth out of nothing," is always listening to you!

X.

GOD'S GREAT QUESTION TO SIMON PETER

"WHO DO YOU SAY THAT I AM?"

A question of faith

MATTHEW 16:13–29

AS FAR BACK AS I can remember, my heart called me toward the sea. My family lived along the shores of Galilee, so I suppose this seaward tug was natural. But whatever the cause of my longings, the sea soon became much more to me than a place where I strained to cast out nets and to haul in fish.

Each time I loosed my boat and launched out into the deep, I expected to experience life to the full. Whether in sunny breezes or stormy squalls, whether in fruitful toil or empty frustration, I knew I would always encounter anew the awesome reality of God and his creation.

The kingdom of the sea also became the arena where I exercised my human calling, much as Adam had before me. This watery realm, still relatively unspoiled by the 'Fall,' became my own Eden where I "exercised dominion over the fish of the sea." This Godward understanding crammed rich meaning into my back-breaking labor. Each night's catch became my daily manna. Each silver-wrapped fish became a gift to me of God's providence.

Oh, I admit that I also found fishing a great escape. Escape from the ever-watchful Roman conquerors of Israel. Escape from the rigid rules of our own Pharisees and Sadducees that bound up the historic faith of our Fathers with damnable legalism and outward shows of righteousness. Escape from the feelings of meaninglessness which permeated our Jewish community now that the voice of God had been silent for 400 long years. Escape from the deadening mundane boredom that expresses itself in the incessant bickering of ordinary men and women. I despised it all. "Not for me!" I vowed.

So, "back to the sea!" became the drumbeat of my life. Back to life as God intended it.

Nothing could possibly lure me away from the sea. Of that I was sure. That is, nothing could lure me away for long.

But rumors caught my ear about a strange man named John who suddenly appeared out in the Wilderness near the Jordan River. Like Elijah of old, people said, John wore a plain mantle of camel's hair girded by a wide leather belt. He existed on simple desert food of locusts and wild honey. Proclaiming a two-edged announcement of "Good News" and "Doom," he cried out in a loud voice like a man possessed with a message not his own. He apparently spoke with such authority that multitudes flocked to him. Some scoffed. But many repented and received baptism. Hence the title "John, the Baptist." Or "John the Baptizer."

Now, given my dim view of the religious establishment of my day, how could I resist going out to see the Baptist? Who knows, perhaps he was Elijah, perhaps even the very Elijah who was expected to precede the coming Messiah. That's what his message of the coming "kingdom" seemed to imply. Besides, I could hardly wait to watch the Pharisees and Sadducees squirm as he unveiled their hypocrisy. And if it didn't happen quite that way, no loss. At least it figured to be a good show.

So I sped out to the desert. I had to see for myself.

I had no trouble in losing myself among the multitudes milling around John, like lost sheep looking for a shepherd. And I heard his words to them, a message that was simple, prophetic, and full of fire:

"Prepare a way for the Lord! Make clear his pathway. The Kingdom of God is close at hand. Turn yourselves around, or you will surely miss it. And once you have turned, let your repentance show in your behavior that which matches what is deep in your heart.

Look! There comes one after me who is more powerful than I, whose sandals I am not worthy to loose. He will not only baptize with water, as I do; he will baptize with fire and the Spirit. In his hand, he carries with him his sifting fork. He will completely clear out the threshing floor. He will gather into the barn the fruitful harvest and gather up the chaff to burn in the unquenchable fire. Therefore, repent and be baptized for the forgiveness of sins."

What was John saying? Make a way for the *Lord*? The Kingdom close at hand? Be baptized for the forgiveness of sins? All this was God-language. I couldn't figure him out. Was John a prophet, or blasphemer? Deranged? Oh, possibly. But no one could possibly mistake his intent.

Certainly John's intent was not lost on the Pharisees and Sadducees. Suddenly John whirled around and unleashed his verbal fire upon our religious leaders. "You brood of vipers," he called them. If I hadn't gasped, I probably would have cheered him loudly, saying, "Rail on, Prophet John!" (I probably shouldn't have enjoyed John's put-down so much, but the thought of undressing those garbed in super-religiosity appealed to my own sense of justice.) "You brood of vipers," John continued, "who warned you to flee from the coming wrath? I say to you, the axe is already laid at the root of the trees. Every tree that does not bring forth good fruit is being cut down and cast into the fire. So produce fruit worthy of your repentance!"

∼

Then John appeared to read their thoughts. "And don't you tell me, 'Abraham is our father,' as if that somehow insulates you from the wrath of God. For I say to you that God can from these rocks raise up sons to Abraham."

Oh, oh! Up to that point, John hadn't exactly been relational. But now he was putting the fat in the fire.

You see, John was attacking the growing rabbinic teaching that the children of Israel, as descendants of Abraham, were exempt from God's wrath because they fell under the umbrella of God's unbreakable covenant with Abraham. So, the rabbis insisted, when accused of sin, all one has to do is to plead God's promise to Abraham. God would then relent and the sinner would to be safe from God's wrath. The unfortunate implication, of course, was that the Chosen could sin with impunity.

And as if that weren't enough, John was affirming something more, something far more revolutionary. Just as God had promised to build a people from Abraham, John argued, God could as easily raise up other sons out of the rocks and build them into a new kingdom—a clear attack on their rabbinic tradition that God chose to build the world on the "rock of Abraham."

Thus, in one slam dunk, Prophet John had thrown down the gauntlet to these religious leaders. He was challenging their understanding of the Scriptures, of God, of the Abrahamic Covenant, of forgiveness, of salvation, of the kingdom of God on earth.

To a simple Jewish fellow like me who loved truth, this was a grand moment. But to a religious professional, it was the 'first shot fired in a war to-the-death.'

When John finished his daily prophetic announcement I walked away in silence, pondering. Every few steps, I found myself shaking my head. Could his news of a coming one possibly be true? My, how I wanted to believe it. I knew this: if the Lord's Anointed were to come, I would certainly flock to him. He would change everything—our Roman rule, our religious leadership, our despairing cynicism. I sighed with longing at such a prospect. "Even so, come!" I prayed.

But for now . . . "back to the sea!" With that thought, my spirit soared and my pace quickened. But I certainly would not forget what I had seen that day. A heavenward "perhaps" had now broken into my earthbound soul.

~

Days, perhaps weeks, passed uneventfully. But I discovered that just the possibility of a new kingdom coming had heightened my senses. With renewed gusto, I fished in my little kingdom of the sea. All the while I kept wondering about the new king and this new dominion. How would he come? How would I know him? How would he rule? And how would I be related to this king and all he possesses?

"Big thoughts for a big fisherman!" I chuckled as I spread out my nets to dry.

In the distance I could hear my brother Andrew cry out as he ran down the road from a day with the Baptist at the Jordan. "Simon, Simon!" Andrew called with an urgency that concerned me. I drew up my tunic into my belt and barreled toward him. "What's wrong, brother?" I yelled. "Simon, come and see! We have found the Messiah!"

The next thing I remember, this stranger and I stood face to face. The man called Jesus looked at me in a way I could never forget. It was he who broke the silence. I remember the first thing he said: "You are Simon, son of Jonah." Well, of course I am. But how did he know? From Andrew? And

GOD'S GREAT QUESTION TO SIMON PETER

then his strange prophetic message continued: "You are Simon ('hearing'), but you shall be called Peter, meaning 'rock.'"

Now, I realize that it may not seem important to you whether I was called "Simon" or "Peter." But in our Hebrew culture, our names meant everything to us. Our names denoted our character, our behavior, our nature. A new name! I couldn't help thinking of Abram becoming Abraham, of Sarai becoming Sarah, of Jacob being transformed into Israel. Aha. Aha! Suddenly I understood. Who had changed their names? Wasn't it God himself? Who else had the power to change our very nature? Wasn't this name-changing-man God's Anointed, the Messiah, the Christ?

After this first meeting, I sought every opportunity to go hear him teach. Each day I'd leave my boat, but each night I headed "back to the sea."

I admit that I kept wondering what my new name really meant. I wanted to keep on "hearing" (Simon). But I had secretly resolved to try to be more "rock-like" (Peter) as well. As it turned out, what a vain hope it was. Alas, I continued to stumble around like a graceless clod through daily life. And in my too-often times of failure, it didn't help to have my weathered fishing partners, James and John, tease me, saying, "Good goin', Rock-y!" At those moments, I wanted to die. I just shook my fist at them.

One morning when I had beached my boat and was washing my nets, Jesus came walking. He was followed by all sorts of bleeding humanity. Because he was so pressed by the crowd, he looked around for a boat so he could put out to sea and teach the multitude from a few feet offshore. Two well-worn fishing vessels sat there before him. I held my breath. And then Jesus chose mine.

When he had finished speaking, Jesus turned to me and said, "Let your boat loose into the deep waters, and then let down your net for a catch."

Do you know what my knee-jerk reaction was? "Hey Jesus, this is my turf. I'm the fisherman here. This is my little kingdom. If I thought your plan would work, I'd have done it already." But I shocked myself because, for once in my life, I didn't voice my thoughts.

Instead I heard myself say, "Master, we toiled all night and caught nothing. But at your word, I will let down the nets."

So I did. And to my surprise, the net came up full-to-breaking. When Andrew and I saw the nets about to give way and the ship about to sink under the load, we had to call for the other boat to come and help haul in the fish. Two boatloads. After a night of nothing at all. This didn't happen in my kingdom!

My reaction then? I fell down at Jesus' knees and begged: "Depart from me, O Lord, for I am but a sinful man." I had just seen something greater. I had heard something greater. This Jesus commanded, and it was so. Somehow his voice had the ring of the voice of creation: "Let there be! And there was!" How could I look upon such a one? I trembled in fear.

But Jesus said to me, "Don't you be afraid, Peter. Follow me! And I will make you a 'fisher of men!'"

A fisher of men? What kind of dominion was that? What kind of kingdom and realm would catch people? Surely that was a greater calling than exercising dominion over the fish of the sea. That seemed to be even greater than the calling given to Adam. Oh, I liked the thought of such dominion.

But the thought of my becoming a 'fisher of *men*' was also ironic. Me, and people? I loved fish; I wasn't as wild about people. For me, a graceless clod, to become "catchy" with people would require a miracle. Aha! Aha! That's exactly what it would be. Just as with the catch of fish, the one who commanded would work the miracle.

How could I resist such an offer? As soon as we brought the boat to land, I left it behind me on the beach. I turned my back to the sea. And I followed him.

∽

As I look back now, I can see how formative these early experiences with Jesus were for me. His twin prophecies—"You shall be called Peter ('rock')!" and "I will make you a catcher of people"—became the dual lenses through which I focused my understanding. Rocks. And people. Little did I realize that rocks and people might possibly be related. That "aha" would come later. But that's getting ahead of my story.

Jesus's invitation, "Follow me!" was just that. Unlike the rabbis, he did not sit down with us disciples to argue the meaning of the Torah. He simply expected us to watch him and to listen to him. At times his approach was frustrating. I wasn't always sure what he was saying or doing. I didn't know exactly what I was supposed to be learning. It was as if he had thrown me into a 'sea' of ideas and feelings and was expecting me to figure out how to swim back to shore.

He asked us question after question. I wanted so much to be the first to get the right answer. I wanted so much to receive his approval. But, graceless and dumb clod that I was, I often shouted the wrong answer. When that happened, I felt awful. What's worse, I always heard 'stage whispers' from my fishing buddies: "Good goin', Rock-y!" Momentarily, I would resolve to try to keep quiet, to listen, to watch.

What I began to hear and see was Jesus—with people! All sorts of people. People I wouldn't have thought he would notice. People who might have embarrassed me. People I wouldn't have wasted my time with. Riff-raff, I called them.

For example, a leper, an outcast, called out for mercy. Jesus stretched forth his hand, touched him, and made him clean. A woman possessed by seven devils assailed him. He freed her from her bondage. A paralytic man sat on a mat in helplessness. "Take heart, son; your sins are forgiven," Jesus told him, and the man leaped to his feet and was whole.

I struggled to understand. If only I could figure out his ways, pick up his patterns, find out the formulae which unlocked his mercy. But the circumstances still defied my logic.

To two blind men, he asked, "Do you believe I am able to heal you?" and he healed them. A woman simply touched the hem of his garment and was healed from her issue of blood. Another time, several men climbed up on a roof of a house where Jesus was teaching, removed a section of the roof, and lowered a paralytic down into the room so that Jesus might touch him. Jesus, seeing the faith of the stretcher-bearers, healed the man.

A ruler came to Jesus, knelt before him and said, "My daughter has just died. But come! Just put your hand on her, and she will live." Jesus went and raised up the child. He touched my own mother-in-law, cured her burning fever, and instantly restored her energy, just because he wanted to.

As you can see, sometimes the healings seemed to be triggered by the faith of the individual, sometimes by the faith of friends, sometimes by the faith of a father, sometimes by his own compulsion to love.

And Jesus seemed to go out of his way to search out those I considered "unacceptable." He called out to a miserable little big-shot named Zacchaeus up in a sycamore tree and motioned for him to come down so that they could have lunch together. Then he found another despised Roman tax-collector, one of Israel's quislings, as he sat at his collection booth; then Jesus called Matthew to be his disciple alongside me.

For the most part, Jesus insisted that his ministry was specifically for "the lost sheep of Israel." But his own compassion often caused him to make exceptions. He healed the servant of the Roman centurion. He honored the faith and tenacity of the Syrian woman by healing her daughter. He even allowed himself to offer living water to the loose-living woman drawing water from Jacob's well in Samaria.

But what shocked me most was that Jesus consistently seemed to treat women with the same dignity that he accorded men. He honored his mother's request by turning water into wine at an embarrassing moment in a wedding celebration. He wasn't at all bothered when a woman of ill-repute approached him during dinner at Simon the Pharisee's house, poured out costly ointment over him, washed him with her tears, wiped him with the hair of her head. While Simon pretended the woman didn't exist, Jesus turned his face away from Simon and turned toward her, saying: "Your sins are forgiven. Your faith has saved you. Go in peace!"

Constantly Jesus was pressed about by the multitudes. And this brought out his special compassion. "Sheep needing a shepherd," he called them. (He always associated sheep with his flock of people!) I'll never forget the day that he fed his hungry 'sheep' on a mountainside—five thousand men, plus women and children. He just kept on breaking the five loaves and two small fish which a little boy had brought for his own lunch. And it became a banquet feast for thousands. Twelve full food baskets were left over. I shook my head in wonder.

From time to time, we disciples became concerned about all the people tugging and pulling at him. So, when little children tried to get his attention too, we stepped in and sent them away. But Jesus reprimanded us. "Let them come. Of such is the kingdom of heaven. Unless you too become as little children, you cannot enter the kingdom of God."

There was that word "kingdom" again! Was he a king? Did he indeed have dominion? His was certainly a voice of authority. Authority over the world of unclean spirits. Authority over nature. Authority over the Sabbath. Authority over sickness, over death. Authority even to forgive sins!

When I saw all his authority put together, it was uncanny. And scary. But there was something I couldn't figure out. All the while he worked miracles and forgave sins, I was still living in the same kingdom I knew. I saw what he did. I participated in his work. But how did the kingdom of God fit alongside the kingdom I knew? I felt a tension. Was I in "the already" or in the "not yet?"

"Come on, Rock-y!" I told myself. "Just close your mouth. Listen more! Perhaps if you hear what Jesus is saying, you will understand." Good advice. I took it.

Day after day, I listened to Jesus in the synagogues, on the hillside, wherever he encountered people. What he taught us seemed upside-down at first. The meek shall inherit the earth? He who saves his life will lose it? Don't be concerned about money or food or clothing? Do your fasting, praying, almsgiving in secret? Blessed are you when you are persecuted for righteousness sake? Be reconciled with your brother even though he may still despise you? Love your enemies? If you want to be the greatest, be servant of all?

Oh, come on! That's not what any of us believed. That's not what we had grown up knowing to be true.

But—if this Jesus was right, then his kingdom would be an upside-down kingdom. In that new kingdom, all the signposts would be pointed in a new direction. And if I were serious about it, if I were really going to be his disciple, then I better start un-learning some things and learning others.

"Aha! Un-learning and re-learning. Let un-truth go. Let truth enter in." (I was both amused and disgusted that it had taken me so long to grasp.) That's what repentance means, isn't it? That's what John the Baptist was talking about too, wasn't it? Re-birthing our understanding. Re-birthing our hearts. Re-birthing the direction of our lives.

That's why the Christ had asked us to follow him, to "catch" this new way from him as one would catch a good infection. And if this Jesus was who John the Baptist said he was, then the Christ would bring us the baptism of fire which would make our re-birth possible. And that would indeed make him the king of the new kingdom which he himself had brought to life.

Oooooh! So that's why the Pharisees and Sadducees and those who have-it-all now began to take up sides against Jesus. That's why when I cheered at the way the Master poured rich new meaning into the Old Testament understandings—first loosing the strictures that kill, then binding them to an ethic of love—the other group didn't like it. That's why when Jesus cast out demons, the group accused him of doing it in the power of Beelzebub. That's why the rich young ruler went away sorrowing. He knew he had to choose between the two kingdoms. That's why the religious professionals rightly didn't like Jesus.

And then other pieces of biblical understanding began to fit together. I began to sing the song of Moses:

> "I will proclaim the name of the LORD.
>   Oh, praise the greatness of our God!
>   He is the Rock, his works are perfect . . .

> Is he not your Father, your Creator,
> who made you and formed you? . . .
>
> [Israel] grew fat and kicked;
> > filled with food, he became heavy and sleek.
> He abandoned the God who made him
> > and rejected the Rock his Savior . . .
>
> You deserted the Rock, who fathered you;
> > you forgot the God who gave you birth."
> > > (Deuteronomy 32:3, 4, 6, 15, 18)

I sang Moses's song often as I walked along. And certain words began to leap out at me: "the rock, who fathered you; the God who gave you birth!" And soon more pieces fit into the puzzle. King David affirmed:

> "The LORD is my rock, my fortress and my deliverer;
> > my God is my rock, in whom I take refuge . . .
> For who is God besides the LORD?
> > And who is the Rock except our God?"
> > > (2 Samuel 22:2, 3, 32)

To the voices of the Lawgiver and the King of Israel were soon joined the voices of the Prophets. Daniel interpreted a vision for King Nebuchadnezzar of Babylon about a 'rock' and a 'kingdom' yet to come:

> "While you were watching, a rock was cut out, but not by human hands. It struck the statue on its feet of iron and clay and smashed them . . . But the rock that struck the statue became a huge mountain and filled the whole earth . . . In the time of those kings, the God of heaven will set up a kingdom that will never be destroyed, nor will it be left to another people. It will crush all those kingdoms and bring them to an end, but it will itself endure forever. This is the meaning of the vision of the rock cut out of a mountain, but not by human hands—a rock that broke the iron, the clay, the silver and the gold to pieces."
> > (Daniel 2:34, 35, 44, 45)

Informed by these and a myriad other texts, I looked again at passages from Isaiah which the Baptist implied that the Pharisees had taken out of context. The theme of the "rock" begins in Isaiah where the Lord describes the coming Emmanuel as "a stone that causes men to stumble and a rock that makes them fall." (8:14). "The *Lord* is the Rock eternal" (26:4) "See, I lay a stone in Zion, a tested stone, a precious cornerstone for a sure foundation; the one who trusts will never be dismayed." (28:16). Isaiah continues the prophecy of God's coming salvation and a new kingdom. In the midst of his long description of the Lord's suffering servant, Isaiah records these words of God:

> "Harken to me, you who pursue deliverance,
>   Who will seek the Lord;
> Look to the Rock from which you were hewn,
> And to the quarry from which you were digged.
>
> Look to Abraham your father
>   and to Sarah who bore you;
> for when he was but one I called him [out],
>   and I blessed him and made him many . . .
> I, I am he that comforts you;
>   who are you that you are afraid of man who dies,
>   of the son of man who is made like grass,
> and have forgotten the LORD, your Maker,
>   who stretched out the heavens and laid the foundation of the earth."
>   (Isaiah 51:1, 2, 12, 13)

Aha! That's it! "The rock from which you are hewn." So, I'm a piece of the rock, am I? Hewn out of a larger rock. But was that larger rock Abraham, as the scribes taught? Or God himself? Since the long Isaiah passage focused entirely on God and his faithfulness, I concluded that Father Abraham was cited as the premier *example* of God's faithfulness. This understanding would square well with the other scriptures. This would also put me on the side of John the Baptist. And this would tie it all together.

Whew! I felt relieved—and excited! Now I would be ready to converse with Jesus about rocks.

Ah, but my glorious display of understanding didn't happen in quite the way I had imagined.

∼

As evidence of Jesus' power and authority increased, so had questions about the source of his power and authority. Reactions began to intensify and polarize.

"He does all things well," the people were saying in joyous praise to God who had given such authority to a man. "Come, see a man who told me everything I ever did," said the woman at the well. "Couldn't he be the Christ?" In Nain, where Jesus raised a young man from the dead, people cried out in awe: "A great prophet has appeared among us; God has come to help his people," echoing names given Jesus at his birth: "Jesus" (God Saves!) and "Emmanuel" (God with Us).

Meanwhile, back at the religious establishment, angry voices grew louder. "He's a blasphemer! Who can forgive sins but God alone?" "What does he mean by his 'Father In heaven'? Isn't this the Carpenter's son?" "Aren't we right, Jesus, that you are a Samaritan and demon-possessed?"

Although I could hardly wait to talk "rocks" with Jesus, I too found myself caught up in the speculation about who he really was. I kept pondering and processing what I knew.

Hadn't Andrew understood from the beginning? "Simon, come see. We have found the Messiah, the Christ, the Lord's Anointed!" Hadn't Nathaniel been so stunned that Jesus saw him under the fig tree before they ever met that he cried out: "You are the Son of God. You are the King of Israel!" Hadn't even the evil spirits screamed out when they saw the Lord approach: "What do you want with us, thou Son of David?"

Thus, the controversy. Hadn't we all seen his awesome dominion? Hadn't we disciples all felt something grow in our hearts? Something real? Something re-birthing us?

While we were walking along near the region of Caesarea Philippi one day, Jesus suddenly turned to us and asked simply: "Who do people say that I, the Son of Man, am?"

"Some say you are Elijah." one disciple answered. "Others say you are John the Baptist." "Still others insist that you are one of the prophets come back, perhaps Jeremiah."

Then Jesus, the master questioner, pressed us one step farther by asking:

"AND YOU—WHO DO YOU SAY THAT I AM?"

What a question! Usually I spoke for the group. But I didn't want to get trapped on this one. So I waited.

GOD'S GREAT QUESTION TO SIMON PETER

Silence. Nothing but unnerving silence. I could hardly stand it. Gradually all the eyes of the group made their way to me as if to say, "Okay, Rock-y. You usually insist on answering first. Now, here's your chance!"

Jesus's question, if I grasped it, took us deeper into the waters of understanding than we had reached before. "Think first, Rock-y," I told myself. "Understand, you graceless dumb clod, before you speak! Surely no human categories stretch far enough to encompass him. So, first think as *big* as you can. Then, think *small*, as small as you can: 'Who is he to *you*, Peter?' Then I was ready to answer.

I took a huge breath, straightened myself up to my full stature, and I looked my Lord square in the eye. And despite my terror of being wrong, I responded in unshaken tones; **"YOU ARE THE CHRIST, THE SON OF THE LIVING GOD!"**

I held my breath. Oh, how I wanted to be right. But right or wrong, my confession felt good. My own emerging creedal statement. My own emerging personal affirmation of faith in the One who called me to follow him.

"Blessed are you, Simon son of Jonah!" the thundering voice of Jesus assured me. "I tell you, flesh and blood has not revealed this to you, but my Father in heaven."

I tried not to let my chest puff up—or certainly not to let it show. But when I heard my buddies whisper in amazement, "Good goin', Rock-y!" I suppose my face beamed.

Jesus looked at me intently and said: "Peter, you are a Rock-Man—a living piece of the rock!"

Then pointing to himself, he continued: "and on *this Rock*—'the Rock from which you are hewn'—I will build my church. And the worst that evil and death can threaten will never be able to prevail against it!"

A loose rock—hewn out of a larger rock. Upon that Rock, the Son of the living God would build a living people of God, from living stones. As Abraham had been called out of Ur and built a people of the Old Covenant, so Christ's church, his "ecclesia", would be called out and built into a people of faith, sons and daughters of Abraham, in a New Covenant now open to all people.

So, this kingdom was becoming more real. But what would it be like? Would Jesus rule this kingdom now? And how?

Looking around at all of us, he said: "I will give you the keys of the kingdom. Whatever you bind on earth will be bound in heaven; whatever you loose on earth will be loosed in heaven."

What did he mean? Would the twelve of us rule on twelve thrones? And where would Jesus be? Were we to establish an appropriate infrastructure for the church? Perhaps. But this much I knew for sure: somehow we living rocks had a crucial responsibility. Christ was entrusting his church to us. *We* were his plan. His only plan.

What a moment! How like Jesus to use this 'non-occasion' to reveal himself and his plans to us as we simply wrestled with his probing question: **"And you—who do you say that I am?"**

But from this moment on, Jesus began to talk about strange things. Talk about suffering. Talk that he would have to endure many things at the hands of the religious leaders. Talk that he must be killed and be raised to life on the third day. Talk that drummed a persistent, morbid theme. Talk that hardly seemed worthy of the Son of the living God.

So I finally pulled him aside and rebuked him. "Never, Lord! That will never happen to you! Surely God will save you from this! This cannot be allowed to take place!"

He whirled around and fired at me, "Get out of my way, Satan! You've become a stumbling block to me. You're not thinking God's thoughts; you're thinking men's thoughts."

Then he turned to the shocked disciples and said: "If anyone would come after me, he must deny himself, hoist up his cross on his shoulders each day, and follow me."

You can't imagine how horrible I felt. I had fallen all the way from "Blessed" to "Satan," in one slam dunk!

I expected the familiar, "Good goin', Rock-y!" But it didn't come. Bless them. I think they shared my deep pain.

∼

Rock-Man didn't do well from this moment on. I didn't behave much like a living stone. More like a rolling stone!

At the Mount of Transfiguration, I so much wanted to be helpful. Alas, I too quickly assigned the same glory to Moses and Elijah as to Jesus. "Good goin', Rock-y!"

Then on the sea one night, we disciples were about to sink when John spotted Jesus coming in the distance, looking like a ghost. I wanted so much to redeem myself. "Lord, if it is you," I cried, "bid me come to you on the water." And he 'bid' me. So I stepped out of the boat in faith, looking to him.

But I quickly became distracted by the angry waves and I felt myself going down. "Jesus, save me!" He reached out his arm to fish me out of the sea. "Good goin'!"

At the Last Supper, I let Jesus take up the servant's towel and basin to wash the disciples' feet. What on earth was I thinking of! And when my "aha" came, I got mixed up all over again. "Wash all of me," I insisted. In my confusion, I almost missed his teaching: "A new commandment I give you, that you love one another as I have loved you."

In Gethsemane, Jesus asked us to watch with him in prayer during his anguish. Alas, Rock-y fell fast asleep.

When the Son of God was arrested, I whipped out my sword and cut off the ear of Malthus. "Put away your sword, Simon! Don't you know that I could call legions of angels if I wanted them?" Ouch! My Lord didn't need me. "Good goin'!"

Worst of all, I had promised Jesus at the Table that, regardless of what others would do on this fateful night, I would never forsake him. But within hours of my rock-like affirmation, I denied my Lord. After my *third* denial, I winced. As Jesus had warned, I heard the cock crow. Just then, my Lord was led in chains into the courtyard. He raised his head until his eyes reached mine. With blood streaming down his brow, he looked at me with such love. I felt horrible. And then they took him away.

Never would there be a chance for 'Rock-y' to tell his Lord how sorry he was and ask for his forgiveness. From the heights of being a Rock-Man, I had slid all the way downhill. The accusing chant drummed louder and louder inside me: "Good goin', Rock-y! Good goin', Rock-y!" I couldn't seem to stop it, and I wouldn't stop it if I could. I was a failure, nothing more. For all my dreams, that's really all I was!

I went out alone—and I cried bitterly.

From a distance I watched the unthinkable occur. The righteous crucified between two common thieves. Above him a crude sign: "Jesus of Nazareth, King of the Jews!" Could it be that I had mistaken who he was? Was he merely man? Or was he the Son of God who walked in the flesh among us?

I thought back to that glorious day in Caesarea Philippi when I had affirmed: "You are the Christ, the Son of the living God!" What had gone wrong? Why all this? But as his agony wore on, I saw him behave more and more un-earthly. In the midst of pain, he assigned the care of his mother to John. In the midst of pain, he asked his Father in heaven to forgive those who crucified him because they didn't know what they were doing. In the midst of pain, in a final majestic gesture of one who exercises dominion, he dismissed his own spirit back to God.

It was all over!

I didn't want to be with anyone. But I didn't want to be alone either. Where could I flee? Where could I find comfort? Where could I get back in touch with God again?

"Back to the sea!" I climbed into my boat once again and rowed out alone to the security of my own little realm.

Numbly, I gazed at the sea from my familiar old vessel that had seen me through many a storm. Hours passed. One day. Two. I bent over the side of the boat and splashed the water. Maybe I should throw myself overboard, like Jonah!

What had gone wrong? Ever since that day when Jesus had said, "Blessed are you, Simon son of Jonah!" things had turned sour. Jesus on a cross, in a tomb! Rock-Man plummeting ever downhill, wishing I were dead too!

"Son of Jonah?" That's what Jesus said. I hadn't paid much attention at the time. Jonah? Or my father, whose name was really John? Was this a play on words? Or, was Jesus pointing me to the sign demanded by the people as proof he was the Messiah. The only one Jesus would give was "the sign of Jonah." The sign of repentance, yes. But more? "As Jonah was three days in the belly of the great fish, so shall the Son of Man be in the bowels of the earth." Three days? *Three?*

Aha! Aha!" I screamed to the howling wind. As fast as I could row, I streaked back to shore. Could it be? The Son of "the *living* God?"

By now it was early morning of the third day. The sun shone. Birds sang. I so hoped I would not be disappointed.

∿

As I ran toward the tomb, I caught up with John who also was rushing to confirm the report of the women. We found the stone rolled away. The tomb empty. The grave cloths folded.

But where was the Lord? My hopes soared. Strangely, so did my fears. Even if Jesus were risen—which, despite my fledgling faith, seemed too good to be true—how could I face him? What could I say? How could he ever forgive me?

When the risen Lord sought me out, I was dumbfounded! I couldn't believe he wanted to see me—Simon, the one who tried so hard but who failed so miserably. "Peter, it is I, the Lord!" I can never speak about that sacred moment!

By now, several of us had witnessed the resurrected Lord. Two friends from Emmaus. Still, we were so fearful that we gathered in an upper room, behind locked doors. Then suddenly the risen Jesus appeared in our midst: "Peace! Divine shalom. All is now complete, made whole, restored, back in balance again." Our joy knew no bounds!

Again a week later, he came. This time Thomas saw the Savior's hands and side, crying, "My Lord and my God!"

What mixed feelings we were experiencing. Joy and fear, belief and unbelief. How could that be? But just as I had affirmed with all my heart at Caesarea Philippi that Jesus was "the Christ, the Son of the living God," I didn't really grasp the full implications at the time. So, rubbed raw by roller-coaster emotions, we were still gripped by confusion.

Yes, Jesus had risen. But what next? Where was he? What did he want us to do? Where was this kingdom to which he had given us keys? What keys? What was going on?

Finally I couldn't stand the impasse. I'm going "back to the sea!" I announced. Thomas, Nathaniel, James, John, and a couple others begged to join me. On the Sea of Galilee we fished and fished all night, and we caught nothing.

Not since the day when Jesus had called me to be his disciple, to be a "fisher of men," had this happened. "It's time for another miracle," I chuckled. Whether a chuckle of faith, or hope, or impossibility, I didn't know. And again came that familiar Voice, saying: "Let down your nets on the right side." "Let it be." He had commanded. And it was so!

"It is the Lord!" John whispered to me. And immediately I pulled on my tunic, and I plunged into the waters to be the first to greet him.

As I helped the others unload the catch, Jesus was already cooking breakfast for us on the beach.

"Simon, son of Jonah, do you love me more than these?" he asked as he drew me aside. (Love, "agape")

"More than these?" I wasn't so sure anymore. And did I love him with the "agape" love he was asking me about? Agape—that selfless love which seeks nothing in return but seeks the highest for the other. "Oh, Rock-y," I warned myself, "this time don't you dare profess more than you can live by."

"Yes, Lord. You know that I am your friend, that I love you ("phileo") with the dearest earthly love I know."

"Simon, do you love me (agape)?" I was hurt that Jesus addressed me as Simon, not as Peter. And I wanted so much to affirm that I loved him with the same love as he loved me. But how could I affirm something I couldn't even comprehend?

I determined to hold steadfastly to my humble, more realistic response again. "Lord, you know all things. You know that I love you every bit as much as I know how."

This third time, Jesus graciously switched the verb: "Do you love me (phileo), Simon?" "'Phileo?' Oh, yes, Lord!"

I saw a twinkle in Jesus' eye. What was he thinking? "Good goin', Rock-y?" I'll never know. His words of response to me were simple, sparse, direct: "Feed my lambs. Care for my sheep. No matter what, just keep on following me."

A gracious three-fold commission for a three-time loser!

"Feed my sheep." "Tend my straying flock." "Look out for my little lambs." I wondered if perhaps these were the simple "keys of the kingdom" he was entrusting to us disciples? Aha! That's what Jesus had told us, "Don't be like the Pharisees, for they slam shut the kingdom of heaven in men's faces. They do not enter themselves, nor do they *unlock* the door to let in those who want to enter." Just help people to love and serve Christ, I told myself.

I vowed to unlock his kingdom to all. We would preach the gospel and tend the flock with wisdom, my brothers and I. It would be tempting to become enamored with power and church structure. But I resolved to adopt Jesus's own priority—loving needy, battered, helpless human beings. Like my Lord, I would stick close to people, to the flock, to his little lambs. As you can imagine, "Rock-y" could never forget how needy, battered, and helpless Jesus's little lambs can be.

A Living Lord! A Living Plan! And now Jesus was transforming his shell-shocked, timid, wavering disciples into Living Witnesses of his Living Kingdom!

∽

At Pentecost, we heard a sound of rushing wind. Flames like tongues of fire appeared. We began speaking languages we had never heard before. We became jubilant. Ecstatic.

A crowd gathered. They seemed confused. Were we drunk?

"Men of Israel," I explained. "We are not drunk. What you see is the fulfillment of Joel's prophecy: "In the last days God will pour out my Spirit on all people, and whoever calls on the name of the Lord shall be saved!"

"Listen, and let me explain. Jesus of Nazareth lived among you. He was authenticated by God through signs and miracles which you yourselves saw. This man was delivered over to you by the purpose and foreknowledge of God. Helped by wicked men, you put him to death on a cross. But God raised him from the dead. We were all eye witnesses. This Jesus whom you crucified, has now been made Lord and Christ!"

Stricken with remorse they asked, "What must we do?" "Repent (be re-birthed), be baptized in the name of Jesus Christ so that your sins may be forgiven and you may receive the gift of God's Holy Spirit," I proclaimed with boldness.

That day, three thousand people responded in living faith. The Living Christ was calling out a people for himself, building his living church. And to my great joy, my Lord was also fulfilling his promise: "Follow me, Peter. And I will (eventually) make you 'catchy' with people, a real 'fisher of *men*!'"

"AND YOU—WHO DO YOU SAY THAT I AM?"

XI.

GOD'S GREAT QUESTION TO THE WOMAN TAKEN IN ADULTERY

"WOMAN, WHERE ARE YOUR ACCUSERS?"
A question of release
JOHN 7:53—8:11

CAN YOU BELIEVE THAT my story is included here? I was hardly a major character of Scripture. And clearly I wasn't any heroine. I was just an ordinary woman. Not worth much in my culture. A woman without even a name. A woman who had committed one of the three worst sins in Israel. A shameful woman!

What happened when I met Jesus is a story that has scandalized the Church from that day until this. Who would have imagined that the holy Son of God would pay attention to the likes of me? And if he did, who would dare have imagined what actually took place?

My story has plagued the Church through the centuries. Should it be included in Holy writ? Should it not? Surely such extravagant grace could not be granted by a holy God to the vilest of sinners. So, embarrassed ascetic copyists of the oldest biblical manuscripts omitted it. Others left a space where they found it, thinking it surely must have been an exaggerated tale inserted by over-zealous, first-century witnesses. Everyone was afraid to proclaim openly what Jesus had told me, lest it give encouragement to those who sinned willfully.

But this too-good-to-be-true story kept on spreading by word of mouth. And by 100 A.D. or so, the tale of Jesus's encounter with me had even found its way into secular literature. So the story's authenticity goes back almost to the days of the last New Testament manuscripts.

Whether my story should be included in Scripture is a question I'll bequeath to the scholars for their theological debates. But what I know, I know! Scandal? Oh yes—mine! But the scandal of grace? His alone.

Mine is an extravagant tale, a rags-to-riches, darkness-to-light, "before-and-after" account of a miserable outcast who, at the worst moment of her life, comes to experience the glorious Kingdom of God. If you are willing to join your heart to mine as I relate my encounter, you too will begin to glimpse the utter scandal of the gospel which is really the "good news" of Christianity.

Here, then, is my memory of that unforgettable day, the story which, through the ages, has simply refused to die.

∽

Ironically, I awoke that fateful day with quiet joy. My heart was full. My joy complete. My spirit light.

It had been a long time since I had slept so well. Tensions gone. Fears erased. Burdens lifted. I felt refreshed. Strong. Like a normal human being once again. Was this "shalom", everything in its proper place? I didn't dare affirm that this happiness was the gift of God. And yet, to me it was! Woman was never intended to be alone, all alone.

Gentle beams of light broke into my room. I lay there quietly on the mat, watching the patterns of dust in the air which the sun's rays revealed. Dust. So invisible. So much a part of our lives, even when we don't realize it. Dust. That unwelcome intruder which covers the clean with uncleanness. Covers the fresh with the residue of the ages. Covers the re-newed with the nagging legacy of the old.

"There's been too much dust in my life," I concluded. I thought back to more pleasant days, days when God's shalom had covered me, days when I didn't worry much about the "dust" of life. I had a husband. Family. Relatives. Relationships which form the wealth of life to the poor. Who could have guessed that, through the unwanted circumstances of life—life's "dust"—they now would be all gone. Dust to dust, ashes to ashes. My glorious past indeed lay dead.

And then a more troubling thought came once again. If my 'shalom' had once vanished like a breath, where had been the Giver of Shalom? I had loved him. I had worshiped him. I had not done much to offend him. So, why was this happening to me, a good woman, a child of God's Covenant?

Such mixed memories and hitherto unspoken wonderings brought chills to my body.

I turned to seek the warmth of my lover's body. I gave thanks for his seeming touch of shalom once again. Thanks to whom? I didn't know. Surely the Almighty wouldn't receive my gratitude. Not from a lonely woman who was committing adultery. Not from a woman all covered with dust!

"Damn the dust! Damn the pain of life!" I blurted out.

My lover roused at the sound of my voice. He reached out. And he drew me close. Within an instant we were rejoicing in each other's embrace.

Amid our squeals of delight, I suddenly heard a rustling outside. I froze in terror. Instinctively I grabbed for something to cover my nakedness. But it was too late.

Into my dusty room, at the first rays of morning light, loud men burst upon us. "Get her! Get her!" I heard them shout to each other. There was a scramble as they grabbed at me. I glanced over to be sure my lover was safe. I saw a bearded man with rough hands lunge at him and thrust him outside. And then, strangely, the bearded one immediately turned around and came back inside.

"Now we've got him," the intruders assured each other with a glint of malice in their eyes.

"Got *him*?" What did they mean? Did they have my lover in custody outside? No, I didn't see any evidence of that.

I didn't have time to ponder. Tears coursed down my dusty face. I pulled my long hair over my breasts to hide my shame. I glanced around for something else to cover me, but I could reach nothing. I was exposed. Exposed physically. Exposed emotionally. Exposed before the Law of Moses.

What happened from that point on is still a blur to me. I do recall how they dragged me, still half-naked, through the rows of houses. Hearing the commotion, all kinds of people rushed outside, rubbing sleep from their eyes. And they stared. At *me!* At my nakedness. At my shame. At the most miserable of creatures under God's heaven.

I had been caught. Caught by the "righteous." Caught by the zealous. Caught by those who wanted to rid the world of dust like me. Caught by those who had the religious duty to put me to death—by stoning. All in the

GOD'S GREAT QUESTION TO THE WOMAN TAKEN IN ADULTERY

name of God. All under the commands of God. All so terribly legal and moral. All so de-humanizing, so horrifying, so unthinkable.

"Behold the adulteress!" my captors shouted gleefully to the growing crowds of the curious. "We took her in the very act! We will rid Israel of her kind."

Until that moment, I suppose, I hadn't thought much about adultery. I certainly hadn't intended to engage in adultery; I hadn't set out to do it. But here I was. And they were right. I had committed the act they termed "adultery." Gradually the horror of my present situation became supplanted with another horror—the prospect of my stoning—and of my death.

I began to imagine how it would happen. There could be no stoning inside Jerusalem, I knew. So these crude, albeit religious, men would undoubtedly march me past the outskirts of town to the place where others before me had met a similar fate. I knew where. Once I had been traveling by there and had watched with disbelief as heavy stones hurled through the air, pelted a frail little woman, knocked her to the ground, gashed her body into a bleeding mass of flesh, pummeled her until her limp body breathed no more life. And then the crazed men just left her there. Birds swooped down and devoured her flesh, assigning her picked bones to return to the dust from which God had first created human beings.

Why, I wondered, couldn't the God of Israel give second chances? Why was he so cruel, so unbending? Oh, I could surely understand how a faithful God could require his people to be faithful to him, and I knew that marital faithfulness was supposed to mirror the faithfulness of God to us.

But such an analogy was far from perfect. Our religious leaders allowed so much inconsistency. For example, why had my captors allowed my lover, a man, to go free? Why did our law allow husbands like mine to give me a bill of divorcement for any and all reasons? How could the law allow my husband, the one assigned to care for my needs, the right to send me away with no way to meet my daily needs? If God had ordained marriage, why couldn't he have ordained its success as well? Why was I the victim of a man's whim? "Where was the greatest sin?" I demanded of God. My former husband's? The married man who had shared my bed? Or mine?

Oh, I was guilty enough, I knew that. I longed so much for mercy. But I nourished little hope of that.

"Have pity, Lord!" I cried aloud in utter weakness toward heaven. My captors just laughed. "Not too likely, adulteress," they mocked me. "Not too likely!"

Our pathway wound uphill and down. I grew weak and faint, exhausted partly by fear. At times I stumbled. But they prodded me to my feet.

Along the way, I became aware of some kind of plotting that engaged the men in whispered conversations. Every so often, someone would turn away from the huddle with satisfaction and utter words much like I had heard at first: "Now we've got him! He can't escape this time."

"Got him?" I was confused. Surely they hadn't confused me with being a man, had they? What could they mean? Whom could they mean?

Then our procession took a surprising turn. Before we reached the Mount of Olives, the men suddenly shoved me toward the other fork of the road. Where were we going?

"Oh, no!" I screamed as the realization hit me. Before us loomed the gold-plated dome. Before us loomed the white marble columns. Before us loomed the mighty stones built one upon another. In triumphal majesty, the righteous having captured the unrighteous, we were heading for the Temple, the house of the Holy God of Israel.

If they were bent on killing me, why not get on with it? Why did I have to face the pious Pharisees and Sadducees? And why under heaven did I have to enter the holy Temple? I wasn't sure I could bear it. I had a conscience. I knew I had committed sin. I felt so sorry I had offended a holy God. Alas, it was too late to change. My hope was gone.

As we neared the Temple, the men jostled me more and more. Perhaps they were getting eager for the moment of stoning. They seemed to be growing more aggressive, more sure of themselves, more disrespectful of their miserable captive, more fixed on reaching the Temple quickly.

We climbed higher and higher. "Who shall ascend to the hill of the Lord?" my captors recited loudly from one of the Psalms of Ascent. And then they recited the Psalm's answer with malice as they ogled me: "She who has clean hands and a pure heart." Their point was clear. They were clean and pure; I was not. They sneered at me. And cut to the core by the biblical reminder, I finally began to sneer at myself. I felt absolutely dirty, inside and out.

The dust of the journey had fixed itself to my moist body. I tried to brush off as much dust as I could before we reached the Temple, but it was a lost cause. My tears had already streaked my filthy skin, and no amount of rubbing helped. Somehow the dust of my life had found its way to the outside of my being where no one could miss it.

GOD'S GREAT QUESTION TO THE WOMAN TAKEN IN ADULTERY

By now we were nearing the place of judgment. I didn't know what to expect. But I feared the worst. The unholy would come face to face with the Holy. Surely the unholy could not survive such an encounter.

If ever "misery" longed for gracious "pity", it was now.

∼

Our solemn procession was nearing its destination. Before me loomed the Holy Temple. I could hear bleating sheep awaiting their time to be sacrificed for the sins of Israel. This reminder increased my inner feelings of shame. "Oh, that my sins could be covered as well!" I muttered to myself, more in resignation to despair than in hope.

The crowd of people bunched together in front of the Temple, all facing the other way. This eased my embarrassment greatly.

Some of my captors bolted into the Temple. Just as quickly they returned, leading a contingent of dour-faced scribes and Pharisees toward me. And that's when I realized who my accusers really were—religious men, scribes and Pharisees themselves, enforcers of the Mosaic Law as measured by the external act alone.

In some strange way, I found myself disappointed. If I were going to be accused, I could at least have hoped that it would be for the cause of deeper righteousness. I could have hoped that my accusers would themselves model deep spirituality. To these men my sin would seem so "black," their own righteousness so "white." How I hated such unfeeling orthodoxy with its goal of condemnation rather than rescue. But alas, I was hardly in a position to bargain with them.

"Behold the adulteress!" I kept hearing them announce.

And thus, these men gradually built my sense of shame. And weren't they shaming me in order to try to establish their own righteousness by comparison? How damnable! Oh, how I wish they had listened to the words of the Teacher from Galilee who said: "Judge not, lest you too be judged." Or, "You look only at the inside of the cup, but inside your cup is full of dead men's bones." Or, "You Pharisees traverse heaven and earth to make one convert, and then you make him twice a son of hell as you yourselves are."

Oh, I was painfully guilty. I admit that! Even so, I found it particularly galling to be accused by "faithful" men whom I knew to be self-righteous "sepulchers." Had *they* no sense of their own shame? How dare they try to establish their own superiority over me by shaming me. If they didn't have the power to put my broken pieces back together again, why did they have the power to condemn me?

Perhaps the things the Teacher from Galilee taught the multitudes were true after all. "If he were here now, he'd surely unmask these hypocrites," I even mused again, more in resignation to despair than in hope.

I watched these men, these teachers of the Law, these self-righteous religious folk, as they barreled their way through the crowd of people facing the Temple. How rude they were, barging their way forward without any apology, just thrusting women aside, forcing their pathway through the mass of human beings gathered there. Even I felt embarrassed for them. And then I laughed at my reaction. Didn't I have enough embarrassment for myself? Why was I worrying about them anyway?

And then came the unexpected moment, an excruciating moment.

As the men parted the crowd, all eyes began to turn toward me. There I stood. Fully exposed. Filthy. Covered with dust. Covered with shame, both inside and out.

Ah, but their stares weren't the worst part. Through the crowd, I began to fix my attention on the One around whom the people had all been focusing. There he sat, leaning against the columns of the Temple with his arms outstretched. The Teacher began to raise his eyes—toward me!

I shrieked in discomfort. "Oh, no! Not *him*!"

Before his eyes reached mine, I dropped my head. Oh, some part of me had indeed hoped he would come to my rescue. But now I knew that he was the last person I wanted to see me. Although I had heard him expound his parables, work his miracles, teach the people, until this moment I had not comprehended the totality of his righteousness. Perhaps it was his stark contrast with me. But suddenly I felt that no two people in one universe could be more different. He, purely holy. I, the vilest of sinners. (If you have ever glimpsed this difference for yourself, you will understand.)

Strangely, this face-to-face encounter with the man called Jesus was both a moment of incredible pain—and of incredible release. I can't explain it. But in that moment I suddenly knew most surely who I was! And I knew most surely who he was! I knew I had nothing I could possibly say. And I knew I didn't have to say anything.

Now, I stood before him, head bowed. Mute. Motionless.

Everyone in the crowd surrounding Jesus strained forward to get a full view of this wretched piece of fallen humanity. They were aghast, yes. But they seemed to be of a different sort than those who had arrested me. From them I felt touches of "humanity," even a hint of pity, I sensed.

Nothing, however, could diminish the grim shame of this never-to-be-erased experience. Can you picture me? Here at the entrance of Jerusalem's Holy Temple. Half-naked before the vast throngs. Hair hung down loose. Arrested for adultery, in the very act. Accused by the pious. Accused on the right grounds. Accused in an unbelievably destructive way. Very much alone! Filthy. Undone. A woman with no name—no personhood—no value—except as an "object of shame and condemnation."

I read nervousness—and excitement—in the excruciating silence.

Then the holy teacher, Jesus, stepped forward to meet my accusers. I stood just a bit off to the right side in the shade, trying oh-so desperately to camouflage my exposed naked body.

"Master," one orthodox man began to speak in a pinched voice revealing his nervousness: 'Behold the adulteress. We caught her early this morning, in the very act." He paused, eyes dancing. I could hear the shocked gasps in the crowd. Already I could feel my life beginning to ebb away.

"Master", he repeated. "I must tell you that we arrested her according to the Law of Moses. As you know, Moses commanded us to stone "such as this one." But we became concerned, Sir, about the difficult situation we now face with the Romans who no longer allow us to condemn our own people to death as Moses instructs us. So, Teacher, what shall we now do? Should we be faithful to the Roman Law, or to the Mosaic Law? What do you think we ought to do to the accused?"

"The accused." Somehow this term had a funny ring to it. Surely this scribe, this teacher of the law, was referring to me. Yet it almost seemed as if he were trying to accuse *Jesus*.

Ahhh! Now I was beginning to catch on! That's exactly what the men said earlier: "Now we've got *him*!" Well! So this is what they had been conspiring about. They were setting a trap for Jesus, weren't they? They were forcing this Jewish Teacher to take a position on The Law. *He* was the accused, even more than I. And I? I was just a convenient object for them to use in setting the trap for Jesus. (Oh, what inhumanity we mortals often commit in the name of religion.)

And what a trap they had sprung. They had crafted their dilemma for Jesus with consummate skill. They well might have "gotten him!"

You see, this Jesus was already well known by the people for being merciful, compassionate, kind. He restored sight to the blind. He raised the widow's son. He healed the paralytic (but on the Sabbath day which brought him the wrath of the scribes and Pharisees). So, how did this new "Proclaimer of Love" dare agree that these religious fanatics could mete out death to a vulnerable woman in order to fulfill the Law of Moses?

If Jesus prevented my stoning, he would alienate all Israel "whose delight is in the law of the Lord," as King David wrote. How could the Teacher ignore such a basic strand in the fabric of our faith, the purity of God and his people as codified in our religious Law?

If Jesus agreed to my death, surely he would alienate the crowds. And not-so-incidentally on the other hand, he would also declare himself against the established law of the Roman Empire?

Such was the ingenious trap. Whichever way Jesus chose, he would surely bleed to death, impaled on the horns of the dilemma they devised! So, as their plan unfolded, now *he* was the accused, as well as I.

"Accused." What chills this word brought to any child of the Holy Scriptures. From the days of Job, we Israelites believed that it was Satan who was the "accuser of the brethren." And just the thought of Satan, the unseen, malevolent one now frightened us. But to "accuse" had another connotation as well. Your modern word "category" comes from this same Greek root. So, to accuse someone was to "consign the person to a fitting category."

Categories are wonderful boxes that help us deal simplistically with reality. Ignore the peripheral differences. Find the common ground. Lop off all that doesn't fit. Label it, file it, forget it! With that accomplished, we simply throw away all responsibility for it. We just forget it. Ah, but how to establish adequate and fair categories for *"judgment,"* that's the problem! Do we judge just by external glance? But what other choice is there for us human beings? Surely no mortal being can see beyond the external. Only the eternal Creator who made us, the One who transcends earth, can see into the heart of a human being created by him. And perhaps that's why God keeps insisting that judgment belongs only to him.

During the accusations, during the framing of the dilemma, Jesus of Galilee listened without uttering a sound. Like me, he stood mute and motionless. He gazed off toward the heavens.

Finally, while everyone else was standing, he stooped down.

With his head bowed, he quietly began to reach out and touch the dust. And he started to write in the dust with his finger. I remember wondering if he had even heard their question. He remained so calm and poised, so untouched by their agenda. He just kept on writing.

Was he trying to cover my shame by lowering his eyes? Probably. What gentleness! What graciousness he showed.

Meanwhile, the men kept prodding Jesus to state his position on the issue they had brought for a decision. "Tell us, Teacher, are we right to stone this creature or not?" Their tones became oppressive, sadistic, cruel. Their voices became louder, more insistent, feverish. Their faces became twisted, more and more inhuman. In time, the mob's imploring began to form a kind of hissing sound, much like that of a snake. They kept on winding around me as a serpent would, circling me in the dust to see from which angle they could best spring their venomous attack. "Hiss! Hiss! Hiss!"

Hearing such sounds, I became frightened on a more cosmic level. It seemed as if these men had somehow lost their humanity. It was as if something from beyond the human realm had possessed them. "Hiss! Hiss! Hiss!" Who was in control of them? And even more disturbing, who was in control of the universe right now?

While these men continued to question him, accuse him, tempt him, Jesus said nothing. And finally, Jesus' silence soon became uncomfortable. Was his silence perhaps designed to increase *their* shame? Surely, if they ever stopped to listen to themselves, they would see what I saw and be embarrassed—even as I was embarrassed by what I saw inside of me. Alas, the mob didn't seem to listen. "Bad adulteress! Bad adulteress!" the crowd kept on saying in an almost chant-like fashion. They couldn't see what they were doing. By shaming me, they were succeeding in really shaming themselves as well.

Finally, Jesus lifted himself up to his full height. He raised his arms and stretched them out horizontally. I glanced up. I rubbed my eyes. Against the strong morning sun, it was almost as if I glimpsed a pole with a brazen serpent crucified on it, as our forefathers witnessed in the Wilderness. Of course I knew it wasn't. There would be no instant salvation for me. This figure was simply Jesus standing there, rising to judge my case.

"All right, I will answer you," Jesus the Teacher began. "And I will also answer you with a dilemma!" The men looked surprised as Jesus continued:

"Go ahead. Stone her according to the Law of Moses!" My heart sank. I nearly fainted. Without a pause he pressed on. "But be sure *you* have clean hands and a pure heart. Let the first stone be hurled by the man who has no hint of sin in him, no act of sin, no thought of sin, ever! Let this person be the first. Then each of you can follow his lead, if you too are pure." Jesus then bowed his head and stooped down to write some more in the dust.

In response, the men immediately began to arm themselves with stones, readying themselves for their holy Mosaic duty to rid all impurity from the camp. They picked up large stones lying in the dust, (rocks probably left over from the former Temple when ours was restored. How symbolic! I was being literally stoned by the law. Thus, they prepared for their task. They began to circle, eyeing me.

Out of the corner of my eye, I kept watching Jesus. He didn't look up. He just kept writing with his finger in the dust. What was he writing? I couldn't read. The Ten Commandments perhaps? No, it seemed to be a kind of list? A writing of charges? Charges against whom? Against these men? Was this a list of the men and their offences? By now, the men seemed to be watching him as well, intently focusing on the ground.

Suddenly, the most elderly man let out a yelp. Somehow he had let his heavy stone drop on his own foot. He yelped as a wounded animal, grabbing his sore toes, then wiping the dust from his hands on his garment, a process which stained the robe noticeably. He limped away, seemingly in great pain. But seemingly also in sorrow and grief. I didn't understand.

And then something similar happened to another old one. Whatever was happening seemed to be related to two things; the weight of the men's own guilt, and the weight of stones. It was as if the stones of judgment they intended to hurl at me became so heavy that they had ended up hurting the very men who had intended to throw them.

These two had departed. Then another left. And another. From the eldest to the youngest they all mysteriously began to leave. My heart leaped with fresh hope. But I didn't dare trust what I didn't understand.

Still the Master remained silent, looking down, until we finally were left with an eerie silence. All I could hear was quiet breathing from the crowd.

Somewhere in the background still stood all those religious men, women and children who had come at the dawn's early light to hear words of eternal truth spoken by the Teacher. But during this amazing encounter, they had somehow faded into insignificance for me.

Now Jesus again lifted himself up. He looked around as if to gesture to all who were watching that the accusers had indeed departed. Then he turned to me. And for the first time during this unfolding saga, he spoke to me:

GOD'S GREAT QUESTION TO THE WOMAN TAKEN IN ADULTERY

"WOMAN, WHERE ARE YOUR ACCUSERS? DOES NO ONE CONDEMN YOU?"

"Woman." Isn't that what he said? He called me "woman!" It had been such a long time since anyone had called me "woman." Wasn't that a word reserved for someone who was a person? Wasn't that the same tender term Jesus used to address his own mother? You'll never know what hope this simple term brought to my fallen humanity. In some incomprehensible way, I thought, this Jesus he must value me. Even amid all my filth, amid all my dust, amid all my sin, he was apparently seeing something else in me that he loved. Yes, he knew I had a "past"—but in his own quiet way he seemed to be granting me a "future!" "Woman!" Yes, I still was. This holy man was confirming it.

"Does no one condemn you?" One by one the scribes and Pharisees, my accusers, had vanished. They no longer stood to condemn me. But I was still here, and I certainly condemned me. How could I do otherwise? And Jesus remained. Surely such holiness as he possessed would have to condemn those like me who act sinfully. What about Jesus? Didn't he condemn me?

I had already felt healing begin in my soul. Not because my accusers had gone, wonderful as that was. More because I had met reality—my own reality of who I was—but greater far was my understanding of this One standing before me who embodied eternal reality! I already felt myself changing. Fears leaving. Self-respect emerging. But even though I was ready to accept my own shame, I still feared the judgment of the Holy One.

How could I answer him? I wasn't sure.

For the first time, I dared look him straight in the eye. Oh, what love I saw! How strange: Love has a right to judge, although it doesn't often choose to do so. Love chooses to change people by its winsomeness. Faced with such love, I decided to trust my life to him.

He knew how much I condemned myself. And I knew his right to judge me. But I gambled that he was more anxious to forgive than to condemn me. So I decided to entrust my life to him.

So, to his question, "Does no one condemn you?" I finally answered with hope born of assurance: "No one, Lord!"

"No one, *Lord*!" I said. To us, the term "Lord" was an ambiguous one. It could be just a polite term of respect, or it could be jam-packed with all the devotion a heart could muster. When I called Jesus "Lord," mine was the outpouring of a soul who had experienced far too much dust and who desperately wanted to be clean again.

As I waited for him to speak to me, I caught myself nervously biting my lip. His would be the final word. Would he set me free? Or, would he condemn me to death? If you have ever wondered how long "eternity" is, just stand where I stood. After what seemed like hundreds of years, the man from Galilee opened his mouth.

"My dear lady, neither do I condemn you!"

Release! He was going to let me go free. But why?

"Neither do I condemn you. You have indeed fallen short of the high calling of God for your life. You have sinned. You know it, and I know it. But that is past. Now you choose how to go on today. You have choices to make for today and tomorrow. So, go and try again. Go—and sin no more!"

Release! Full release! I came to Jesus expecting to die. I left him expecting to live—today, and forevermore! If that isn't grace, I don't know what is.

But I fully heard what Jesus said to me. He offered me no cheap grace. He condemned my sin. That's why he could permit no more such behavior. Nor was his release of me a release for all eternity. Quite the contrary. He clearly implied to me that there would be another day, perhaps a long while from this moment, when I would indeed be judged for the deeds of my life. But in the meantime, I was now starting fresh again. My slate was wiped clean. I could choose to write a beautiful new life on my fully washed slate. If I were willing to choose this better way, I could still stand before him guiltless. Clean. Pure. Released. By his grace alone, he was granting me a second chance to choose my better path. And isn't precisely the pity for which I had prayed for on the road?

Changed. Grateful. Jubilant. Free. I headed back home.

Head held high, I hurried toward my little house, past those in the crowd who didn't understand, past my curious neighbors who had earlier seen me marched off toward the city gates. And a few hours later, I pushed boldly past the sore-footed scribes and Pharisees when I came back to the Temple, all cleaned up, to offer to God my sin offering of barley, as required by the Mosaic Law for those who commit adultery.

Again I heard the bleating of the sheep in the Temple area. If only there were a way for human beings to be cleansed once and for all without the constant sacrifice for sin. As I blinked away tears of contrition, I looked up to see Jesus across the courtyard. "Behold, the Lamb of God who takes away the sin of the world," the Baptist had prophesied. An unbelievable thought. And yet, it had been an unbelievable day!

∼

John's Gospel leaves my story unfinished, as is the story of all of us until that final day of accounting.

But I assure you that I used my second chance well. How could I not respond to his faith in me? I had no choice. I had to follow him, serve him, love him with all my heart.

My journey from this point on wasn't as carefree as you might imagine. I encountered these same unfeeling, orthodox men again and again. No, they weren't after me anymore. They were now stalking Jesus. "Now we've got *him!*" became their ongoing theme. Once they even took up rocks to stone Jesus for blasphemy. "Hiss! Hiss! Hiss!" But the Teacher somehow miraculously escaped from their midst.

Unfortunately, the misguided efforts of these religious zealots didn't end there. These same "blind leaders of the blind" continued to push and shove until they had their way. Finally they succeeded in their plot. They took Jesus, scourged him, mocked him, and finally condemned him to death. "Hisssss!"

Why Jesus? Why the holy one? Why not me? 'Twas I who deserved to be scourged, mocked, killed. I was the guilty one. Not he. Oh my God, not Jesus!

I watched with horror as the good-man, the God-Man, the merciful one, the one who had extended pity to me, was nailed to a cruel cross. Crucified at the insistence of these miserably self-righteous men. Crucified between two common thieves. And then I heard those unearthly words uttered by Jesus from the agony of the cross. Looking down at these self-proclaimed moral watchdogs who had conspired against him for so long, he cried out:

"Father, forgive them. They really don't know what they're doing!"

Words too gracious for a mere man. When I heard this, I remembered what Jesus had told us: "As the serpent was lifted up in the Wilderness, so must the Son of Man be lifted up." And, "If I be lifted up, I will draw all people unto me." And he did!

Through his death and resurrection I came to love him more and more, this God who releases us from our sins, from our failures, from our powerlessness, from our self-condemnation, from our falling short of the mark of "God's high calling."

No one cheered louder than I when the Apostle Paul captured this truth for all generations: "There is therefore, now, *no condemnation* to those who are in Christ Jesus!" But what about our accuser? My biographer, John, later gives us his God-given revelation in the final war of the worlds: "The accuser of the brethren is cast down." There's no one left to accuse us, no one left to condemn us! And isn't that the ultimate answer to God's great question to me:

**"WOMAN, WHERE ARE YOUR ACCUSERS?
DOES NO ONE CONDEMN YOU?"**

"No, one, Lord!"
"Neither do I condemn you! Go! And sin no more!"

My Friend of Today, I trust that you find this story "Good News!" A story about the God who, instead of condemning us, loves us into repentance. A story about the God who, instead of condemning us, liberates by his grace the saint trapped inside the sinner. A story about the God who, instead of condemning us, keeps on giving chances to those who admit their guilt and turn to a new life. A story about the God who, instead of condemning us, enjoys rescuing us. A story about the God who, instead of condemning us, gives his life for the most unlikely people! Sinful people. Hurting people. Dusty people. People like me. And you?

Amid the dust of your life, may you too encounter Jesus, the one who alone can offer you release. May you experience the lavish grace of God freely given to the unworthy, the good news which is 'the Scandal of the Gospel.' And surely I can attest that if the Son shall set you free, you shall be free indeed!

XII.

GOD'S GREAT QUESTION TO MARTHA

"WHERE HAVE YOU LAID HIM?"
A question of hope
JOHN 11:1–57; 12:1–11

"MARTHA! HURRY! LAZARUS IS fading!"

Sister Mary's scream, however, did not bring me near. Instead I bolted through the open doorway. Down the path I ran at breakneck speed. My frantic steps stirred up the thick dust, causing me to gasp for breath. I coughed. I wheezed. I blew dirt from my nostrils. By now I was nearing the road. Shielding my eyes from the setting sun, I squinted hard.

Where was he? I couldn't believe he hadn't yet come.

As soon as we had realized how terribly ill our brother was, Mary and I relayed the news to Jesus. We dispatched a messenger to the other side of the Jordan where Jesus was staying with his disciples. Our word to him was simple: "The one whom you love is sick." We didn't elaborate. We didn't demand. We simply gave him the information. We felt sure that love would respond.

Now, I searched the desert road for the hundredth time. Through the creeping shadows, through the dust raised by travelers hurrying to destinations before nightfall, I again sought some sign that the Master was coming. But I saw nothing. No hint of approaching movement. No far-off puffs of dust. No promising humps on the horizon. No Jesus.

I cradled my face in my hands. How could it be? Chills coursed up and down my miserable body. The anguish of not finding the one I was expecting to see left me paralyzed, stunned. And in these terrible moments, hope escaped.

How long I lingered there, I don't know. When the shock of reality of the empty road finally hit me, I simply turned away, turned toward home.

"Oh! Lazarus. I must get back to Lazarus." I realized with a jolt. I took off in a frenzy. I managed only a couple of strides toward our stone dwelling before I heard Mary's sudden wail. Lazarus was already gone.

I kicked the ground. Why on earth had I run to the road instead of being at Lazarus' side when he died? I kicked the ground again, but I was really kicking myself.

I reached home breathless to find Mary kneeling over our brother. His hand lay limp in hers as she still caressed it. Already his color seemed to be draining away. As I looked into glazed eyes staring vacantly at me, I came face to face with the grim specter of death in a way I never had before. I groaned. In an act of finality, I reached over Mary's shoulder and closed my brother's eyelids. I slumped down beside my weeping sister.

With Mary's wail and my flurry of activity, our neighbors now swooped in on us even before we could catch our breath. While Mary and I sobbed our grief, friends and relatives gathered around to comfort us. In age-old sounds of mourning they began to wail hysterically, venting their sorrow at full voice to show how very much they too loved and honored Lazarus.

Thus began our neighbors's ministries of kindness toward us. I remember, for example, watching one woman as she quietly turned over my cooking vessels. (While we remained in deep grief, we would not be allowed to prepare food.) Later, friends brought hot dishes they prepared just for us. Mary and I received them outside our house of mourning. We hardly felt hungry, but we agreed to nibble enough to keep us going. Then we slipped back inside. I felt a bit awkward in the house. Because of the late hour, the body of dear Lazarus would have to remain with us in the house until morning's light.

Once our friends drifted back to their homes, my sister and I hugged each other and cried some more. Then I blew out the lamp and sought the solace of sleep. We were alone. Alone with our own thoughts. Alone with our own pain. Alone with our own evening prayers to God. I recited mine with strangely enlightened new feelings: "Into your hands, I commit my spirit."

"Into *your* hands!" Isn't that what Lazarus would have prayed a couple nights ago too? Just a couple days ago he had been so healthy. Then this raging fever invaded. And by today—it had happened with such dizzying speed. I still had trouble absorbing it. I glanced over at Lazarus lying on the reed-strewn ground. My first odd thought was that he was asleep. Maybe I should go over and shake him to wake him up. I started to rise. Ah! I had already felt him. He lay pale, cold and rigid. No life remained. It was all over. Somehow I had to face that, to accept that. But it might take some time, I knew.

Lazarus hadn't suffered long. For that, I was grateful. Yet I had so desperately hoped that he could cling to life, painful though it be, just long enough for Jesus to come and heal him. What a vain hope that had turned out to be. Jesus hadn't come. Not to Bethany. Not to Lazarus. Not to us in the most urgent hour of our lives.

And why? Why hadn't Jesus come? How could he stay away when my brother was dying? How could the Savior desert his friends?

Just now, a noise caught my ear. Could it be? I jumped up and tiptoed over to the window to peer out. My heart began to thump. For an instant, my anticipation soared. "Even now." But no matter how hard I strained my eyes through the dark circular opening, I could see no one. No one. I heard myself groan as I kept gazing through the window.

Along the roadway, streams of light bathed the quiet earth, drawing my gaze heavenward. In the dreadful silence of blackest night, the stars still shone. Even in my grief, I found myself smiling back. Where was Lazarus now, I wondered. In Sheol, the abode of the dead? Probably. But someday perhaps even with God himself! That was my hope—and my dream!

This flicker of hope enabled me to dare think again about this brother of mine whom I adored for so long and with whom I had forged such an unbreakable link in my life. He was so quietly faithful. Dear as anyone I knew. Loving. Giving. Persevering. And God-fearing. I'm sure that's what bonded Lazarus, Mary and me close, even when our strongly diverse personalities threatened to drive us apart at times.

I stretched my memory back as far as it would take me, and Lazarus was always there. Sharing my plans, sharing my dreams, sharing my secrets. He always mirrored back to me who I really am. Struggling alongside me. Rejoicing alongside me. Always interweaving his heart and soul tightly with my own. My brother. My friend. My lovely friend!

But he was gone. I would never see him again. But I would never forget him. Not brother Lazarus!

With these painfully bittersweet thoughts, I fell into an exhausted and fitful sleep. After a short night, we must arise early to prepare his cold body for burial.

∾

In the morning, my real mourning began.

I stretched a bit when I heard the rooster crow. Then I awoke with a "thud." My bravery of last night had ebbed away. Trembling now, I opened my eyes. Yes, there still lay Lazarus' dead body. I thought I was prepared to see it, but the stark reality of my brother's death suddenly seemed to frighten me in a new way.

This was the most difficult death I had ever faced. Inevitable as I knew death was, I could never have anticipated the enormity of death's ripping power, death's robbing power. Into our peaceful lives which always seemed so normal to us, that unwelcome intruder of death had suddenly snatched away our 'shalom.' And even as it was immediate, it was so final, so terribly final. So irreversible. I vainly struggled to find a way back again. I felt utterly helpless.

Through gentle rays of dawn, I mindlessly watched the gnats circle the corpse. In one sense, how very natural. In another sense, how inhuman! "Who ever thought up this thing called 'death,'" I wondered. "Surely not a loving God!"

At the mere mention of Jehovah, my eyes again overflowed with tears. Didn't the Almighty understand how much my brother meant to me, to us? So, didn't he care about all three of us? Our house was silent enough—but I heard no answer.

All I heard was the sound of Mary awaking and beginning to cry. Today would be harder for her too. "Take courage, sister," I comforted her. "Who knows, perhaps Jesus will still come, even now." She just sobbed all the more.

I began to wonder why I had ever suggested such a thing. Yes, Jesus had raised the dead, just as Elisha had long ago. But they had raised those who had just died, not someone like my brother who hadn't twitched a muscle in hours. Ach! That was much too painful a thought. So, I rushed outside to escape my inner conversation.

Our neighbors were also rising. Soon they began their lovingly protective fussing over us, first urging Mary and me to take some nourishment. We tried. But even though we couldn't eat much right now, it felt so merciful to have these dear friends care for us in such intensely practical ways.

For me, the most difficult part came when I heard them say, "Now we must prepare the body for its final resting place." Some had already brought spices and bandages. Others returned to their houses for supplies. Mary and I brought out the linen, the preservatives, the ointment, and the tender treasures we had set aside for this unthinkable day.

With efficiency and poetry of motion, the group of women worked to anoint and preserve Lazarus's body. Mary followed some of their many suggestions. I helped just a little, then made a quiet exit.

I decided to wander outside with no particular plan except to flee the scene of death. Gradually I made my way down to the road. Once more, I scanned the horizon. "Even now!" This time I did see puffs of dust. I was too afraid to hope, but I did wait there on the chance that it might be Jesus.

As the figures drew nearer, I could see them better. The dust apparently was stirred up by a group of professional mourners from Jerusalem coming to join us in expressing our grief on the way to the gravesite. I turned away in disgust. Not at them. More at my own disappointment.

Within a couple of hours, busy hands had completed wrapping the body in bandages and had slipped Lazarus into his "traveling gown." They hoisted him off the floor and onto a litter they would use to carry him to the tomb. As a last gesture, I laid the final linen cloth over my brother's face.

Mary and I took a couple of long, deep breaths to ready ourselves for the funeral procession to the tombs. What a sorry mess we were. No sandals. Torn, unkempt hair. Rent, soiled clothes. Dirty all over. But no matter. These were signs of deep mourning. So, out the door we marched. We women would go first. We believed that, since woman first led man into sin in the Garden, the women should be the first to face sin's consequence, death, at the grave.

I can't call to mind much of what happened along the burial route. I do recall the shrieks and wails that kept building in intensity until my head ached. And I vaguely remember my friends' consoling me in differing ways.

Only one moment do I recall vividly—the fork in the road. Try as hard as I might, I couldn't resist one last look toward the desert before we turned for the tombs. I hesitated at the crossroads, scanning the distance for this final time. Where was he? Even now, if he were to come, there might still be a chance, I thought. But there was no sign of him, even now.

I again kicked the ground.

And then a strange thought hit me. Perhaps Jesus had never gotten our message. I wriggled loose from the embrace of friends, and I searched out our messenger. "Didn't you give him the news?" I demanded. "Surely if he had gotten our message he would have come."

"Believe me, lady, I gave him your message just as you told it to me," he replied.

"And what did the Teacher say to you in reply?" I asked.

"Only one thing," the messenger reported. "Jesus promised very clearly: 'This illness will not end in death. All this is happening for the glory of God, so that the Son of God may be glorified by it.' I know that's all he told me, sister."

At least he'd gotten our message. I whirled around from the desert road and, with neck bowed in resignation, I now headed for the tombs.

Surely Jesus must have intended his words to encourage us, I reflected. But by the time the man had returned with the message, my brother had already breathed his last. And these words of Jesus which would ordinarily have breathed promise, now fell dead upon my heart.

Anger? Disappointment? Confusion? I was feeling all of these. And more. I was gradually beginning to realize that the "more" I was feeling was a profound sense of betrayal by Jesus. Jesus, longtime friend of Lazarus. Jesus, my unfortunately *absent* friend.

"There's nothing more cruel than the betrayal of trust," I murmured to myself. "Not even death itself."

I lifted my eyes. Before me stood the rocks from which the burial cave had been carved. Someone had whitewashed it so that the many travelers to the Passover Feast in Jerusalem couldn't miss it. We surely didn't want those on pilgrim-age to become "unclean" by accidentally touching the sepulcher. Across the mouth of the cave, a huge flat stone would be used to seal it tight.

When the mourners finished wailing and beating their breasts, several friends gave speeches to honor Lazarus' memory. This unexpected outpouring of reminiscence and gratitude was touching and tender. And meaningful. But I also found it excruciating. So, I began to fidget and fuss. "Hang in there, Martha, soon it will be over," I counseled myself in my usual parental tones. And it was so.

When everyone at our house who wanted to speak had done so, I motioned to one of the men. "Roll away the stone!" Several strong fellows helped him tug and pull and push at the circular stone set in its groove. In a few moments we heard a chilling creak. Then grinding sounds. Then a low, steady rumble as the giant stone inched away from the tomb's entrance.

We all gasped in horror. The death stench was putrid.

With the stone fully rolled aside, I could see that the cavern contained several shelves carved out, three on each side and two along the rear wall. A center passageway gave access to those carrying in the next corpse.

The men gently lifted Lazarus from his litter and transferred him to a shelf in the back. "Depart in peace!" we shouted together in farewell.

Then once again the sounds of the men's grunts and groans mingled with the squeaks and moans of the stone as it creaked in its rocky rut and was finally locked into its tight position. When we heard the final thud, we knew it had reached its mooring.

With the sealing of the tomb, there was total silence. Nothing more remained to be said. It was all over.

As if by some signal, the crowd quietly moved to form two lines at both sides of Mary and me. I grabbed my sister's arm, patted her in comfort, and led us with heads bowed through the double cordon of mourners. Not a word was spoken. In gracious sensitivity, they left us alone to deal with our own very personal sorrow.

Never had I felt so very much alone! What an agonizing ache I felt inside. What an unfathomable loss! Our grief was indescribable. Lazarus was dead and buried. Our dear Lazarus was gone.

I felt completely shattered. Confused. Set adrift. My world suddenly turned upside down. My reality ripped apart. Somehow I couldn't even call to mind who I used to be and what I used to do before this tragedy struck us. I felt hollow inside, everything that used to be inside me had been swept out; no feelings, no emotions, no hunger or thirst remained. Everything was gone . . . except this damnable pain, a nagging pain for which I could find no relief.

If only Jesus were here, I found myself longing! But Jesus wasn't here. He hadn't cared enough to come when Lazarus was so sick. Even if Jesus had come today, perhaps we still wouldn't have had to bury his body. I couldn't believe our dear friend would treat us this way. Not the one who had so freely opened the eyes of the blind, who had enabled the paralyzed man to leap for joy, who had sent the Gadarene's demons cascading headlong off the cliff in a herd of swine. If Jesus had come for *these* people, why not for Lazarus? Why not for Mary? Why not for me? Why not for those he loved?

As we stumbled through the doorway of our home once again, we faced the many symbols of our mourning. All of our furnishings were turned upside down to portray the upending event which had so violently brought chaos to our lives. So, Mary sat down on a makeshift stool. I strangely preferred the hard ground, the "dust."

Each of us dealt with our own grief. Mary spoke few words, as did I. What was there to say? What was there to do? I couldn't even cook in my own house.

I kept mulling over the events of the past two days. Each tragic turn. Each step of mourning. Each dashed hope.

"No, No!" I argued with myself. "Dashed hope" was far too mild a phrase to express what I felt way down deep. I felt quite betrayed—betrayed by Jesus! Betrayed because he didn't come in time, yes. But more than that. I felt betrayed because he had lied to us! Hadn't he told the messenger, "This illness will not end in death." Humph! Just a nice, encouraging sentiment! But the brutal fact was that Lazarus died. We had just buried him. We had just locked a dead Lazarus in the tomb.

"It is too late! It is too late now," I repeated to myself in hushed tones. "You are too late, Jesus. And what's worse, you lied to us! You said that his illness wouldn't end in death. Oh, you probably said it out of very good motives, I can imagine. But nonetheless, you lied to us." Indeed, Lazarus died.

And with such a disturbing thought, night was descending, the blackest night I had ever experienced, night that refused to lift all through the next day.

∼

By today, Lazarus' face may be decomposed enough that his spirit which had been hovering above him (since, we believed, death could no longer recognize him) would depart. Like any good Jew, I knew that by this day there was no more hope. Lazarus was gone, really gone!

At daybreak, I arose without a sound. How I slipped away unnoticed, I'll never know. I didn't mean to worry the mourners by my absence, but I couldn't let that stop me. I had an important mission.

Late last night I'd heard the news. Jesus was finally headed toward Bethany. Fine. *Now,* after all hope is gone, he decided to come back. Through the night I kept bouncing back and forth between anger and joy.

By morning, I was frantically propelling myself down the desert road to meet him. In my resentment I kept muttering, "You are too late, Jesus." What I would say when we met, I had no idea.

Down the path, a lone figure approached. I couldn't quite make out who it was. Jesus? No. Not even now.

"Martha!" the figure greeted as he ran. It was Thomas.

Soon Thomas was overwhelming me with bits and pieces of conversation from Jesus's lips. He repeated Jesus's promise, "This illness will not end in death." He quoted something about "twelve hours of daylight" which conjured up my memory of Jesus's words, "I am the light of the world." Someone said to his disciples something about "being glad for your sakes that I wasn't there, so that you may believe." Something about Lazarus's being "asleep" and about Jesus's "awakening him." My ears perked up. But then I heard the Master correct the misunderstanding of his disciples, saying plainly: "Lazarus is dead, but I am going to him." Strange words. What could they mean now?

All the while Thomas was speaking, he kept glancing around furtively, his eyes darting. He whispered his fear that the Jews would keep trying to stone Jesus. "We had hoped he wouldn't return to Bethany," Thomas admitted. "But when Jesus insisted, I urged the others: 'Let us go too. If he's hell-bent on getting himself killed, we might as well go to our death along with him.'" Amid such despair, I still admired his loyalty. (I guess!)

"That's enough from me, Martha," Thomas interrupted himself. "Come! Jesus is waiting for you. I'm sure he has words of comfort for you." Ach! A nice sentiment!

Well, when I finally faced Jesus, I didn't have to think. Out of the depths of my broken heart, I simply blurted out: "Lord, if you had been here, my brother would not have died!"

The Master looked surprised. Even pained.

As my words drifted back to me, I shuddered. In one sense, I heard a grand affirmation of trust, but in another, a grand affirmation of despair. It was so confused, so intertwined, so jam-packed with violently opposing thoughts and feelings. I was really reproaching him: "Jesus, you could have worked a miracle. But you didn't! And now it's too late!" I shrank back, chagrinned. Why had I ever come? But I had. And my coming to him in itself was a profound statement of faith, even now.

"Even now!" I took a deep breath to measure my words. And in his gracious silence, I continued my hot-and-cold message. "*Even now*, Lord,

I know that God will give you whatever you ask." Then I stopped speaking, exhaled a bit, and smiled, obviously embarrassed.

He took my hand. He looked me straight in the eye. And Jesus voiced his assurance to me: "Your brother will live again!"

Brushing aside the echo of another empty sentiment, I began to realize that in some ways he spoke truth. So I reached for the highest statement of faith I could find, and I responded: "Yes, Lord, I know he will rise again. He will. On the *last day!*"

Again the same puzzled look spread over his face. "Martha, my dear, listen to me. I tell you that I am . . . !" Like Moses standing before the burning bush, I felt as if I was hearing God himself reveal his name. And Jesus continued. "I am the Resurrection—and the Life! If someone believes in me, he shall live, even if he dies. And if he believes in me, he shall never die." Martha, my friend, in the midst of your intolerable pain, can you believe this?"

"Yes, Lord! I can. I can. I believe you are the Messiah, the Son of God, whom we've been expecting."

I looked up with pleading eyes. In my heart I was asking, "Are you saying that it's not too late, Lord? Are you telling me that, no matter what, there's always hope—even now?"

He grinned his approval. "And what about Mary? Where did you leave her? Don't you think she should join us in our hope—'even now?'" He waved me on my way. And I streaked back down the road toward Bethany with feet bringing my sister "good news."

∽

Totally breathless my sister and I returned, leaving the other mourners trailing far behind. Jesus stretched forth his hand to Mary. She fell down at his feet, as she often did when he visited us. Weeping, she cried, "Master, if you had been here, our brother would not have died!"

I struggled to repress a laugh. Two such contrasting personalities. But an identical response! Our pain hadn't been so different after all. Our inner questionings had followed the same trajectory. The exit point from our shattering wound? Just alike.

Seeing Mary cry, along with the mourners, wrenched a heartfelt groan from our friend. Jesus wept!

And when Jesus regained his composure, he asked us the oddest question. Odd, because the answer seemed so obvious to us:

GOD'S GREAT QUESTION TO MARTHA

"WHERE HAVE YOU LAID HIM?"

Hardly had he finished, when I began to describe for him the location of the tomb. Then I stopped short. Surely that wasn't what he was asking. He wouldn't need my information. Not this one who had seen Nathaniel under the fig tree. So our surprising-Jesus must be probing, searching me deeper.

I don't know how to explain it but suddenly time stood still. In a flash of insight a little more truth entered in, tumbling in, thought after thought.

"Where have you laid him?" he asked. A simple question. But his question seemed to have no end. Its implications, profound. Its application, transforming! Questions like these, for example:

Where did hope disappoint you?

Where have you abandoned the heartache, the mess?

How did some part of your life become so useless and painful that you finally had to lock it out of sight?

What broke apart so badly that you had to disassociate yourself from it?

In front of which dead relationship have you rolled a stone—your brother—your sister—your friend?

Why did you conclude it was too late?

Can you really keep your unresolved grief locked up in the burial caves, or do you have to keep trudging back there day after day?

What aspect of your struggle most needs my breath of life, my resurrecting power?

Where, my friend, is the place of 'death—for *you*?

What, my dear lady, do you wish me to do for you?

What do you hope for most?"

"WHERE HAVE YOU LAID HIM? WHERE HAVE YOU LAID HIM? WHERE IS LAZARUS? AND—WHERE ARE YOU?"

Until this moment, I hadn't realized that Lazarus wasn't the only one who had died in Bethany. I had too! So had Mary! We had allowed our brother's death to become our own.

Into the decay of my own tomb, I could feel the fresh breath of life enter. I could feel the healing begin. I could feel the first-fruits of God's shalom. Yes, Lazarus was still dead. Yes, I still desperately missed him. But I, Martha, was now coming alive. Still in pain. Still in confusion. But I, Martha, was finally willing to open up my own tomb, finally willing to start tackling my future.

I glanced at Mary. She too was beaming. I shared the glint in her eye as I read her thoughts. In response to his penetrating question, "Where have you laid him?" we borrowed a phrase that the Teacher used with his disciples. So Mary and I replied as one: "Come and see, Lord!"

Come, Lord, let us face the scene of death together. Come, share our sorrow. Come, help us make sense out of this. Come, show us how to bury our grief. Come, lead us to shalom. Come, make our life worth living once again!

Jesus wept. Some of the Jews whispered to one another, "See how much he loves Lazarus." But others chose to remain skeptical: "If he opened the eyes of the blind, why couldn't Jesus have kept his friend from dying?"

∽

"Roll away the stone!" Jesus commanded with an air of authority that startled us all.

"But Jesus," I piped up, deserting my fleeting statement of faith in the Christ, "it has already been four days! The odor surely will be overwhelming."

Again came his puzzlement. "Martha, didn't you hear me when I assured you that if you believed, even now you would see God's glory? Or will you keep insisting it is too late?"

I had no answer. I couldn't imagine why he wanted the stone rolled away. Did he want to look one last time on the face of his friend? I shook my head. I hated to see him be disappointed, as by now surely Lazarus's face might be rotted away beyond recognition.

Despite my warning, the men rolled away the stone.

When the creaking and rumbling ceased, Jesus slowly lifted his face heavenward, away from the scene of death. And he began to pray. "Father, thank you for always hearing me when I pray. I know you do, but those gathered here do not. So I am praying aloud to enable them to understand that you have really sent me."

Then—with a voice appropriate to the last trump—he shouted out my brother's name. "Lazarus! Come forth from the burial tombs!"

"Come forth?" Was he serious? I held my breath. My eyes strained into the dark cavern. I desperately scanned the scene for a glimmer of movement.

And then in the flick of an eyelash, I thought I saw something move. Or did I? Yes! But what? Who?

Shuffling out of the burial tombs, a figure staggered forward. Inching his way. Struggling to keep his balance, with all of the bandages circling his arms and legs. Knocking into the stone shelves, his head still wrapped.

"Lazarus?" we gasped. Laboriously, the mummy nodded.

Stark silence reflected our incredulity, our awe! And when we began to realize what was happening, we cheered to highest heaven. Some dropped to their knees in gratitude to the Father. Some fell at the feet of the Savior. Some danced and sang. Some just expected it. Oh how I envied them!

Oh, my! I should have trusted his word. Who but Jesus dares unseal a tomb after four days? Who but Jesus rolls away the stone? Who but Jesus calls forth the dead? Who but Jesus breathes life into what is already becoming dust? Who but Jesus has the power to resurrect a corpse—or a deadened soul?

Meanwhile, a living Lazarus stood there before us. Wrapped. Still immobile. Waiting for his "unveiling."

Seeing our stupefied inaction, Jesus became both teasing and practical.

"Well, folks, you were the ones who bound him up. Isn't it time for you to release him? Loose him! Strip away all that holds him back. Let him breathe again. Let him become part of your lives once more. Loose him, and let him go free!"

I rushed to help rip away his wrappings, yanking and tugging at them. But all the while, I kept my eye peeled on the One whose voice could wake the dead.

Now the brother who once lay so cold, so pale, so rigid stood before us. Alive. Strong. Robust. Resurrected! We hugged. Tears flowed. Words failed. Shalom came to Bethany. To Lazarus. To Mary. To me. To us all.

For days I kept on shaking my head. I kept repeating the reminder to myself, "It's *never too late!* There is hope—even now!"

You know the rest. Word of Lazarus's open tomb spread, heightening the frenzy of the religious leaders in Jerusalem. So these leaders plotted to kill Lazarus in order to still the voice of the people who wanted to make Jesus king.

At the dawning of Passover week, Jesus then left Bethany, setting his face toward Jerusalem. Instead of walking the two miles from Bethany to the Holy City, this time he chose to ride. Riding to dramatize his Messianic claim, yes. But riding on a humble donkey, a symbol he was coming in peace, a signal he was coming as a very different kind of humble Messiah than we were expecting.

Multitudes ran to greet him, throwing down palm branches on his path. Their shouts became more and more insistent. "Hosanna! Save us now!"

And then, seemingly less than a week later, just as insistently, they shouted "Crucify him!"

I watched the unthinkable events unfold with a growing premonition of his fate. Although the circumstances differed radically, Jesus seemed to be heading as inexorably toward death, just as Lazarus had, I feared. Again, I kept hoping desperately that someone would intervene before it was too late. But no one stepped forward. Not the disciples. Not the multitudes; they chose Barabbas instead. Not a prominent believer like Joseph of Aramathea. Not one of us. Not I. Not even God.

"My God, my God, why have you forsaken me?" a suffering Jesus implored heaven from the cross.

Although I kept looking for the *"even now,"* nothing forestalled the inevitable. I watched as the soldiers pierced Jesus' side. Blood and water flowed. He was gone. Jesus, this one who had so recently raised Lazarus, now died!

Again, reaction was polarized. A centurion confessed: "Surely this must be the Son of God." But others chose to be more skeptical: "If he saved others, why can't he save himself?"

So, once again, weeping women now anointed Jesus's body for his burial. Mary, bless her, kept clutching the empty container of nard that she had poured over Jesus' feet just days before. "You're doing this in anticipation of my death," he had said. So, obviously Jesus knew then. But we let ourselves hear him. And now it was too late. Too late! Indeed, Jesus, too, lay in his grave.

Once again, the dark night of grief descended.

And then early one morning, the first day of the week, came news of another open tomb. At first his followers didn't find this very good news. We all became frenzied. Where had they taken the body of our Lord? We saw no hope. It was simply too late!

Or was it?

Now, as I huddled with the disciples in an Upper Room, I heard strange words coming from Simon Peter and also two friends from Emmaus. "I have seen him," the three said. Jesus is alive!" And suddenly I knew they were telling the truth. *"Even now! Even now!"* Again, when it indeed seemed too late, the Son of God had burst forth from the tomb. And on the third day!

Who had ever heard of someone being raised from the dead? Who indeed.

"O death, where is your sting? O grave, where is your victory?"

For forty glorious days, we fellowshipped with our risen Lord. Marveling. Listening. Learning. When the moment came for his departure, he led us out of Jerusalem, back toward Bethany. There he blessed us. "Be willing to lay down your lives in witness of me," he charged. I worshipped him, but some still doubted. Then in a cloud, he ascended. From Bethany on earth, to the Celestial City somewhere in "the great by-and-by." From the earthly home he so often visited during his ministry, to his Father's eternal dwelling above. "Even so, come, Lord Jesus!"

Come, Lord! Resurrect my simplistic priorities. I look back and can't believe how I thought I knew exactly how it should all work out. But the same Jesus who raised my brother also refused to come at my command. The same Jesus who raised my brother refused my pleadings to prevent his death. The same Jesus who raised my brother allowed me to suffer the dregs of grief. The same Jesus who raised my brother took the time to "resurrect" *me* first. The same Jesus who raised my brother later allowed him to die. The same Jesus who raised my brother allowed himself to die on a cross for you and me. Easy answers? Hardly! So why not let your Lord decide for you?

Come, Lord, and resurrect my dying physical body. Despite these dramatic incidents, I realize that I have seen only two bodies raised—only Lazarus and Jesus. No one else. And I knew others who died and remained dead; for them, it was indeed too late in one sense. And yet I still believe Jesus' promise: "Whoever believes in me shall live, even though he dies; and whoever believes in me shall never die." As I reflect on Jesus raising Lazarus, I can only conclude that ultimately not even physical death can frustrate the work of God. Meanwhile I watch Lazarus die, and then die once again. Meanwhile I watch my friends die one by one. Meanwhile I watch history march only one direction, toward the grave! Yet the resurrection and ascension of Jesus assure me that death isn't the end of our story either. Because our Savior indeed lives, one day I too shall be raised incorruptible.

Come, Lord, and resurrect my lifeless soul. I've often wondered whether I could ever have grasped Jesus's great and transforming power, except for our experience with Lazarus. Would we have ever believed it if

Lazarus had not come forth bodily from the tomb? Probably not. But now I can begin to grasp a deeper level of truth that Jesus can yet resurrect those hopelessly dead in their sins, granting us life that partakes of the eternal, even in this lifetime. This, I've seen many times—Mary Magdalene—Zaccheus—Matthew—even me!

Come, Lord, and resurrect *me* amid all the 'deaths' of life. I am discovering that so often my inner restoration hinges on my willingness to come to Jesus and admit to him (and to myself) where something has died within me. Where have you laid it?" he asks me once again. And I try to show him. I call: "Come and see, Lord." Then, into the putrid hollows of my existence, he breathes new life once again. He calls me by my name. He removes the stony seal from my living-grave. He calls me forth from all my "burial tombs." He looses me, and lets me go free! Has this happened to you?

Dear Martha of Today: May the one who demonstrated at Lazarus' tomb that he is indeed "The Resurrection and the Life," breathe his transforming power into the furthest recesses of your own tombs of death as well. May he renew you. May he enliven you, imbuing you with fresh hope for others, even for yourself!

XIII.

GOD'S GREAT QUESTION TO SAUL

"SAUL, SAUL, WHY ARE YOU PERSECUTING ME?"

A question of discernment

ACTS 9, 22, 26

WHEN ASKED TO SHARE my story along with the others, I was so pleased. Indeed, I thought my life *should* be detailed here. Yet I must warn you in advance that my tale has a terrible side. You see, my early history is hardly like those of the pious God-worshipers whose lives you have just read. No. Not at all!

In my early adult years, I tried in every way possible to defame Jesus, to unmask him, to discredit him. I hated this Jesus fellow with a passion. Indeed, my intense persecution of Jesus (and all of the super-righteous ones of Jesus's early days) proves this. What would you in the modern world have dubbed me during these years? If you will pardon my "French," I'll admit that, in my fanatical early persecution of Jesus, many Jesus's followers called me names akin to today's "son of a bitch!" And what's worse, at the time, I was so proud of that. So, prepare to meet a vastly different person than those whose stories you have already read. In all honesty, I must share with you from the outset the horrible dregs of my early and mid-life days. Later, you'll discover why.

∼

I, Saul, was born a child of two worlds. My mother and father were devout God-fearing Jews from the tribe of Benjamin. But as Jewish citizens of Tarsus, we lived outside Israel, as did so many Jewish people of the dispersion. Thus by birth, I, Saul of Tarsus, became not only a son of the Jewish Covenant but a citizen of the Roman Empire as well.

Every time I heard my mother call me "Saul," I remembered that my parents named me after the greatest of all the tribe of Benjamin, King Saul, first monarch of Israel. Later when I heard my friends refer to me as "Paul," I couldn't forget that I was also living among the increasing population of Gentiles now living in Tarsus.

As I grew toward manhood, I found Tarsus absolutely fascinating.

Hundreds of years before I was born, the people of Tarsus built by hand a broad stone highway called "The "Cilician Gates," ten miles inland from our nearest seaport. This allowed commerce to flourish much more easily between Tarsus and Europe, then back to us here in the isles of Calatia and Capadosia. Thus Tarsus, capital and key city of Cilicia in Asia Minor became over time a bustling trade center. Tarsus soon became an increasingly vital trade route between east and west, both by land and by sea.

Because our own harbor, located just ten miles inland from the Mediterranean Sea was such a protected site, Tarsus also became a valued port for anyone seeking a wealthy and welcome harbor to unload their opulent goods for purchase. So we in Tarsus were always welcoming fascinating foreigners from afar. These strange new merchants brought us their very best. As you can see, we people of Tarsus were hardly denied any of the best goods, from the finest cities of our world.

But our "safe haven" was not always quite so safe. Because of our convenient location, we in Tarsus suffered unfortunate times as well. We were hardly immune to the voracious aspirations of many a tyrant abroad who sought to destroy Tarsus, or at least to rule over us.

So, we were hardly some little backwater "ville." We in Tarsus were delighted to become a more vital part of our increasingly larger world.

Although replanted here in Tarsus, we fleeing Jews felt fortunate to continue our worship of the awesome God of our Fathers, just as Jewish people in Jerusalem had always sought to do. Of course we were aware that many other competing faiths and philosophies surrounded us here. But no matter. Here, in our own Jewish Temple in Tarsus, my family and I rejoiced once again we could worship the true God of our Fathers to whom we resolutely pledged our allegiance. Here again, we faithfully recited the sacred

Mosaic Law recalling those historic "Ten Commandments" that Jehovah God revealed to Moses so long ago.

From my youth I lived by our age-old traditions, scrupulously obeying all the laws of Holy Scripture as interpreted by our Jewish Priests and the Pharisees. We were scrupulous about God's laws about filial piety. Laws about ritual cleanness. Laws about preparing food. Laws about the Sabbath. All 1521 of them! Burdensome? Oh, yes. But what a light burden it would be if, by obeying these laws, I could be deemed righteous before God.

So, because of my Jewish heritage, I sensed very early that perhaps I was "called," indeed destined, to become a Jewish rabbi. Eventually this "destiny" of mine caused me to make my way back to Jerusalem. There I would sit at the feet of the great Jewish scholar/teacher, Gamaliel, for several years at the School of Hillel. And that's exactly what I did.

∽

These were exciting, but unsettled, days for us "strict Jews, God's faithful ones." At least, as a young zealot, this is how I perceived some of our people's growing frustrations with our once-zealous faith.

You see, with the last of the prophets, we Jews assumed that the God of our Fathers had ceased speaking to us. That's because, for 400 years now, we had received no fresh word from God to us. Yet, we still clung to 'the Jewish Law' that, we all believed, contained everything that we Jewish people needed to do need to obtain God's favor.

But, since we assumed that God was no longer as present and active in our world, serious Jews like me must be all the more committed to following the sure light God had already given us. So I too vowed to be all the more punctilious in fulfilling the "ten Commandments" that God entrusted to Moses. Fulfilling the Mosaic Law became my heartfelt response to the age-old question of needy humanity, "How can a mere man like me ever be counted righteous before God?"

As one who strictly obeyed God's laws, I could be very sure that I could proudly stand before Almighty God on that final "Day of the Lord."

Alas, since our God had been so silent for the last 400 years of Israel's redemptive history, various usurpers of the faith were even now making use of this religious vacuum to serve their own political ends. Many a zealous religio-political movement among us had already flared and fizzled. How sad! And yet, most of these startups were hardly worthy of our great heritage as the strict Jewish faithful with our roots (and our boots) firmly planted in the sacred law of Moses. Anyway, that where I, Saul of Tarsus, stood. And that's where I, Saul of Tarsus, would stand forever.

And we faithful Jewish adherents faced still another challenge. Among the many new religious movements these days, one particular teaching about our Jewish faith began to alarm me. This emerging "faith teaching" struck me as being inconsistent with my own very strict Jewish legalism. If we Jews were to allow this unfortunate teaching to remain unchecked, I greatly feared that this could spell danger for the historic faith of all our Jewish people. Already one self-taught heretic, a young Israelite Jew aptly called "Jesus of Nazareth," was teaching some very strange, new-fangled truths.

As a Pharisee (a 'separated one'), you see, this was my heartfelt response to the age-old question of needy humanity: "How can a man be righteous before God?" By being a strict Pharisee who strictly obeys God's Divine Law, I *knew* that I would stand in good stead before the Almighty on that final 'Day of the Lord.'

Of course, since God (I believed) was no longer as active in the redemptive history of Israel, various usurpers through the years had already tried to take advantage of this religious vacuum to use for their own ends. Many false prophets appeared and disappeared. Many a zealous religio-political movement had already flared and fizzled. How sad! I considered them hardly worthy of our great heritage of Jewish faith rooted in its Sacred Law of Moses. Among these many challenging religious movements, one particularly alarmed me. It grew up in a way that appeared to be inconsistent with my own strict Jewish legalism If we Jews allowed this teaching to remain unchecked, I feared that it could spell danger for the traditional historic faith of our Jewish people. Some of our own people in Israel had already named this challenging new faith taught by Jesus, "The Way." *"The Way!"*

Here in Tarsus we had already learned that many of our Jewish brethren back in Israel were beginning to believe in Jesus, this dangerous upstart. And as this Jesus-fellow continued his tantalizing ministry, some Jewish believers even dared to view this Jesus-chap as perhaps God own anticipated "Messiah" for whom they had been waiting so long. Oh, my! Why, oh why, I asked myself, don't people stop and think once in a while. Don't they notice, for example, that this so-called "Holy One" surrounds himself with sinners? This in itself should clue them in. Why, this supposedly "holy" guy even breaks bread with sinners. Eats with them. Now, what genuinely 'Holy

One' would ever consider doing such obviously unholy things? Surely not I. Surely not Saul of Tarsus!

As I pursued the matter further, I began to see that these "Jesus people" had also begun to accept the odd notion that God is somehow alive and accessible to us human beings today. So, perhaps we might call this new faith a kind of "fellowship, or cult, or healing ministry." How very sweet. And, imagine this, friend. Theologically this group stresses God's enormous "*love*" for us all!

Well, after more than three years of this Jesus-fellow's ministry, Jerusalem's soldiers finally arrest this beloved Jesus and bring him to trial before Caiphas (our Jewish High Priest) and the Sanhedrin. That day, Jesus stands all alone before them. And our High Priest, Caiphas, asks Jesus to "clarify" exactly who he is. Then he presses him one step further by asking him "Are you the Christ, the Son of God?" At this question, a holy hush descends upon our entire hall. How quietly, but boldly, Jesus replies: "It is just as you say," Jesus responds! And then this Jesus-fellow goes on to make matters even worse for himself, by adding:

"I say to you that in the future you will see the Son of Man sitting at the right hand of power above and coming in the clouds of heaven!"

Well, I guess Jesus finally condemns himself that day by inserting the Prophet Daniel's early vision of a heavenly figure who will come one day with all of the power and authority of God himself. I assume that Jesus now supposes himself to be this heavenly figure of authority. How dare this Jesus, just one of us common folk, blaspheme in such a before all, I ask you? What heresy! Everyone there that day heard Jesus's bold affirmation that he is God's own son as apparently was earlier prophesied. And this time, we all hear it from Jesus's very own lips.

Well, with Jesus's own unbelievable declaration that day, my own emerging war against this Jesus-heretic is suddenly propelled forward. And with utmost urgency.

You see, I've come to the conclusion that we faithful simply can't allow this imposter to destroy the historic faith of the Jews. We really can't. And with this ardent declaration, I now vow to dedicate all of my fervor to destroy Jesus the heretic and his innocent-sounding message about "THE Way." Right there and then, I determine to do everything possible, either legal or illegal, that I possibly can in order to crush out completely this damnable new-fangled faith so clearly spawned by this theological upstart. I determine to hunt down all his followers and see that they are bound, chained, and then jailed by our authorities, either here in Israel or in the cities and countries where I may ferret them out. I vow to destroy them all.

Even my nickname, "Saul the Zealot," will begin to terrify them, and then to silence the growing number of followers of "Jesus, the Christ." So I vowed to travel anywhere, indeed everywhere, to decimate the growing following of this imposter to our precious Jewish faith. I'd even travel, I'd even be willing to go back to the land from whence I'd already come—back to Israel itself, if necessary to fulfill my vow.

Years ago, when Jesus and I were both Jewish youngsters, we two received similar traditional religious teachings at our two very different and separate synagogues. So, you might expect that this fellow Jesus and I may likely be very much "on the same page" in our theological thinking. Well, as you've seen for yourself, "Perish the thought!" Over a several-year period, I continue to see that Jesus-fellow and his non-strictly-Mosaic theology emphasis could quite easily become very slippery, very dangerous. That's why I continued to voice, and to spread, my own strong support of our historic and very strict "Mosaic Law" throughout my adopted land of Tarsus. And hopefully very soon this would also be true in Jerusalem itself.

My increased inquiry into Jesus's new faith eventually brought me to the follow tentative conclusions:

First: I discover that, although Jesus and I both believe in One God, Jesus now claims that 'God is a unity/unit, a fellowship of at least the Father *and* his Son. But still just *one* God, mind you Now, figure that out! Can't Jesus count?

And then this self-important Jesus also asserts that he himself is the second person in this sacred new God-ness. Another way of saying this perhaps is that Jesus is the second member of the one God! And Jesus claims that all of this was written down long ago in the Sacred Writings Well, so says the Jesus-fellow. I myself have read the same Scriptures and I haven't happened to read all this myself, even though Jesus and I both pledge allegiance to the same Sacred Writings. Indeed, I see all of our historic sacred writings as full backing for my total allegiance to worship Almighty God alone.

As for my own theology, what I want is so simple. I personally want only to look lovingly upon the face of "God, my Father," to look upon the face of my God (singular God) who reigns above us all. Yet, when Jesus talks about all of this with his own followers, he shockingly stretches his own importance way too far, even to the point of declaring this quite audaciously and plainly:

"He who has seen *me* has seen the Father!"

(John 12:45)

Balderdash! That's damnable heresy. Can anyone believe this?

Second: Early in our lives Jesus in Israel and I in Tarsus both chose to abide by the Ten Commandments and the basic rabbinic laws. So, I naively supposed that we held all this in common. But, oh no! Many of Jesus' followers were there on days when Jesus himself issued his very own God-like commandments, or simply to correct our own offensive way of restating the various commandments. And again I notice that so many times Jesus simply restates the people's common view of things, then adds his own divergent command beginning with the now-familiar: *"But I say to you . . . !"* What amazing arrogance that takes. And, of course, what heresy he utters.

Third: All of my life, I've sought to obey every single law, every single precept, every single part of the Jewish Law. I truly believe that, by my total obedience to all God's sacred law as revealed by Moses, I am now thoroughly qualified for God's salvation. (I affirm once again that I really do keep all of God's laws to perfection.) And because I remain so strict in my obedience (and by doing many extra noble deeds), I feel very confident that God will receive me at last. Perhaps he may even receive me with lavish appreciation and approval.

Yet this Jesus-fellow apparently doesn't see the saving value of my strict obedience to the Mosaic law. This Jesus seems to think that my strictness in obedience doesn't profit me at all. It profits me nothing? Nothing at all? I become irate when he doesn't think that my careful obedience is good enough. Poor misguided Jesus says that all of us are apparently still dead in our sins. Is that possible? No! And then this Jesus fellow goes on to tell us (and get this!), that all of us need a "Savior" who will himself pay the ultimate sacrifice by his own death, on behalf of each one of us. Supposedly, by shedding his own blood in death, Jesus will, thereby, cancel out the many sins of believing followers. I suppose that Jesus may be stuck on all those Old Testament passages (hundreds of them) about "our life as human-beings as being located in the blood." After all, that's why all of us ancient Jews offered abundant "blood sacrifices for our sins."

And Jesus's heresy hardly ends there.

When the John the Baptist affirms to all that Jesus is indeed "the Lamb of God," who takes away the sins of the whole world, Jesus simply accepts John's statement as truth. Later, Jesus adds about his anticipated sacrificial death that, by offering up his blood sacrifice for us all, he thereby opens up access to heaven for every one of us who truly confesses his/her personal sins and who trusts this Savior's (Jesus's) redeeming work on his/her behalf. Now I ask: what intelligent person is going to believe this wild promise from this mere man? Not me. Not Saul of Tarsus!

From then on, Jesus and I (Saul) both try even harder order to "sell" to the masses our two divergent points of view. I keep emphasizing my "strict Mosaic obedience and self-sacrifice" for all of my sins (of which I may be aware.) Meanwhile, Jesus keeps emphasizing how very gracious and loving this God is to all those who *believe* in him and *trust* in him and in his Son's death for us on the cross. Unfortunately, Jesus and I never get a chance to debate these divergent views in public. So, you will have to decide for yourself who's right on this important doctrine.

All of this shows you why I am so doggedly determined to rub off all of the rough edges from Jesus's destructive ideas and teachings before they can possibly spoil historic Judaism, both here in Tarsus and in Jerusalem. And since I'm always sent off on assignments in new places, I, Saul, can make very sure that these newfangled ideas that Jesus teaches on how we can obtain God's grace-filled salvation do not survive around there, or here, or elsewhere for very much longer. That's my daily commitment.

Already our more rigorous religious leaders are banding together to safeguard our historic Jewish faith. Our religious authorities, even now, are said to be pulling many strings with the Roman authorities in Jerusalem to let the proposed crucifixion of troublesome "Jesus of Nazareth" to go forward. They are doing precisely what leaders must do to stop this absurd kind of teaching, before this newfangled kind of pseudo-faith gets further out of hand.

But then, Jesus's disciples even now seem to be trying to outwit these naïve elders and high priests. You see, Jesus's followers very recently made up some fantastic story about the dead body of Jesus, the publicly crucified one, now having somehow disappeared from his own grave. They even say (and get this!) that this dead man now comes back to life after having already appeared "alive in the flesh" several times to a few disciples and then others after he rises from the grave! Now, who is going to believe this? Surely not I. Not Saul of Tarsus!

At the same time, I do find it strange indeed that Jesus's formerly wavering disciples suddenly became very different indeed. They're now confident. Bold. Unshaken. Powerful. Surprisingly even speaking in hitherto unknown tongues. Even working "miracles." Persuading both Jews and Gentiles alike. And this causes me to wonder once more about what could possibly have transpired to cause such a vast turn-around in his slow-to-believe disciples.

Hardly a day now passes that I don't hear new reports of this spreading movement of "The Way," especially among those living outside of Jerusalem who can't be set straight as quickly as by our own religious authorities here.

Oh, my! I must stop briefly here to catch my balance. So much change! Just look first at the silence of God for 400 years since the apparent conclusion of the Holy Writings. Then, look forward and see the dawning of this radical new "Way" being proclaimed by Jesus of Nazareth, a fellow who blatantly calls himself 'the Son of God.' And now our third radical change is the growing dispersion of our own Jewish people living here to go to nations far beyond Israel. Obviously our people are getting too far removed from our center of religious orthodoxy in Jerusalem for dispersed professional religious leaders like me to influence them properly, quickly helping them to contain this dangerous "Jesus" heresy.

Indeed, the dispersion of our Jewish people is now swelling to rather large dimensions. Some estimates place four and a half million Jews scattered throughout the Roman Empire, in the cities of Europe, Asia and North Africa. Now in fact, more live outside Israel than live within her borders. In Egypt alone reside some one million Jews. In two of Alexandria's five city districts, Israelites form the majority of its inhabitants. As far away as Rome, Hebrew communities spring up, virtually without any contact with the Holy Temple in Jerusalem that is fully intended to be the center of their Jewish faith. What a huge change. Can you believe that?

That's why Israel's religious leaders are now scrambling to recapture their influence and control over these vast numbers of dispersed Jews. Thus, our Jewish Elders are urging all foreign Jews, such as my family, to make family pilgrimages back to Jerusalem at least once a year so they can celebrate the feast days among their own people (and "incidentally" to participate financially in our Temple program.)

And, in order to reach those who can't come back here to our homeland, our Temple officials are quickly dispatching Pharisees like me to go wherever these dispersed people can be found. In cities far and wide, we apostles of Judaism will monitor the faith of Israel's sons, and even try to proselytize non-Jews toward accepting our more historic Jewish faith. All this is a very ambitious and creative program. Exactly what we most need.

Of course, as a Jew from birth and a citizen of a Gentile city since birth, I knew I'd really be ideal for just such a mission. Yes, I, Saul, would gladly move heaven and earth to restore religious order, to help root out these misguided people of "The Way." I would gladly pour out my own life if necessary to recapture the historic faith of my fathers, to champion fully the Law of Moses as fundamental to our core faith. And thereby, not too incidentally, I will prove to everyone that I am as much a zealous son of Israel as anyone who lives within her borders.

∾

Meanwhile, Peter and his band of Jesus-followers continue to meet together each day in the colonnade of the Temple. There, they persuade throngs of men and women to embrace this dangerous Jesus-fellow as the saving Messiah. So successful are they that even folk from the towns circling Jerusalem now daily bring in their sick and demon-possessed to these disciples, hoping they will lay healing hands on them. And at our Temple these days, some visitors even hope and pray that that the shadow of Peter may fall on the infirmed as he passes by, thereby healing them.

At last, to deter the swelling increase of these Jesus people of "The Way," our Jewish High Priest has no choice. He demands that the Apostle Peter and his entire group cease teaching in Jesus's name. And when our staunch religious leaders then drag these same lawless disciples of Jesus before the Sanhedrin (Israel's high court of Elders), defiant Peter haughtily claims his rights by insisting simply, "We must obey God rather than man."

And Peter hardly stops there. Now he is boldly proclaiming to all that the God of our Fathers has in fact already "raised Jesus from the dead and has exalted him to be reigning Prince and Savior at his right hand."

Hearing Peter's bold declaration causes our Sanhedrin II group to erupt in fury. So they quickly seek to seize many of Jesus's followers and to put them to death. But at this very critical moment, my venerable old theology teacher, Gamaliel, quickly rises to his feet. With his years of wisdom, he urges his fellow members: "Send any Jesus's followers outside so we can discuss this matter fully." And because the Sanhedrin greatly values Gamaliel's sage advice, they quickly agree.

Gamaliel then offers quite a speech, a surprising speech, to these smoldering religious leaders. After reciting our present religious situation in non-controversial terms, this dear venerable man concludes:

"Therefore, in this present case, I advise you: Leave these men alone.

Let them go! For if their purpose or activity is of human origin, it will fail. But if it is from God, you will not be able to stop these men; you will only find yourselves fighting against God."

By the time Gamaliel finishes, I can feel my blood boil. While my mentor's speech calms down the council, it totally alienates me. Why on earth is Gamaliel arguing for reason and caution? How can he even raise the possibility that Almighty God "may have already impacted for good" the lives of these unlearned heretics? Why can't he grasp that, at this time of national tension, his gentle wait-and-see attitude betrays our righteous cause? How dare my venerable old teacher barter away the full truth for what seems to me to be mere expediency? As you may have guessed, I am once again growing rather annoyed. And I am stating this very mildly indeed.

Immediately I storm out of the proceedings. I probably look as if I have fire and smoke figuratively pouring out of my ears and nostrils. Once again, I call down God's curses upon such unrighteousness. And I make a fresh vow before heaven that, even if no one else is willing to protect the honor of God, I will. And nothing will stand in my way. Not ever. No, never!

And so, when Sanhedrin II seizes a heretic named Stephen and drags him before the council, I listen so very intently. Fortunately some officials had the foresight to bribe the court witnesses, coaching them how to testify against Stephen.

These witnesses falsely quote Jesus as saying: "I, Jesus, will destroy this Temple and overturn all at the customs passed down to us from Moses." Fortunately the conveniently purchased testimony of these two false witnesses should seal Stephen's fate. I agree that Stephen should probably be silenced. So what, I ask myself, if the truth isn't quite as they choose to report it?

Stephen continues his long side argument to prove that this Abrahamic Covenant between God and man actually preceded the Law of Moses. But then he presses his argument too far. He concludes his comments by attacking our religious leaders for killing Jesus, "God's Righteous One," just as they had killed all the prophets before him.

Understandably, a wee bit of chaos ensues. And with the self-preservation instincts of deeply wounded animals, the entire Sanhedrin II leaps up, abandoning their seats in an attempt to lash out at already bleeding Stephen.

Yet, even while they all continue to growl and glare at him, Stephen stands there quietly, seemingly unmoved by all the hubbub. With each new breath, the dear soul appears to draw fresh courage and strength from above. And just then, the most eerie thing happens. I wish you could have seen it for yourself. But I can tell you that young Stephen's face does really begin to glow until it looks to be "the very face of an angel." And as this accused one begins to lift his countenance toward heaven, he suddenly cries out to all: "Look! I see heaven open. And the Son of Man is standing at the right hand of God!"

An "open heaven?" An ascended Jesus in the very seat of heavenly power? To any devoutly strict Jew like me, that is sure blasphemy, of course.

But, then, I suppose that's precisely what I should have guessed might come from such a super-holy Stephen.

Of course, Jesus had already prophesied to Caiphas that he, the High Priest himself, "will see the Son of Man standing at the right hand of God in glory." And already Peter had testified at Sanhedrin I that in fact Jesus is now risen above to be "exalted Prince and Savior." Once again, here is faithful Stephen in Sanhedrin II still trying desperately to insist we keep alive this unbelievable Jesus-myth.

As you might imagine, most of our Elders were completely startled, each one frantically rushing to cover his ears in an attempt to block out Stephen's obvious heretical statements. These Elders rush forward "as one body, with one full voice" toward a totally serene Stephen, seemingly at full peace. The crowd together drags him outside, all the way past Jerusalem's city wall. And there, just before the final coup, each Elder first throws down his fine garment. And where does he throw his garment? At my feet. At the feel of Saul of Tarsus. At the feet of the most prominent zealous hater of Jesus and "THE Way." So, why do they worry enough to first throw down their garments, I ask myself? Oh, I see. Because their fine garments, their fine priestly robes are deemed so holy, they must never become stained with blood (as they very well could be with the 'sinner's blood' now streaming from a bleeding Stephen.)

These prominent Jewish Elders, fully enraged, now hurl giant stones in a swift volley at the target, each Elder now very much hoping to help stone Stephen to the point of death.

GOD'S GREAT QUESTION TO SAUL

Although bleeding and near death, this "Saintly Stephen" keeps up his godly charade all the way to the end. Even while this young blasphemer is breathing his last, he drops to his knee and begins to pray something quite angelic, perhaps patterning his words after Jesus's final words on the cross:

"Lord, Jesus, receive my spirit. Forgive my tormentors. And lay not their sinful acts toward me back against them."

And with this unearthly utterance, heretical Stephen "falls asleep." And all the while I stand there right alongside his tormentors. And I, Saul, am quietly consenting to his death. Without much pause, however, I realize to my great satisfaction that now we won't have to worry about Stephen's powerful testimony in any possible future court proceedings.

As I reflect more on all of this, I'm becoming increasingly aware that our strict Jewish High Priest here in Jerusalem, may well be pleased with my special part in these proceedings as I faithfully safeguarded all of the priestly robes as the frenetic faithful moved to rid us of our nation's troublemaker. And strangely, all of this unexpected turn of events now give me my longed for opportunity to press our High Priest right away for letters introducing me to all of our Jewish synagogues scattered rather widely in foreign lands. With the High Priest's much-needed official blessing, now at long last I'll be able to root out hundreds of scattered followers of "The Jesus Way," bringing them back bound in chains to Jerusalem's prisons to suffer for their gross idolatry.

My life now seems to be proceeding very well, exactly as I have hoped.

Stephen's death whets my appetite and that of other Jewish loyalists. We can now envision how it may now be possible to destroy even more of our God's enemies. We strict Jews fully agree to expand our efforts, to ferret out and destroy all remaining zealots of this self-proclaimed "Jesus the Christ." After all, the very purity of our own faith is at issue. No, "God's truth," that's at issue!

Having now done all I possibly can to restore traditional religious order here in Jerusalem, I look passionately ahead to pursuing my exciting and crucially important, brand new assignment abroad as an official emissary of Israel's High Priest. In my pouch I carry his own official letters of introduction to each of these areas, including its synagogues in Damascus. There my orders are once again to seize any and all followers of Jesus, to make them my prisoners, to bind them with chains, and to deliver them to our High Priest for judgment for all their heresies, to suffer endlessly in Israel's secure prisons.

Once I leave here, my journey, largely on foot, will extend from Jerusalem to Damascus, Syria, a difficult journey stretching over several days across the hot and vast desert sands. Each daybreak, of course, I will rise to thank God for this great privilege of serving him on such a vital mission to safeguard Israel's historic Jewish faith Never do I recall experiencing such absolute purity of purpose. Nor such unbridled joy in my work.

If it takes the rest of my life, I vow, I will surely eradicate the memory of this "Jesus of Nazareth" from the face of the earth. What an arrogant deceiver he was, I can't help recalling. I can't even imagine someone calling himself a deeply holy man and then so blatantly go and eat with sinners. This man gave us God's authoritative commandments, but then, all on his own authority, boldly added: "But I say unto you . . ." A man who pictured our jealous Jehovah God suddenly as some soft and forgiving father who thinks nothing of shamelessly embracing his own very wayward son. Who so often whizzes past our historic Mosaic standards. Who condemns the gloriously righteous among us as "whited sepulchers." How ridiculous! What a simple fellow this Jesus was. I can't help but laugh in derision at the enormously naïve faith he tried to force on us.

With all of this recent wild idiocy settled, I, Saul the Zealot, can at long last begin to make my way toward Damascus. There I can use my sealed orders to arrest, to chain, to bring back to our prisons, these horribly misguided people so glued to that Jesus fellow and "THE Way."

∽

Whew! How miserably hot it's getting here in the desert. Can I possibly continue, I wonder of my miserable self? But then I, Saul, God's faithful zealot, pull myself up just a bit higher. I try to persuade myself, saying, "Endure just a few more hours of the angry sun before it retreats at long last in the twilight." And while this good advice seems like an enormously encouraging thought, right now the painful reality is that this blazingly hot day has, as yet, not even reached noon. Our promised soothing sunset is as yet very many hours away. Ah, well. I guess I must force myself to continue braving the way ahead.

I comfort myself with a hopeful thought: "After this very long night I will soon reach the end of this hot journey, and the beginning of my new holy mission. My ever burning goal of arresting more and more faithless

GOD'S GREAT QUESTION TO SAUL

ones, making them my prisoners, then bringing them in chains back to Jerusalem is now fully in sight."

∼

But a very, very strange thing happens on my way to Damascus.

Still on this blazingly hot Damascus Road, just short of my objective here in Syria, when I least expect it, I suddenly find myself under siege. By "under siege" I mean that all kinds of intense beams of light from somewhere are suddenly assaulting me from every side. These flashing beams of ranging colors appear to be refracted through some unseen giant crystal prism. Huge streams of light flash radiant rays of violet, purple, indigo blue and green, with yellow, orange and red. Reaching all around me now, fully embracing me, together they form the most unapproachable light I could even possibly imagine.

I freeze in unexpected terror. My knees buckle weakly. I instinctively slump to the ground, urgently grabbing at my cloak to shield my eyes against the insistently searing brightness all around me.

When I can breathe more freely, I begin to grope all around me, just hoping to feel anything familiar. A bit later, I try valiantly to cry out to for my travel servants, imploring them to help me. But, alas! My paralyzed throat cannot find its own voice. Half-crazed, I now squeeze my eyelids tight. I don't dare look outward. I can't possibly imagine what kind of fearful reality could possibly be out there, that I could encounter so innocently or, worse, that might suddenly pounce upon my face from "out there."

Now in this setting, far away from my rabbinic studies back home, the prophetic words of Isaiah suddenly blaze into my troubled consciousness.

"The people who walked in darkness have seen a great light. Those who live under the shadow of death, upon them has the light shined."

Oh, fine! Just what I don't need, these unsolicited comments from some ancient and irrelevant Scripture. Right now, I desperately want to cry out.

"Oh, calm down, old Saul," I seek to quiet myself, "you're sounding a bit hysterical right now." So I try to relax a bit more. Yes, for sure I surely have seen a great, great light. (Actually, like nothing I even before imagined, let alone encountered.) But, of course, this old Isaiah passage hardly applies to me, does it? Does it? No! Surely I am not "walking in darkness" or living "under the shadow of death." So, all of this must be but the hysterical working of my subconscious mind living under far too much heat plus an overload of stress.

Then one more quotation assails me. Again a word from Isaiah 60: "Arise, shine! For your light has come. And the glory of the Lord is risen upon you."

Oh, my goodness! But can God's own 'Holy Light' possibly be shining down especially on me? Can that perhaps be true? On *me*? Is it just remotely possible that the Lord of the Ages is perhaps intending to bless me on my way to Damascus? Has he perhaps come here to bless and even to please me?

Excitedly now I manage to leap to my feet. I virtually rip away the protective cloak from my eyes. And I bare my countenance upward toward heaven in order to receive the full experience of this dazzling light that God surely brings to me today to bless his lifelong servant in ferreting out those dreadful Jesus followers.

Soon I fully open my eyes. And what an unbelievably rude shock awaits me.

Just as my now prayerful eyes begin to open toward the dazzling light . . . instead, absolute blackness stretches endlessly before me. What, oh what, has happened?, I ask myself fearfully in my confusion. Where, oh where, is God's glory that I had so naively expected? So, where is he hiding the dazzling light of his presence? Has the God of the Ages suddenly departed from me? Even before he blesses me? Oh, no! No, no, no!

Picture me standing there. Suddenly with no light at all. With no blessing at all. Not even with much evidence of God anywhere near me.

Just then I hear a voice, a voice unlike any human voice I've ever heard. Pure. Thundering. Inviting. Gracious. Sweet. Surely this could only be the voice of God himself! And his voice is now calling me by my birth name given to me way back in Tarsus so long ago:

"SAUL, SAUL, WHY DO YOU PERSECUTE ME?"

I am stopped dead in my tracks. What? Me? Persecuting God? I'm stunned. I'm caught flat footed in surprise. Oh, not so much by the voice itself. Rather, by this very strange question God is now asking of me.

How can God possibly think that I am persecuting him? All the time I'm feverishly searching out and destroying God's enemies. Even now. Surely the God of Moses remembers that I was the very first one to give my consent to the death of God's late blasphemer, Stephen.

GOD'S GREAT QUESTION TO SAUL

Here on the Damascus Road, I discover that I haven't stopped to take a good long look at myself for quite a while now. I don't even want to look. But over time, I do. And what "marvelous" sights do I see in myself right now? I don't even want to look. But in time, I do. And what do I see as my present reality?

"Behold" ("take a good look at") this once mighty Saul of Tarsus. Now running madly here to chain up all those ungodly believers in Damascus. Right now, both confused and stunned. I'm bewildered both by God—and by my present enemies. I'm fully blinded by the light I just encountered. Suddenly cowering in despair. My own reality suddenly upended. My once sacred assumptions shattered. My lifelong sense of reality shattered and dwindling toward bankruptcy.

As I struggle further with God's revealing questions to me on the Damascus Road, I can feel a sickening emptiness beginning to grow inside of me, a huge chasm that just aches to be filed. Finally from the uttermost of my being, I turn fully toward the one whose voice is confronting me. And with the desperate pleadings of a long lost child, I cry out feebly to him, "Who are you, Lord?"

Then a voice speaks to me so softly. "Who am I, you ask? Oh, Saul, dear Saul, I am Jesus! Jesus whom you are persecuting."

The conversation that began with God's blinding light and thundering question on that road to Damascus then continued over several years, revealing more and more truth to me. I listened carefully as Jesus, the anointed one sitting at God's right hand, continued his answer to my earlier question of him.

"Who am I?" you ask. "I am Jesus whom you are persecuting! For a brief time, I came to earth at the will of God. My Father sent me here to save sinful mankind from all of its deadly ways. An angel named Gabriel announced my birth over a common stable in Bethlehem with this life-changing message for our lost world: 'For unto you [all of you] is born this day in the city of David, a Savior named 'Jesus Christ, our Lord.' Saul, is it remotely possible that, as yet, you haven't received this important heavenly announcement?"

And my delayed response: "How can this possibly be true?"

You can see how badly stuck I, Saul of Tarsus, have been for so very long. Despite God's gracious unveiling of his own Son to me just seconds ago, I instinctively return to my age-old question: How can our one God ever share his glory with another?" What a predictable response from Saul of Tarsus!

In the following silence, I now begin to recall the quietly simple words God uttered when he created this earth: "Let us make man in *our* image, after *our* likeness." And these similar words recorded by the Psalmist seem to add their own testimony:

> "The LORD says to my LORD:
> Sit at my right hand
> until I make your enemies
> a footstool for your feet."
>
> (Psalm 110:1)

Oh, my goodness! So, then, all of this "Father, Son, Holy Spirit" teaching is really true? My God is indeed *one* God—all three of them? So from the very beginning, this Jesus has been with God all along? And the Holy Spirit too? And even more surprising: This God (with three separate entities) has unveiled these crucial facts to our faith in our already-given Sacred Writings? And still, I (with so many others) have managed to miss all of this prophecy? So then, I, Saul of Tarsus, have in fact been "spiritually blind" for a very long time even before I became physically blind here on this Damascus Road!

Strangely, this new-found light revealed from above now begins to unlock Jesus's earlier words to the Jewish High Priest, and of Peter's testimony before Sanhedrin I, and finally of Stephen's dying vision when his last words revealed: "I see heaven open, and the Son of Man standing at the right hand of God." What a joy it is for me to understand all of this at long last.

Now I sense that I'm just on the verge of discovering many more huge and exciting new truths.

So, indeed I now know that Jesus really is who he claimed to be all along. He did indeed rise from the dead and ascend to rule in power with his Father, reigning at God's right hand, along with the Holy Spirit as well. So the gates of heaven are now flung open wide to accept all of us who believe in the Savior.

Even I, Saul of Tarsus, have finally seen and heard the Lord of glory for myself, right here on the Damascus Road.

GOD'S GREAT QUESTION TO SAUL

And strangest of all I, Saul of Tarsus, now called an Apostle named "Paul" here in Israel, can join with my old adversary, the Apostle Peter in affirming:

"Jesus you are indeed the Christ, the Son of the living God!"

"I am Jesus whom you are persecuting." Before me, I still see pictured the tragic scene of Jesus hanging limp on the cross, nailed there by people just like me. Sincere, righteous, "good" people. People who likewise long to worship God, but as yet don't quite know him to whom we belong. For so long, I, like them, had it figured out all wrong. And so many of us living today are people charging full speed ahead, yet still heading a full 180 degrees away from the truth and reality. We are people who may decide, for whatever reasons, simply to kill what we ultimately can't quite understand fully for ourselves.

Oooh! Then comes the "ouchiest" part of all. If I, Saul of Tarsus, am just like them, then haven't I in effect also participated in Jesus's death? You see, if I had been there at the cross at that time, wouldn't I have consented to his death, just as I later consented to dear Stephen's death? So then, isn't it my own sins, my hatred, my very misguided zeal that also hammered those wretched nails into Jesus's hands and feet, just as I orchestrated deaths for so many of his followers? Oh, I can plead ignorance. Even innocence. But I surely know that I am as guilty of Jesus's crucifixion as if I'd been there personally and did nothing to stop it. Now I, Saul, must confess to my great shame, "I really am the 'chief of sinners!'"

What will God do with me now? I deserve his wrath. But I sincerely hope for his great mercy.

∼

Then comes God's gracious surprise!

Oh, can you believe this? This same Jesus whom I have persecuted for so, so long, now calls out to me once again. He calls out to me on this hot and dusty Damascus Road with an amazing brand-new plan for my life—in his own service. Listen to my great God for yourself, and marvel at his amazing grace:

> "And now the LORD says—he who formed me in the womb to
>   be his servant . . .
> It is too small a thing for you to be my servant
>   to restore the tribes of Jacob

> and to bring back those of Israel I have kept.
> *I will also make you a light for the Gentiles,*
> *that you may bring my salvation to the ends*
> *of the earth."*
>
> (Isaiah 49:5, 6; emphasis added)

With joy renewed, I leap to my feet. I open my eyes. Although it is now mid-day I still can see nothing, except for the light now focused on heaven. Now blind, I call out to my travel companions to help me on toward Damascus. No longer will I be searching out more prisoners for the Lord. Instead, I am now his very grateful prisoner. No longer a prisoner of darkness, although my physical blindness remains painfully real. Rather I am now becoming a prisoner of God's enormous love shown toward me.

To this wonderfully grace-filled Triune God, this unique "Three-in-One" I gladly pledge everything I have, all of my energy, indeed all of my life and being. I now fully belong to Him.

I, Saul of Tarsus, once avowed enemy of THE Way, has finally seen the Light!

~

With friends leading me by the hand, I now joyfully take my first faltering steps along the road. I gradually learn to walk more by faith, rather than by sight alone. How strange, I reflect: It was precisely when God's light overwhelmed me on the Damascus Road that my God's light first showed me just how very blind I had been all along.

With my eyes made fully alive by faith, fresh new light streams into my soul, illuminating the pages of Scripture. Now I see truth that I never could have seen while in my darkness. God's light now clarifies all of my earlier misunderstandings.

Words suddenly come to mind from the book of Isaiah that seem to describe a blind man very much like me:

> "We look for light, but all is darkness;
> for brightness, but we walk in deep shadows.
>
> Like the blind, we grope along the wall,
> feeling our way like men without eyes.
>
> At midday, we stumble as if it were twilight;

GOD'S GREAT QUESTION TO SAUL

Among the strong, we are like the dead.

(Isaiah 59:9, 10)

That's exactly how I behave in my own blindness. But now I also can affirm with Micah: "Though I sit in darkness, the Lord will be my light" (Micah 7:9).

For three days in Damascus I stay at the house of a friend. I cannot eat. I cannot drink. I cannot sleep. For three days I could do nothing but pray to God and to ponder all that is happening to me.

What I know most surely is that I, Saul, am radically changed. My whole perception is being radically transformed by the God who continues to encounter me with such loving insensitivity that I can no longer avoid his goads. This ever-loving God has completely turned me "round right."

After three days of fasting, prayer and meditation, I hear a knock at my door.

There I meet a very dear man named Ananias.

"Brother Saul," Ananias assures me, "the Lord Jesus who appeared to you on the Damascus Road has sent me to you—to restore your sight—and to bestow on you his Holy Spirit." Ananias then places his hands on my blind eyes. Something like scales fall off. Once again I can see. And best of all, I can see many more spiritual truths than I could ever see before.

So, my physical sight is restored. But my even greater joy emerges from the sight and insight granted me from above, God's gracious gift of perception. It was as if for many long years I had been looking at a picture consisting of two images, one white one and one black. But until the light shined from above on the Damascus Road, all I had been able to see was the black image in the picture. Now, suddenly, this gorgeous white image burst forth from its formerly black prison. And from the moment I first glimpsed it, I knew most surely that this glorious white side of the picture is the one its Great Artist had hoped all along that I would perceive. (Only those who have experienced this can imagine what I'm saying.)

By his mercy, he led me from darkness into his marvelous light.

∽

With my sudden about-face on the Damascus Road—my "conversion experience"—I feel a need to withdraw from people and to retreat into the desert for a little while. There I can reflect on all I have seen and heard, can explore its meaning for the rest of my life, and then can interpret its significance for as many others as I can possibly reach.

There, I gradually begin to bring into sharper focus the startling beams of God's light I had just seen on the Damascus Road. In stumbling words, I begin to articulate what I can now see so much more clearly.

First ray of light: I finally grasp that it is God who seeks man, not man who seeks God. My God is indeed the "Seeking Father" of Jesus's parable who ever scans the horizon for the homeward turn of his erring child, then rushes to embrace him afar off and to restore him to God's fellowship, much as the Father, Son Jesus, and the Holy Spirit have already done for many of us.

Second ray of light: I discover that the old and strict Mosaic Law that I followed so zealously since youth had actually failed to earn me the favor I sought from God. Although I still follow the Law as unerringly as I can, and although I do everything I know how to please God, he could only see me as his persecutor on that day we first met each other on the Damascus Road. Without God's gracious intervention on this road far away from my home, I now know that I never could have perceived him on my own.

Nor am I alone in my confusion. If our own teachers of the Law, the finest and most righteous people of my day (according to the Law) have now condemned God's Anointed One to death on a cross, then they have been fully as blind as I.

And consider this. Jesus's own disciples have not followed my strict Mosaic Law nearly as zealously as we Pharisees understand it. Yet, against our own scribal tradition, haven't they performed healings on the Sabbath? And it is they, not I, who perceive that Jesus truly is the "Messiah" sent here from God. They are the ones with whom the Christ is clearly standing in solidarity.

Now I can see that the "Law" (as I had once understood it) had never been intended to make us righteous. That's clear. The Mosaic Law's twofold role was simply to guide us daily, and then to serve as a catalyst to demonstrate to us our great need for Jesus Christ, our rescuing savior. Only when I turned from darkness and responded in faith to God's love in Christ did he declare me righteous before him. Now at long last, I understand. True righteousness is a pure gift to us from our life-giving God.

Third ray of light: So, if God (Father + Son + Holy Spirit) accepts us by our faith, (apart from the meticulous "righteousness" of the Law) then an even more glorious truth comes bursting forth. Those Gentiles, whom

I once thought to be so far off from God, can now, by faith in Jesus Christ, become acceptable to the holy God of Israel. So, this God of Israel can be, indeed he must be, the God of the whole wide world.

Further, if a person is justified freely by faith in Christ, in contrast with the works of the Law, this means that even I, a former zealot against the Christian faith, can now freely take this 'Good News' to anyone, anywhere. To both Jews and Greeks. To slave and to free. To the Holy Temple in Jerusalem, and to the marketplace in my native Tarsus. To everyone I meet. Everywhere. God's great salvation is now readily available, by faith, to all. *All!*

Fourth ray of light: I stumble upon the amazing truth that God is no longer as silent and aloof as I had once thought. Once again our God acted decisively and redemptively in human history in the person of Jesus Christ, God's own Son.

Like the disciples, some others also recognized the coming of the Christ as the in-breaking of God himself into our world. But for the rest of us, for all the light we thought we had, we in fact continued to walk in darkness with our eyes blinded by the "god of this age."

Meanwhile, this glorious Messiah whom we were seeking had already slipped into our world incognito. Born in a manger. Friend of sinners. Crucified on a cruel cross. No mighty political figure who rules from a throne, but rather a man who pours out his own life for sinners, and "by whose stripes we are healed."

All during his life, we didn't know who he really was. We thought he was of no importance. But the truth still remains that, whether we understood him or not, we didn't know who he really was. We "esteemed him not." Yet, "God was in Christ reconciling the world to himself."

We learn that, one day in the future, all things will indeed be put under our Savior's feet. But until this "day of perfection," even though the victory of salvation from sin has already been accomplished by Christ Jesus, the earth itself still groans in travail, convulsing as if still giving birth to a renewed world and a fully renewed people of God.

Meanwhile, in these latter days inaugurated by Jesus's birth, death and resurrection, we Christ-ones remain on earth as citizens of two warring kingdoms: the kingdom of God, and the kingdom of this world. So, we still wrestle with the ambiguities of living in the "already" as well as in the "not yet," living with evidences of power as well as with powerlessness, and experiencing some of the first-fruits of Jesus's resurrection while at the same time despairing of our fickle earthly wills and decaying bodies. And yet, through vibrant faith in Jesus Christ, we also live in full expectation of God's presence with us now, throughout our lives, and then forever more. Jesus himself tells us, " I will be with you to the end of the world and to the end of the age." What a lasting comfort and joy!

～

Dear Saul of Today, as I've described to you my own very human struggle to come to grips with God's great question to me on the Damascus Road, I hope I have also stirred up your own heart and helped to deepen your own faith. If so, this will please me greatly.

As you know, I'm also an evangelist sent from God. And now, as I'm called "Paul the Apostle," I'm asking you to get to know me better. You've followed my dramatic change from "Saul the Zealot" to Paul who spreads Christianity throughout the then-known world. How do you feel about this? For example, do you adamantly want to remain just as you are right now? Or are you open to change, to grow, to betterment? Are there heights of joy that you've never reached but still want to? Or do you so delight in yourself right now that you want to remain exactly as you are at this moment?

These are meddlesome questions, I know. But fortunately someone meddled in my life, for which I'll be eternally grateful. So I'm simply asking: "Now that you've read my story, indeed now that you've read all of our stories, what difference, if any, will this make in your life today. Ponder this a bit further, won't you?"

On behalf of each friend whose story you have read here, I now close with a benediction—literally a "good saying for a good life"—just for you!

May the God of creation who first commanded, "Let the light shine out of the darkness," now make his light shine into *your* heart too, granting you the light and knowledge of God's own glory as seen in the face of his Son, Jesus Christ." AMEN.

P. S. My new friend, from now on, please feel free to call me, "**Paul the Apostle**" because , with God's help, that's finally who I became as I served my Lord .

Of course, if you want to know all that I later became (and did) as the "Apostle Paul," just pick up a copy of the New Testament and turn to the book of "Romans."

I'll gladly meet you on its pages!

POSTSCRIPT

"Seeing, then, that we are surrounded by such a great cloud of witnesses to our faith, let us cast aside everything that gets in the way, and the sin that holds us back. And let us run with expectant, creative hope the race that is set before each of us—looking unto Jesus, the initiator and fulfiller of our faith. He did not pull back from the Cross. Quite the contrary! Because of the joy that awaited him, he endured death on the Cross, despite the shame. And now he reigns at the right hand of God . . .

Therefore lift up your tired hands. Strengthen your shaking knees. Keep walking in the way he has shown you, so that your wounded foot may not cause you to stumble, but instead be healed!"

(Hebrews 12:1, 2, 12, 13)

www.ingramcontent.com/pod-product-compliance
Lightning Source LLC
Chambersburg PA
CBHW071441150426
43191CB00008B/1191